The Courtship of E

THE
Courtship
OF EVA ELDRIDGE

*A Story of Bigamy in the
Marriage-Mad Fifties*

Diane Simmons

University of Iowa Press ~ Iowa City

This is a true story based entirely on some eight hundred letters and other primary documents, on site visits and interviews, and on archival and library research. However, since there are those who still live with the legacy of these events, the author has undertaken to protect their privacy. For this reason the names of people and places—mostly small towns—have sometimes been changed, and in a few instances the nature of relationships has been altered slightly.

University of Iowa Press, Iowa City 52242
Copyright © 2016 by the University of Iowa Press
www.uiowapress.org
Printed in the United States of America

The University of Iowa Press is a member of Green Press Initiative and is committed to preserving natural resources.

Printed on acid-free paper

Library of Congress Cataloging-in-Publication Data
Names: Simmons, Diane, 1948– author.
Title: The courtship of Eva Eldridge : a story of bigamy in the marriage-mad fifties / Diane Simmons.
Description: Iowa City : University of Iowa Press, [2016] | Includes bibliographical references and index.
Identifiers: LCCN 2016008500| ISBN 978-1-60938-461-6 (pbk) | ISBN 978-1-60938-462-3 (ebk)
Subjects: LCSH: Eldgridge, Eva. | Bigamy—United States—Case studies. | Single women—United States—Social conditions—20th century. | Marriage—United States—History—20th century. | United States—History—1945– | United States—Social conditions—1945– Classification: LCC HQ535 .S46 2016 | DDC 306.810973—dc23
LC record available at http://lccn.loc.gov/2016008500

Designed by Kathleen Szawiola

Perhaps intentions were never honorable.

MARGARET HICKEY, Chairwoman,
Women's Advisory Committee of the
War Manpower Commission, 1942–1945

The only truly acceptable pattern in
American life is marriage.

MARGARET MEAD, *Life*, 1956

For Eva and Grace

Contents

Acknowledgments

❦

This project was supported by a PSC-CUNY Award, jointly funded by the Professional Staff Congress and City University of New York. Support was also provided by the Borough of Manhattan Community College in the form of sabbatical leave. Thanks to the Oregon Historical Society for the use of newspapers, oral histories, recordings, and photographs, and to the Canadian National Library and Archive in Ottawa for sharing military records. Thanks to the American Anthropological Association for permission to use the epigraph by Margaret Mead. Thanks to the individuals who were generous with their assistance, especially Bob LaDu and Therese Klein in Portland, Dom Driano in Seattle, Pam Navrat and Tom Sandwell of the Harvey County Historical Society in Newton, Kansas. Thanks to those friends and writers who read the first draft: Meredith Sue Willis, Michael Harris, Jason Trask, and Deborah Clearman. Special thanks to Jessica Papin for her belief in *Eva*. Thanks as always to my husband, Burt Kimmelman, for his support and particularly for his companionship on numerous research trips. Above all, thanks to those who played a role in this story and were willing to share their memories with me.

Introduction

By now I am intimate with the letters that once were Eva's, and over the last several years I've been living in them as a kind of alternative life. But it took a long time to open the first envelope. Though I've spent most of my life as a reporter and writer, prying into the thoughts and deeds of others, this time something held me back. Something that felt a lot like fear.

For one thing, everything about the letters seemed to resist intrusion. For decades they and their secrets had been safe, hidden away in the arid eastern Oregon attic where I found them after Eva died, naming me, a family friend, executor of her estate. The letters, some eight hundred of them, were bound together—collected into fat packets and tied with loops of tightly knotted kitchen string. So it was impossible to simply pick up one or two and glance casually through. If I was going to read them at all, I had to break in. I had to get a knife and cut the graying but still sturdy old string that had done its job so valiantly all these years.

When I began, I was hoping simply to get a glimpse of an era, the heady and passionate years of World War II. I was drawn by the return addresses from Italy, North Africa, and "somewhere in the Pacific." But as I started to read, I found I had stumbled upon a remarkable story of transformation and betrayal—and a puzzle yet to be solved.

As I read, a creepy sense of voyeurism became overpowering. The letters, I realized, *smelled*. It was not necessarily a bad smell. But the paper had stored scents of these long-ago lives: the sweat of World War II infantry fatigues; the residue of Eva's cigarette smoke; the aroma of face powder and perfume that had seeped in from a dresser drawer. I learned how emotionally draining it can be to hold in your hands letters that in some cases had delivered life-shattering news, some blotched with tear stains, some with a handwriting slanting so crazily that the words lie almost prostrate. As I read, I could not help imagining Eva, holding these same pages in her long thin fingers.

Could I really bear to intrude on so many private moments?

Still, could I *not*?

Why had they been so carefully saved all these years if not to be found someday and their remarkable story told?

PART 1

Three decades earlier, on December 20, 1930, the Hotel Boise had opened to tremendous fanfare. The white, art deco "skyscraper" was ten stories high, the upper floors set back in wedding cake style. Its luxury, the *Idaho Statesman* declared, was equal to that found in any great metropolitan hotel. All that day, thousands of Idahoans toured through, gaping at the Egyptian-style curlicues that topped the doorways and at the elegant lobby, which, according to *Hotel News*, resembled nothing so much as the lounge of a French luxury liner. That evening, five hundred leading citizens in evening attire—the ladies sparkling with jewels—attended a dinner-dance in the Crystal Ballroom. Don Keith's Spanish Ballroom Orchestra had been brought up from Salt Lake City, and the event was broadcast on a San Francisco radio station.[1]

Now, on a March evening in 1958, the Hotel Boise is no longer in the headlines, though it's still the swank place in town. The Crystal Ballroom is still the largest in the city, and the hotel bar is the unofficial meeting place for the city's elite. During the legislative session, many of the lawmakers live in the hotel, walking back and forth to the capitol a few blocks away.

Boise goes to bed early, though, and by ten P M activity in the hotel is winding down. At the cigar stand just inside the grand entrance, a woman whose golden-red hair is done up in a sleek roll closes out her cash register. It's Eva; she's thirty-five, attractive and slim, several inches taller than average. Her Tareyton Long is balanced on a silver ashtray as she restocks the gum and packs of cigarettes that have been sold since she came on shift at three. Though she's working, she's attired as though for an elegant evening out, wearing one of the cinch-waist dresses in deep forest green that set off both her slim figure and her redhead's complexion. Her feet are long and thin, and she always wears open-toe, open-back high heels.

Besides being a classy looker, she's nice to everyone, merry and fun; she has a way of looking into your eyes as if the two of you are about to burst with some hilarious secret. As a result, she's popular around the hotel. The waitresses are always stopping by to yak, and the bellboys like to hang around the cigar stand, kidding about this and that. Their kidding though is just in fun, to pass the time between calls. Everyone knows she's married to Vick, the hotel's handsome new chef. The guests, of course, don't know about Vick; but Eva is wearing a diamond-studded wedding ring on her long slender finger, and if anybody starts to get cute, she makes sure not only that they see the ring but that they realize they've been shown it.

She's been married a year, almost exactly, and she is deeply, deeply in love. She's so in love that she's downright mushy. At every holiday, she gives Vick the gushiest greeting card she can find.

Eva is lucky to have landed tall, good-looking Vick, the waitresses think. But she's a sweetheart and she deserves it. Besides—she's had a tough time. Before Vick showed up, it was clear to the practiced female eye that under the merry exterior she was lonely, even a little frightened. And no wonder. As anyone who goes to the movies is constantly reminded, being single in the 1950s is a terrifying experience. Motion pictures are full of pathetic, often desperate single women. By now the jaunty career gals of an earlier time are pretty much gone. In 1940 Rosalind Russell was a fast-talking reporter who just couldn't trade the newspaper game for a husband and a bunch of kids.[2] But by 1955 Russell is playing a woman so terrified of becoming a spinster school teacher that, swallowing tears and pride, she goes down on her knees, begging her reluctant gentleman friend to marry her.[3]

There's good reason for this desperation, as the movies also show: single women can be alarmingly vulnerable, subject both to remarkable brutality and assumptions of criminality. Susan Hayward, for example, plays a young woman who likes to kick off her shoes and dance with sailors; her only real crime is that she's too good of a pal to a couple of low-life guys. She gets the electric chair all the same; and just to underline the point of what can happen to a girl, the movie shows her being strapped in for execution. The restraints force her legs apart, and the newsmen jostle to get the best view.[4] Even a demure good girl, like Anne Baxter in *Blue Gardenia*, loses her invisible shield of protection when her fiancé dumps her. Now she's fair game for a heartless womanizer, and when she tries to defend herself, she too ends up facing a capital charge.[5]

No, it's terrible to be single, especially as you head onto the downhill side of your thirties. You may feel "young and carefree," a recent magazine article warned unmarried women. But soon you'll be "middle-aged Sad Sacks," and it'll be too late to get "husband insurance."[6] So, of course, everybody is glad to see Eva settled and so happy.

Since tonight is one of Vick's nights off—they can never get exactly the same schedule, though Eva has tried—she puts on her coat to walk the five blocks home. Before leaving, she visits the ladies' room to smooth her hair, touch up her lipstick and powder; she wants to look good for her man, who'll be waiting up, reading one of his magazines. They'll sit and smoke, have a cup of coffee. They'll put Perry Como on the hi-fi. Neither of them has to be at work until three the next afternoon.

One of the bellmen holds the door, and Eva steps out onto Eighth and Bannock. The night is chilly, and she walks briskly along the nearly empty streets, up to Jefferson, and then four blocks over to the little basement apartment that was Eva's before they got married and Vick moved in. It's small, just a bedroom, front room with three street-level windows, and a nook of a kitchen. Maybe they'll look around for a house eventually, but for now it's cozy, the perfect little love nest.

As Eva steps onto her block, she sees that the brand new '58 Mercury she and Vick recently bought on time—dark blue over robin's egg—isn't in its usual place in front of the house. She tries to remember: did he say something about taking it to the garage? She walks faster, clip-clipping along the dark sidewalk, and she is glad when she sees the lights shining from the apartment windows. She walks down the cement steps at the side of the house and taps on the door. She waits a minute, then, her toes too cold to wait for the big lug to unfold himself from the couch, lets herself in with her key.

It takes only a few seconds in the neat little apartment for Eva to see that though the lamps are on and everything looks perfectly normal, Vick is not there. She stands in the living room puzzled. She knows he likes to go out. Sometimes he gets antsy on his night off. But why didn't he pick her up after work and they could have gone somewhere? There aren't many places open this late in Boise, but there are a few. She goes to the phone to see if Vick has left a note on the pad or jotted something that would show what had come up, but nothing is there. She puts her hand on the phone, but that doesn't make it ring, doesn't put Vick on the other end explaining where he is and why. She thinks of calling the different places that might be open this late but doesn't want to come across as the nagging wife.

Now she begins to worry that she may have *already* nagged a little. She's thinking how Vick had been a bit moody in the last few days, quiet, and how she worried he was getting sick. She was afraid it was something about the lung problem he'd had for years. She'd urged him to see the doctor, but he hadn't wanted to and hadn't wanted to talk about it. Stop asking him if he was OK, he'd finally said. Not mad. Just telling her. And she had. But now she's worried. Could he be peeved that she tried to get him to go to the doctor? Tried to tell him what to do? Could he have just gone out alone to teach her not to nag? But he's never been peeved before, not even once. He's never done anything even the slightest bit thoughtless or inconsiderate.

She goes into the bedroom again and stops still; the framed wedding pictures are gone from the dresser. After a moment she steps to the closet and opens it to see her own collection of dark green and midnight blue dresses on the right; on the left is an empty space where Vick's slacks and jackets had hung. Back at the dresser she opens the drawers that held his underwear and socks and the one where she put his shirts as they came packaged from the laundry. The drawers are empty.

Her heart racing, she goes back to the closet. Vick's jackets and slacks are still not hanging on his side. All of his things are gone except for the soft green sweater she gave him for Christmas. It's on the closet shelf, folded neatly. There too is the shoe box where he keeps his check stubs and so forth. Also in the box are the greeting cards she has given him. She knows he kept them because she once peeked to see.

Eva sits up smoking all night. She has no one she can call, not a living soul she can tell. For one thing, she can't bear for anyone to know. And anyway, she's sure that no one—none of their friends—would take it seriously. Everyone was always teasing them for being such lovebirds.

Whadja have, a fight? The girls would say. Don't worry, he'll cool off. He's out driving around. He didn't just *leave*. But they hadn't had a fight. They'd never had a fight or even an argument. There had never been a night when they didn't sleep in each other's arms.

She doesn't call her mother, Grace, who still lives on the farm in the eastern Oregon mountain valley where Eva grew up. She can't bear for her mother to know that something terrible has happened. Again. Eva knows she has put her mother through a lot since leaving the farm in 1943 to go to a war job. Though she and her mother are close, Eva is aware that she hasn't turned out at all as her mother had hoped. She knows Grace has worried and prayed over her so many times. Now it crosses Eva's mind that this new blow might be more than her mother can stand.

As the light breaks, she sleeps for a couple of hours, slumped on the couch, hugging the green sweater in her arms. Around ten she phones the manager at the hotel. She wants to ask if Vick, who is scheduled to work this evening, has called in. But when the manager answers, she hangs up. She waits until three when Vick would be starting his shift. Then she calls the kitchen and asks for him.

"He hasn't come in yet, Eva," one of the other cooks says, recognizing her voice. She hangs up and calls the assistant manager. Her mother is sick, she tells him. She and Vick have to drive over to eastern Oregon. He'll have to find someone to replace them both for a few days. The assistant manager doesn't like it; it's pretty short notice. She says she's sorry but it can't be helped.

Eva has to do something. She makes coffee and sits down at the little kitchen table with the only thing that's left her: Vick's shoebox of papers and other small articles. She takes each item out and studies it, looking for something, she doesn't know what.

⁓ The shoebox, too, has come to me in Eva's things. And as I open it, looking for clues, I begin, as I expect Eva would have, with the orderly, rational-looking book of check stubs on a Boise bank. It begins mid-December of 1956, the month Vick arrived in town, a few weeks before he got on at the hotel and the two of them met.

Vick has a messy, scribbly hand, and for some reason he always seems to be using a blurry pencil. But by now Eva can easily read his writing. And though she has not had occasion to look at his check-book before, she sees that he fills out the stubs fully, giving check number, amount, date, and item, then subtracts the check amount to arrive at the new balance. In the first month he's in town, he's carrying a balance of about two hundred dollars, and most of his checks are for five or ten dollars, made out to a restaurant or bar, often a place called the Torch Café. Eva knows that when he first got to Boise he lived in a furnished room over on Idaho Street, and she assumes he was eating his meals in restaurants and paying with a check. Ten dollars is a lot for one person to spend in a Boise restaurant in 1956 with a steak dinner at about three bucks and beer thirty or forty cents. But he must have written the checks for more than the bill so he could get cash back and wouldn't have to bother standing in line at the bank.

She sees that he paid fifty-seven dollars a month rent for the furnished room where he lived when he first arrived. It seems like a lot. Eva's rent is only forty a month. But maybe at the house where Vick stayed, the lady was doing the cleaning, washing the sheets and towels, even doing his laundry.

Going on through the stubs, Eva sees that Vick paid fifteen dollars for a pair of shoes at C. C. Anderson's department store and made several fifteen-dollar trips to the doctor for his lung condition. She worries again that something could have worsened with his lungs and for some incomprehensible reason he couldn't tell her what he was planning to do about it. She feels sick to think he's somewhere suffering and can't let her know.

She keeps turning the little green stubs and comes to January 25, 1957. On this day he noted a ten-dollar check for "jewelry down payment." She sees another "jewelry" entry of $125 a week later. Eva knows this is her diamond wedding ring, and she puts down her head and sobs.

Eventually, however, there is nothing to do but light another cigarette and turn back to the check stubs and the scrawly handwriting that has become so dear. In March, after their marriage, there are no more checks written to the Torch Café. Instead, the checks are for the normal things a couple spends money on: $6.33 to the telephone company, $6.80 to Idaho Power, $11.05 for groceries at

Albertson's. The everyday expenses hearten her a little. It's so clear that they were a happy married couple and that this is all some terrible misunderstanding.

She stops to rack her brains: is it possible he told her about something he had to go do and she simply forgot? But she can't think of anything, and the hotel hadn't been notified that he wouldn't be at work. She turns back to the stubs. Getting to July, she sees an entry in her own neat hand. Apparently she had grabbed his checkbook to pay fifteen dollars owed to Stewart Photography. Yes—the wedding pictures.

At the bottom of the box, she finds Vick's green-on-olive master sergeant stripes. He'd shown Eva these with pride. Surely he would not willingly have left his stripes behind. Though she has seen the stripes before, Eva has not seen a postcard from the Veterans Administration, sent to Vick at an address in Washington, D.C. The postcard dated March 1953 notifies Vick that his VA records have been forwarded from the San Francisco office to the Washington, D.C., office. Though Eva had known Vick was from California, near San Francisco, she had not known he had ever lived in Washington, D.C. He's eight years older than she; at forty-three, a man like him has been around, of course. Still, she's surprised he wouldn't have mentioned living back East.

The military card gives Eva another idea, one that is frightening and at the same time a bit desperately hopeful. Could his moodiness and his disappearance have something to do with his experiences in the war? Eva doesn't know many details of his service, only that he'd been in a tank unit in Italy and had seen a lot of things. He'd hinted that he'd had to do things that he found distasteful but that he didn't want to talk about. It was all ancient history, he'd said.

Eva, as it happens, has had her own searing experience with what combat can do to a man. And now she is remembering a recent movie where a married man who loves his wife is haunted by flashbacks of wartime experiences that he cannot share with her. She remembers too another movie from a few years back where a shell-shocked vet believes he killed his wife and flees, even though he has no memory of the act and really did not commit the murder.[7]

Could it be something like that? Could Vick be wandering around, lost and confused? Could he have forgotten his name and where he lived? But if he has the car, doesn't he have the registration with his name and address? If he has the wedding photographs, wouldn't he see the name of Stewart Photography in Boise stamped on the back? Couldn't he call up Stewart's, describe the photographs, and ask who had ordered them?

Knowing him, maybe he is just being too stubborn to follow these clues. Maybe he is too stubborn to go to the police or a hospital to ask for help. She could imagine that maybe. What she can't imagine is that he would knowingly frighten her so. He is so good and kind, so gentle and understanding. So very, very loving. But if he can't remember, then he doesn't know what she is going through. She finds a little comfort in the idea.

Putting the things back in the box, Eva notices two small scraps of paper that seem to have been torn from magazines. She sees now that they are both the same advertisement. Both have been torn out in the same careless way; the top and the left margin are missing. Still, she can make out that the ad is for discount diamonds and that you can send for a free catalog of diamonds "from $25 up to $5000."

It's not so much the words that hold Eva or the idea of discount diamonds; it's more the partial picture of a woman who appears at the top of the ad. Her face and arms gleam pale against a dark background, and she is embracing a man who is only seen from the back. Because the ad has been carelessly ripped, you don't see the top of the woman's face, but you see her thin, white fingers, one with a diamond wedding ring. The fingers are spread. One hand clutches the man's back, the other is in his smooth dark hair. You see the curve of her jaw and the beginning of her chin. You see that her head is thrown back and her lips are parted in an expression of ecstasy.

The woman, Eva thinks, looks like her. Not just the long fingers and the clean jaw line, but the expression as well. Did Vick think so too, that he would tear the same ad out twice?

It is not until an hour later that Eva, back at the little kitchen table with a new pack of cigarettes, absently turns one of the little clippings over and sees that she has been looking at the wrong side. For on the back of both clippings is another advertisement, this one neatly torn out along the lines. The ad is headlined "Fun in Mexico," with a second line, "Retire on $150 a month."

In the fine print, the ad invites readers to come to an American-English colony, Posada Ajijic, on Lake Chapala, where they will find three hundred and sixty-five days of sun a year and dry temperatures of sixty-five to eighty degrees. Houses rent for ten dollars a month with full-time servants and cooks costing seven to ten dollars a month. Or if you prefer, you can maintain a luxury villa with servants and all expenses for two hundred a month. Here in Mexico, the ad goes on, filet mignon is fifty cents a pound; and gin, rum, and brandy are sixty-five cents a fifth. Gas is seventeen cents a gallon. Here you'll find "no fog, smog, confusion, jitters. Just serene living among considerate people." To learn more about this opportunity, you could send two dollars to Robert Thayer, manager of Posada Ajijic, at a post office box in Jalisco and allow two weeks for full details to be airmailed back.

Instantly, Eva is certain this is where Vick has gone. She doesn't know why he has gone to Mexico without her or why he couldn't tell her, but she is sure this is where he is. Could it be for his health, his lungs, or just because something was making him nervous? Could it possibly be as some kind of surprise for her? He knows she has always yearned to travel and that she loves warm climates.

And now Eva, so weary with fear and dread, seizes on the idea that she will soon get a call or a letter from Mexico telling her to get her family on the train and come on down. She's known Vick for only a little more than a year after all. Maybe there are still aspects to him she doesn't understand. Maybe this is how he does things, thinks of something and then just up and does it. It certainly didn't take him long to decide he wanted to get married.

Her mother won't like the idea of her in Mexico, Eva knows, but she will just have to get used to the fact that this is how Eva and Vick live. Her mother has to realize that they are of the generation that came of age during the war. For better or worse, they're used to quite a bit more excitement than the folks at home. And now, almost happy, Eva goes into the bedroom, puts on a fresh nightgown, and hugging the green sweater, falls asleep.

But the next morning, as she finds herself alone in the double bed, the idea that Vick has gone to Mexico to prepare a surprise for her doesn't gleam as brightly as it had the night before. Still, it's all she has. Eva tells herself she has to have faith, that this is a test of her love. At the same time she knows she can't just sit and wait to hear from him. She'll go mad.

༝ Eva never learned to drive, which is unusual. She grew up in the same mountain valley as I did, where most farm kids were driving at twelve. But Eva was young during the Depression years, when vehicles were scarce. You rode a horse, I suppose, or you walked. Or you just stayed home. Then at twenty-one, Eva left the farm and went across the state to the city of Portland, where public transportation was available for the thousands of war workers. And, of course, tires and gas were rationed, so there wasn't a lot of joy riding.

So now she starts trying to figure out how to get to Mexico by train.

In the papers that have come down to me I have Eva's jotted notes, the little scraps of paper showing what she was learning, what she was considering. It looks as though she called the railroad station and was told the closest she could get to Lake Chapala is Guadalajara. Eva noted this down. The price of a one-way ticket would be $118.80. For Eva, who made about $150 a month, it was a lot of money. And, of course, she had bills and her rent. And, as she must have been realizing, she would have to make payments on the new car alone.

Instead of getting on a train for Guadalajara, Eva writes the first of a series of letters, addressing them to Vick in care of Robert Thayer at Posada Ajijic. She drafts the first letter on yellow scrap paper, then edits with cross-outs, additions, and a few changes in sentence order before recopying onto airmail stationery. Her approach in this first letter has been carefully thought out. She feels that she is fighting for her life, and everything depends upon what she is able to communicate to Vick. The energy, effort, and passion with which she writes makes it clear that she has convinced herself the letter will find him in Mexico.

Though in the first paragraph she speaks of her love that is so deep and true that it can be "only vaguely" described in words, the main job of the letter is to make a case for why Vick left, a case that does not allow for the possibility that Vick has simply walked out. Her own pain is barely mentioned. Rather the letter portrays Vick as a man who is heroically battling unimaginable personal suffering. Eva doesn't say exactly what this ongoing battle entails but does write, "I've often wondered if you were so hard and lacking in heart that you could go through what you have unscarred. Years of war, loneliness, sickness, and the loss of most of your family. Now I know that you have normal human feelings & that it couldn't help but affect you as it has thousands in one way or another."

In addition to portraying Vick as locked in a struggle to overcome unimaginable pain, she portrays herself as the one at fault, a woman so selfishly in love that she could not understand what her man needed. "I must have been a miserable failure as a wife or you could have felt like you could have told me of your past, your problems or the way you felt. Perhaps I was so blinded by my complete happiness with you that I saw nothing else." And yet, she was not completely unaware: "I felt so close to you in one way & yet always as if something was between us."

It is her great failing, she writes, that she could not detect what this "something" was. And she realizes now that she was doing and saying all the wrong things, talking about "settling down, getting a house, my family, having a baby." Meanwhile, Vick was "doing nothing but putting in such long hours, working hard, and then coming home to an empty apt. Darling, you are a wonderful man, anyone else would have flipped under it months before."

And now Eva offers a plan. First, she will "sever" her relationship with her mother. "I don't want her words of advice, her financial help, or her well-meant kindness. All I want is you." Second, she doesn't really want to settle down, doesn't care about all the things people are supposed to have. She needs "no home, no family, friends, or so called worldly possessions. All I need or want is you. I love you more each day. Darling, just let me go with you, wherever you go & whenever you go and I will spend my life trying to make you happy."

Maybe they can get a "cheaper car & a little house trailer" and hit the road together, living a life that replicates their honeymoon tour through the West, a time she remembers as the happiest in her life.

In the next weeks, she writes half a dozen such letters to Vick, sending them off to Mexico in care of Robert Thayer. One letter is written on March 10, their first wedding anniversary and "the day that has more meaning to me than any other day in my life." For this letter, Eva goes to the post office and pays thirty cents for a special delivery stamp. But by the next letter, Eva has undergone a slight change. She has realized that she doesn't want to cut her mother off after all. "It was just that I didn't want anyone around if I couldn't have you. And I couldn't help feeling that if I hadn't had family you would have taken me with you."

Throughout the weeks of letter writing, Eva holds onto her scenario: the blinded-by-love Eva failed the suffering Vick. But Eva, if she could be given another chance, could learn to love him in the way he needs. Only in the last of the letters does she falter. "The one horrible thought is that maybe you never really loved me. But I cannot believe it. I could not have loved you so much if my love had not been returned. Neither could you have been the wonderful husband you were for a year if you hadn't cared."

No. It just can't be that he never loved her.

℘ I know what Eva wrote in these letters to Mexico because they all came back to her in Boise, with a big blue fist stamped on the front of the envelope, the thumb pointing up to the address of Mrs. Virgil Vickers, Boise, Idaho. On the envelopes someone has written, "*no conocido*" and "*no reclamada*." Eva saved the letters, and they have come down to me unopened.

Eva gets other mail that spring, including a letter from one F. W. Parker at the Loss Recovery Section of Pacific Finance Company in Los Angeles. The case of the missing Mercury has apparently been referred to him from the bank in Boise. Parker has obviously been in communication with Eva, and he has to have picked up on her desperation as she tries to find Vick. But Pacific Finance is not paying Parker to go into the human aspect of the thing, even though he's dealing with a woman whose husband has deserted her and left her with—among other things—a big payment on a car she no longer has.

No, Parker's job is to hound whoever he has to hound to get the car back. In a letter dictated to his secretary, he suggests that Eva may not be on the level and at any rate isn't trying hard enough. "If

Mr. Vickers was released from the service with a medical discharge as stated by you, it would appear that you would not have much trouble in relocating him. The service of the Red Cross is available to you." Accordingly, he directs Eva to present the case to the Red Cross immediately and to then advise Parker of the person she has contacted and the location of the office. Also, she is to authorize the Red Cross to release any information to Pacific Finance Corporation. Finally, she is instructed to send a letter of compliance in the enclosed postpaid envelope.

As I read F. W. Parker's condescending letter, I cannot help being glad to see the postpaid envelope flutter to the floor.

After weeks of waiting, Eva finally does get a letter from Mexico. It's not from Vick but from Robert Thayer, typed on onionskin paper under the letterhead for "Posada Ajijic, Ajijic, Jalisco, Mexico." On one side of the letterhead is a drawing of a man at a typewriter; on the other side is a figure in a beret standing before an easel, paintbrush in hand. Thayer writes that he is aware of all the letters Eva has written, of the telegrams she has sent, and of the calls she has attempted to place. From all this Thayer understands that "the matter is urgent to you." However, "Virgil is not here. I haven't heard from him, nor do I know where he is. As a matter of fact, I haven't heard from him in years." Thayer appears to wish to soften this, adding, "Virgil wrote me some long time ago that he had married, so in a sense I am acquainted with you." He signs himself Robert H. Thayer, Mgr. Posada Ajijic, Ajijic, Jalisco, Mexico.

For Eva, this must have seemed a thin ray of hope. At least she has reached someone who knows Vick; but as I study Eva's notes, I see that nothing ever comes of the Thayer connection, and I have come to believe Robert Thayer's letter is strangely, a fraud, a red herring across her path.

First, I don't find anybody who knew Vick calling him "Virgil."

Second, when the Pacific Finance goons find Thayer—Eva has apparently given them his name and the Ajijic address—he claims, as the company reports to Eva, that he never knew a Virgil Vickers.

Third, when I type a few lines from the Posada Ajijic ad into a search engine, I end up on a site offering retirement advice. Here, somebody has scanned in an article from the 1950s that gives tips on ways to generate income in cheap and sunny foreign countries. The article holds up a man named Bob Thayer as a success story, describing how he runs ads in many American magazines and how he makes "an excellent income with little expenditure of time or effort." It's all perfectly legal, the write-up assures, though reading between the lines you suspect that there is probably no Posada Ajijic and quite likely no information packet sent by return mail. What Thayer is doing, the article hints, is making a living off the two dollars people send in.

Finally, Thayer's claim to feel "acquainted" with Eva because "Virgil" wrote him "some long time ago" saying he was married will soon come to seem painfully comic. I'm guessing that Thayer had never met Vick but, as a small-time con man who didn't want any trouble, thought it best to give the distraught wife a little something to get her off his back. Then when the car company dicks showed up, he still didn't want trouble and had to change his story: he'd never heard of the guy.

For somebody in such pain, Eva is very industrious and is doing pretty good detective work. But I think she missed something in Vick's shoebox. I missed it too at first, something that looks like an unimportant piece of junk mail, a letter to Vick from the Frye Motor Hotel in Seattle. It's dated February 21, only a few days before Vick's disappearance, and addressed to him at the Jefferson Street apartment in Boise. The form letter inside invites the addressee to present an enclosed "commercial discount card" when registering at the hotel to guarantee a special businessman's rate.

At first I assume it's a general solicitation, though it does seem a little strange that the hotel would have him on some list and write to his home address. Does a chef really travel for business? It's not until I pick up the little plastic "commercial discount card" for the second or third time that I notice it has bumps on the back. Turning it over, I can just make out the embossed words: "Mr. Virgil Vickers, Western Auto Supply, Boise, Idaho."

Vick, I realize, reinventing himself as an auto supply dealer, has inquired about the discount and is preparing a move not to Mexico but Seattle.

Though I'm twenty-five years younger than Eva, I knew her through her mother, Grace, a widow who lived on a little farm near my family's place; and when I was five or six, I would sometimes walk to her house to get a sack of the big brown eggs she sold. This was about 1953, and Grace lived alone; neither of her children had come back to Wing Valley after the war. When I went for eggs, she would invite me in for one of her big soft sugar cookies with the raisin in the middle. And sometimes, if I could be reverently careful, she brought out the funny old toys that had belonged to Eva and her brother: Eva's china-headed, cloth-bodied doll and Aub's wooden train—the flecks of red paint showing its former brightness.

When I was a little older, Grace would let me look through her photo album. In one snapshot, Eva and Aub are each cuddling a rabbit as a dozen more crowd around their bare feet. Eva is a pretty girl, her hair neatly bobbed and held back by barrettes. Though the photo is black and white, you can tell that while Aub is a blond, Eva's hair is a light red.

Sometimes too Grace let me look through a little flowered box filled with dozens of letters in small brown envelopes. These were from a boy, Dave Johnson. His father, Grace told me, had been the agent at the railroad station down on Snake River some twenty miles away, and Dave wrote his letters on the funny, brown Union Pacific stationery. I didn't see the point of boys then and couldn't think why Eva had filled her nice flowered box with all these ugly, brown letters. But the little flowered box is another one of the things that has come down to me. And now, I try to catch a reflection of seventeen-year-old Eva in the letters from twenty-year-old Dave, the boy to whom, in the last months before the war, she would be engaged.

✑ In 1940, when the letters begin, there is no phone service down to the tiny hamlet of Hayes, where Dave lives, so he has to write Eva with plans for his visits up to the more populous farming community of Wing Valley. Part of the planning, which usually revolves around a high school ball game or a dance, is to make sure that Eva realizes she's going to the event with him.

His letters are full of humorous conceits. In one letter notifying Eva that her response to his last missive is long overdue, he writes on the envelope, "This is Ye One and Only 'Hint' that I have ever written to: Miss Eva Eldridge, RFD, Wing Valley, Oregon."

He comes across as an energetic, take-charge kind of kid. Maybe he has to be since he's trying to organize things from his outpost on Snake River. In a note planning the one-hundred-mile round trip from Hayes through Wing Valley and on to the county seat of Baker he writes, "Eva: Be ready about 7:30 or 8 tomorrow morning. No excuses for being late—want to get there for morn matinee."

Dave, as the son of a professional man—rare in this farming area—would have been viewed as a catch. For one thing, in the Depression years, the child of a salaried man would have had a level of material comfort not available to the children of what were basically small subsistence farms. For another, ideas about possible careers would be more obvious to a boy like Dave than to Eva's classmates, who, until America entered the war, seldom saw anybody do anything but farm. Of course, in this day and in this spectacular, mountain-ringed valley, farming is considered a fine and free occupation, a life spent under the blue dome of heaven. Still, the Depression years have shown everyone—especially those trying to make it on a small acreage—how vulnerable the seemingly independent farmer is to forces beyond his control.

But it is clear that it is Dave who pursues Eva, complaining that she doesn't write often enough and that she keeps "beating around the bush" about some date or other. The letters also show Dave making himself agreeable to Grace. In one, he wonders if there's anything she would like him to pick up when he goes to the county seat next week. In another he speaks fondly of her lemon cream pie.

Reading Dave's letters now, I turn to Grace's photo album, which has also come down to me. I study the one picture of Eva and Dave from this time, the two of them standing rather stiffly in front of Grace's lilac bush. Eva is nearly eighteen, a high school senior in a homemade white dress with puffy cap sleeves and a tie sash. She is pretty and she knows it, but she isn't bold or conceited. A sweet-looking girl, she stands with her hands laced demurely together. Dave, dark-haired, a big dimple in his chin, stands a couple of feet away. They must be going somewhere important—Eva's prom I expect—because he is wearing a jacket and tie. His arms are crossed with the awkwardness of a boy posing for his girlfriend's mother. Still, his head is back a bit, and his gaze is steady and confident.

Grace, looking down into her black box Brownie, is undoubtedly happy. This, everyone is pretty sure, is the boy Eva will marry, probably quite soon. She is young, but then Grace herself was married at nineteen, a mother at twenty-one. The young couple, both devoted to family, will probably locate nearby, and Grace will be able to help out with the grandchildren that should soon arrive. As Grace looks into her camera and waits for the perfect expression to flit across Eva's face, she has every right to believe that Eva's future is set and that it will be all a devoted mother could have hoped.

That summer, six months before Vick would arrive in Boise, Eva was living in the little basement apartment on Jefferson Street. Grace worried constantly that Eva was alone and that she was working in a hotel where any sort of people could come in. She fretted so much about Eva having to walk home late at night that I remember actually dreaming of her trudging for long, cold hours in high-heel shoes, wending her way through the narrow, brick-walled streets that I must have assumed would make up any urban scene. Probably because she worried so much, Grace would often drive over to Boise to visit for a few days. Once that summer I was invited to go along.

It was not unusual for me to go traveling with Grace; she didn't like to make the drive to the county seat of Baker alone. Once we had visited the drugstore or the courthouse or wherever her business took us, we had our treat: lunch in a dinette with plate glass windows where we could watch the Bakerites passing by. Always frugal, we would each order soup and then cups of tea, taking care to preserve our tea bags so they could be reused in the second pot of hot water the waitress did not mind bringing.

Driving to Boise was a much bigger deal, a daylong trip, and in the excitement Grace seemed to forget herself. We stopped for lunch in Weiser, Idaho, and she bought us both hamburgers deluxe and a pineapple shake, divided into two glasses.

When we arrived, I was surprised to meet the real Eva. Having known her mainly through the keepsakes, I suppose I thought of her as a child like me, only a little older. So I was amazed to see that the little girl was a grownup woman with an abundance of red-gold hair, an exotic smell, and a merry conspiratorial wink.

Once there, we settled into Eva's bachelor life with—it seems to me now—astonishing ease. Evenings, Grace and I stayed up reading or looking at magazines until Eva came home from her job at the Hotel Boise. When she arrived, we still didn't go to bed but sat up for another hour or so drinking cups of tea and talking about this and that. Then—unheard of—we all woke up late and didn't have our breakfast until almost eleven.

I loved everything about Eva's tiny apartment, especially its utter bareness. In my own life on a hundred-year-old farm, our barn was full of old stuff from pioneer days. And, of course, our house was filled with the necessities of a family of five. But, aside from her dresses and shoes and a couple of handbags hanging on the closet door, Eva had virtually nothing. In her doll-sized kitchen were three cups, a little teakettle, a couple of cereal bowls, three spoons. In her tiny refrigerator there would be a bottle of milk and a wrapped-up piece of something—cake, steak, chicken—she had brought home from the hotel. On the kitchen shelf was one box of Grape-Nuts and one box of tea bags.

Grace must have been scandalized. But I, who did not yet understand the peril single women were in, was charmed. The freedom of it! No refrigerator full of leftovers that you had to think how to dress up and serve again. No stacks of pots or pans to be washed. And, of course, there was no washing machine. How different from our lives at home where, on laundry day, we hauled an old wringer washer into the kitchen, hooking it up to the sink. It took until suppertime to wash the five or six loads, jam the sopping clothes through the wringer, and lug the heavy tubs out to the clothesline in back. But Eva didn't seem to *have* dirty clothes except for her underwear and stockings, which she washed in the sink and hung on the towel rack to dry.

After we had eaten our Grape-Nuts and lingered over our tea, Eva would begin getting ready for work. Grace said I shouldn't get in the way, but Eva said she liked having company. So I would sit on the bed, watching her do her hair and touch up the red nail polish. Then came the hard part, drawing on the tawny eyebrows. When the eyebrows did not come out right, she had to cold cream them off and start all over again. How she wished, she would say, that she had pretty dark eyebrows like mine instead of her own useless white ones.

Sometimes she would forget getting ready for a minute or two, grab a damp comb, and have me sit beside her, twining my hair around her fingers until it fell into ringlets. What a lovely curl, Eva would exclaim; how silky! Then magically, in Eva's oval dressing table mirror, I was transformed, pretty, a girl with enviable qualities that I had no idea I possessed. Eva fussed over me in this way, I assumed, because she had no children of her own and therefore wasn't worn out from taking care of them all the time. Not having children was, I knew from Grace's murmurings, a terrible thing. To me though, it didn't seem so bad.

At around three o'clock, we would be ready, and Grace and I would walk Eva to the hotel. Then Grace would go out to look at the things they had in the Boise stores while I got to stay with Eva for a couple of hours, sitting on a high stool in the cigar stand. Here I learned—once Grace had gone—that Eva's exotic aroma came from the cigarette that was usually burning in her silver ashtray. I had never seen a woman smoke; I was shocked and impressed. And, as Eva seemed to understand, I didn't have to be warned not to tell.

In my memory, the cigar stand was a place of pure delight. There we were in the bright bustling heart of the fancy Hotel Boise. There I was with beautiful, shining Eva, who was clearly the darling of the place and who introduced me to everyone as her little friend from home. I could have all the Lifesavers I wanted off Eva's shelves, and when the jocular, dressed-up men stopped to buy a cigar, they sometimes gave me the paper ring for my finger. Now you have to marry me, I remember one man kidding. Well, I wittily kidded back, I'll see.

As it grew later, Grace came by to pick me up, and we walked the six blocks back to the apartment through Boise's wide and quiet streets, a walk that was, to my rather disgusted amazement, vastly shorter and safer than, say, my walk to school across a field where I had barbed wire fences to crawl through, ditches to jump over, and the ever-present threat of bulls appearing out of nowhere.

Seeing what Eva's walk home was really like, I began to think Grace's worrying was a lot of silliness. What I couldn't have understood, of course, as I watched Grace fret and pray about Eva and her life in Boise was how much the two of them had already been through since the spring evening in 1940 when Eva and her boyfriend Dave posed for the prom night photo. Every expectation Grace held would be overturned, and during the next few years Eva would change beyond recognition.

1940–1942 ✑ Wing Valley

Though Europe is already at war in that spring of 1940, America is not. The boys are still at home; Eva's brother, Aub, is still farming with their father, Wes. But as the summer progresses, Dave begins to talk about going up to British Columbia and enlisting in the Canadian Army. At war with Germany for almost a year now, the Canadians welcome American volunteers. Dave isn't the only young man to consider traveling north to enlist; for many, ground down by the hardships of the Depression, the offer of room and board and the chance of travel and adventure seems like a pretty good deal.[1]

Dave's parents object to this plan, as does Eva. But he has a supporter of sorts in Grace. Dave has apparently sat down with her and, as he writes Eva, "told her everything." Besides telling Grace of his thoughts about enlisting, he's also told her that he has given Eva a ring and is waiting to see if it "would mean anything or not." Grace, who is clearly fond of Dave and—only forty-two herself—perhaps a little flattered to be sought out, sides with him. She gives him advice she will surely come to regret: Eva shouldn't be allowed to "make up" Dave's mind for him. He has to do what he thinks right. And by November Dave has begun his service in the Canadian Scottish regiment.

In letters, he and Eva are still arguing about his decision, and it seems he has stopped writing for a time, as he is sure that she would get along without him "just fine." He has seen girls since he's been away, he informs her. Still he writes, "Damn it all, to be quite frank about it, I haven't kissed a girl since leaving the States."

He tries earnestly, if a bit contradictorily, to make her understand why he had to join up. "Eva, you know that I love you, but before I can consider a future life of any sort, I want to be sure in my own mind that I will not have to leave a family to fight a war." Since it seems that he is likely to see "some time of military service," he has decided on the Canadian forces. He feels that America will avoid war and fears that enlisting in the United States would result in "training in a great deal of theory." The Canadian forces, on the other hand, "would offer active service, a chance to get actual combat training."

Though no one else in her family has been to college, Eva is an intelligent girl, and now, with Dave away, she goes off to Eastern Oregon College. As she mentions in a letter, she might like to be a teacher for a few years before, it is assumed, she becomes a wife and mother. Neither Grace nor Eva would have imagined any other future for her. For one thing, it's all the women in their family have ever known. For another, here ten years into the Great Depression, women's role in the home has grown in importance; they are seen as the glue that holds the family together. Even when the men can't earn much, women, especially farm women like Grace and Eva, can sew and garden, keep chickens and rabbits, finding a way somehow to clothe and feed the family. Though she did not believe in complaining, for example, Grace once mentioned that throughout the Depression she sewed her nightgowns and underclothes from bleached flour sacks.

Then too, the Depression has brought out hostility toward women who work, especially married women, who, it is believed, deprive another family of a livelihood while delivering a blow to their own husbands' self-esteem.

But it is deemed acceptable that Eva could teach here at home as she waits to marry. And so she goes off to college. Once there, however, she finds she cannot do the work. A childhood bout of rheumatic fever has compromised her eyesight in a way that can't be corrected with glasses, and while she can see to read, she has to squint and hold the page up close. It doesn't take much of this to give her terrible headaches. The college reading is an impossible strain and may even have damaged her eyes further. So the family takes the extraordinary and expensive step of sending her to Chicago by train, where she can be fitted with a pair of early contact lenses. Now her eyesight is improved, but the hard lenses can be worn for only a limited number of hours a day; overuse can cause dangerous infection, and as a result she cannot do much close work. College is clearly not possible, and she returns home.

In Canada, Dave is becoming increasingly enamored of the military and preoccupied with the studies that he hopes will land him a commission. The military will be his life, he now writes Eva. It will be a good career because it is something that will always be needed. Despite good grades, however, he doesn't get a commission. Still he seems happy to have been assigned to the Eighth Armoured Regiment as a signaler, or wireless operator.

"Not bad," he writes. Though he still expresses love for Eva and is keeping her "little blue dress clip" for luck, his ardor seems to have cooled. He wonders who she is going out with and writes that he "can't expect" her to wait. In March, plans for a leave fall through, but it seems that Dave is not completely without companionship. There are, he writes, "some American girls in town. They are much nicer than the Canadians. They can laugh and still be grown up."

In summer of 1941, as the Nazis launch their invasion of Russia, Eva, still at home with her parents, turns nineteen. Dave writes that he will be leaving for England in September. The little blue dress clip, he says, has broken. Then there is a gap in the correspondence. Some of Dave's letters to Eva could have been misplaced, I suppose, but the packets of letters are so carefully saved and neatly bound that it doesn't seem likely. Since I don't have Eva's side of the correspondence, I don't know what has happened. Have they broken up?

In November he writes again. "Remember me? I'm the fellow who was going to forget you entirely. It can't be done. I don't know whether I'm glad or sorry." Still, he has more than Eva to think of. He is training to be a motorcycle dispatch rider, "rather tricky with a goodly amount of thrills and spills." While Dave has his thrills, Eva waits at home. What, I wonder, does she tell herself that she is doing as the boy she ought to have married by now is living an adventurous life far away? Does she say that she is "waiting for Dave"? But who is Dave now? He claims that he is still "in love." But he's clearly being changed by experiences of a sort she can't even imagine.

Then it's December 7, 1941. In the West, the first news flash comes right before noon, and Eva and Grace, rushing home from church to get Sunday dinner on the table, wouldn't have had the radio on. But they get the news soon enough, and the next day Eva's brother, Aub, and the other young men in the Valley go to Baker to enlist. By spring of 1942, they are all gone, spread with astonishing speed to different parts of the globe. Local boys—who from the "just-friends" tone of their letters show they understand that Eva is spoken for—are writing from California, Iceland, England, and "somewhere in the Pacific."

Aub writes from Texas, replying to Eva's latest letter in which she has told him of going to a high school basketball game and the senior play. Though he's spent his boyhood going to the same school events, now, far from home for the first time, he marvels at what it must be like to "go to something like that where you know everybody there and all about them." She's told him, too, of her activities around the farm, and Aub writes, "I can just picture you cleaning up the yard and doctoring old Snap's ears. Guess you haven't changed much." For his part he's been having a bit of unspecified fun with "some little Mexican girls." He just got paid and is enclosing a "ten spot for you to get a new pair of shoes with or some dope for Snap's ears if you want. Anyway have some fun with it."

I get out Grace's photo album to see snapshots of Eva at this time. In one picture, she is kneeling in the barnyard, the chicken house and other ramshackle outbuildings behind her. Behind those is a wooden fence. In the near distance is a slightly crooked telephone pole and then the low foothills that guard the valley. Behind the foothills rise the high mountains. As she kneels, she is surrounded by a dozen sheep. Her face still has its adolescent roundness, the broad forehead and fine eyes. The red hair has darkened and is pulled back from her face. She gazes at the camera, only half smiling, one arm resting on the woolly back of the nearest sheep.

Here there are no thrills and no spills. Is she the only young person in the world to whom nothing at all is happening?

1942 ∽ "If the Fair Sex Were to Replace Men"

Then, in the chill late winter of 1942, a strange lady pulls her car into the Eldridge barnyard and picks her way through the mud, around to the front door. She is a respectable, official-seeming person, and she has come to find out if there are females in the household who are over eighteen and who might consider helping in the war effort. The lady—one of six thousand registrars now fanning out across Oregon—is part of a first-in-the-nation effort, organized by Portland clubwomen, to survey the ability and willingness of women to fill the labor shortage left by men who have gone into the service.

This idea is not altogether new. In 1941, Eleanor Roosevelt visited Great Britain and, when she returned, reported that women were working with a will at jobs usually held by men.[1] British women have in fact been called up, and as war draws closer, this option is studied in the United States. But the idea of drafting women draws immediate protest, and Roosevelt rejects it. Instead, he urges that local, state, and city authorities begin voluntary enrollment drives. Oregon is the first to step up.[2]

Understandably, it is hard for people to grasp the enormous change that is about to occur. All anyone has known for years is that jobs are desperately scarce. How could they be expected to realize that within a few months the opposite will be true, that jobs will go unfilled and workers will be desperately sought?

In early 1942, it is not obvious that this great reversal is underway. Though many men have already left their jobs to join the service, some are still at home.[3] And the fear of unemployment remains strong; in January of 1942, for example, thousands of men mob a Portland hiring hall on word that there are jobs at new shipyards. The men refuse to disperse, the *Oregonian* reports, "even when told over loudspeakers that the new yards aren't even built yet."[4] And when the newspaper runs a story about the city's first female taxicab driver—"She's comely. She's petite. She's vivacious. And incidentally she can handle a car"—the taxicab union up in Seattle immediately announces that only male drivers will work in *their* jurisdiction.

But within a few months, the nationwide supply of male workers has dwindled alarmingly. And the labor shortfall is expected to be particularly severe in Oregon—for the coming of war has precipitated a shipbuilding crisis. Many ships are being lost in the Atlantic, and the chairman of the Maritime Commission has declared, "We are in a war of transportation . . . a war of ships. It's no damn sense making guns and tanks to be left in the U.S." President Roosevelt has concurred, demanding that the United States, now turning out fewer than one hundred ships a year, must immediately build twenty-nine hundred new vessels. To build the new ships, the number of shipyard workers must increase dramatically, from one hundred thousand to seven hundred thousand.[5]

Portland, Oregon, at the mouth of the Columbia, only eighty miles from the Pacific Ocean, has been identified as a prime location for shipbuilding, and now plans for vast new shipyards are in the works. But Portland—along with her sister across the Columbia, Vancouver, Washington—has been mainly a commercial center for the surrounding ranching and timber operations. Only about fifty thousand of the city's three hundred thousand residents work in industry.[6] Where will all the new workers be found?

To address this problem and in response to the call for women to volunteer, the clubwomen of Portland have announced a door-to-door canvas of the state's females. Perhaps because the question is still such a delicate one, *Oregonian* editors do not place the story amid the war news but in the women's section, where it is flanked by engagement announcements and instructions on how blackout drapes can be made more attractive. Readers are assured that the survey is not compulsory and is designed purely to appeal to women's patriotic sentiments. When the information has been gathered a month later, it is announced, again on the women's page, that 302,000 Oregon women have been registered and their skills listed.

Apparently among those reading the women's section are editors at a shipyard newspaper, the *Bo's'n's Whistle*, which responds to news of the survey with a full page of cartoons mocking the very idea that women might enter the all-male environs of the yards.[7] This page is headlined: "During the past few weeks the fair sex have been interviewed and classified for defense work—the scenes below are what might take place if the fair sex were to replace men in the plate shop." In the drawings, female ninnies—all are buxom and leggy unless they are saggy grannies in aprons and spectacles—are given speeches such as "These little hammers sure tire me out!" "Say Gertie, will a quarter inch drill make a half inch hole?" and "Oh dear! Now I've broke my high heel off. Darn those holes![8]

Despite such views, the idea of women filling in for men is being increasingly promoted, and within a few weeks newspapers around the country run a wire story lauding the Oregon women for "blazing a new trail" not to "gold and rich bottom soil" but to "women power." Though the "croakers" said voluntary enlistment would never work, the story declares, the Oregon women have proven otherwise, canvassing in "cities, on farms, beside rivers, and in virgin forests where 'stump' ranchers built cabins." One registrar reportedly reached snowbound communities by riding sixteen miles on horseback. Another flew to a remote community by chartered plane, registered the women there, and was back at her own fireside by evening. It is further reported that the survey found women very receptive. One woman stated, "I'm a good shot and can carry a 50-pound pack along with the best of men. I want coast guard duty."[9]

To reach Eva out in Wing Valley, however, no treks on horseback or chartered planes would have been necessary; in these arid hills, snowfall is scant, and in February the registrar could easily drive the fifty miles from the county seat in an hour or so. Grace, of course, cannot be spared from the farm and does not participate in the survey. Wartime privation means that farm animals and produce are every bit as important as during the Depression years. Grace is busy with her chickens, her orchard, and her immense garden. But Eva and the interviewer sit down at the dining room table. Eva lists her skills: cooking, sewing, cleaning. Also she has tended farm animals and can drive a horse-drawn hay wagon. She does not know how these experiences might help the war effort, but the registrar assures her that every sort of skill will be needed. And for the first time Eva could wonder if there may be some role for her in the great struggle that has taken Dave and Aub and so many others.

By March of 1942, Dave is in England and has transferred from the Canadian Army to a U.S. Army infantry unit. By now he has gotten his first taste of the "actual" warfare he was hoping for. His convoy from Canada was attacked by German planes, though the RAF drove them off. The food on the ship was sickening, the fish filled with worms. His mail was lost, though some of it was "reclaimed from the sea." He got a Sunday School paper—sent by Grace no doubt—and something from Eva, but the ink was "almost washed out."

And he hints of seeing things that he won't describe, horrible things. Later he will disclose that he experienced the bombing of Bath, one of the so-called Baedeker Raids, as the Germans bombed landmark sites in reprisal for raids on their own historic cities. In Bath, tens of thousands of buildings were destroyed and hundreds killed. Now Dave's letters have lost much of the cocky tone that they held earlier, and for the first time, he begins to write longingly of home, remembering picnics on the river and dinner at Eva's house. But even as he begins to portray home as an ideal and unchanging place, he also makes a prediction that is truer than he can realize. "No one will be untouched when this war is over."

The war news is dire. Hitler controls most of Europe, and Germany has signed a pact with Italy and Japan so that the Axis extends around the world. After much debate, the Allies decide to invade Europe through Italy. In November, to position the Allies for an assault on Italy, Americans and Canadians land in North Africa. Dave Johnson is among them, though he tries to keep this alarming information from Eva. His parents know, however, and share the news with Eva's family.

At first, big, empty Africa might have seemed better than flaming England, and it does not seem to be immediately apparent to those at home that American boys are about to go into their first major battle in the European theater. Grace wonders in a letter what on earth Dave could be doing in Africa, imagining him perhaps on one of the motorcycle escapades he has written of. And maybe, at first, North Africa really *does* feel better to Dave than bombed-out England. For one thing, it looks a lot like eastern Oregon with brush covering the dry brown hills. Though the huge invasion is a logistical nightmare and most of the soldiers are sleeping on the ground, the Americans are initially upbeat; censors tell journalist Ernie Pyle that many of the boys are writing their folks that they expected to be home by April.[1] But the picnic soon ends, and it becomes clear that nobody will be going home any time soon.

Though the men on the ground could not know, the desperate fight in North Africa was to be a crucial early harbinger of Allied success. It is here, Rick Atkinson writes, that "Allied soldiers figured out, tactically, how to destroy Germans; where the fable of the Third Reich's invincibility dissolved."[2] For this to happen, however, it was necessary for American soldiers to become "killing mad." North Africa is "where the hard truth about combat was first revealed to many" and, through them, to the folks at home. One soldier writes to his mother, "It is a very, very horrible war, dirty and dishonest, not at all that glamour war that we read about in the hometown papers. . . . For myself and the other men here, we will show no mercy. We have seen too much for that."[3]

For Dave too, the true horror is beginning. On December 14, Eva gets a letter with a New York City postmark and the inside address "Somewhere." Dave will soon be on the move, he writes, though the place he gives as his destination has been snipped out by the censor leaving a neat rectangular hole. He makes an effort to comment on her news from home but writes, "Home seems unreal." Then there is a gap in communication. In March, Dave writes that he has gotten a package from Eva. She has sent food, a wallet, her picture, and a "little blue string." The last has sentimental implications that Dave seems to understand. The guys "fell on the food," he reports, and the censor has allowed the comment "What we get at the front isn't much." Also included in the package was some religious literature, contributed by Grace, something about putting faith in God in difficult times.

"There's no God over here," Dave writes.

By April he's still at the front. He can't tell her much though he "has permission to say" that he sleeps in a foxhole and that the food is warm. His letters now seem to veer seriously off-kilter. A long, rather peculiar discussion of the respective merits of the private letter versus V-mail is followed by the information that he has to burn all of her letters after he reads them as "anything found on me would tell the enemy something."

He describes beautiful African sunsets, then adds, "But even the wrath of man is beautiful to behold. Can you imagine the quiet of the night being torn asunder by the screams of a broken woman and suddenly hear the whistle screech of flying bits of metal and have the world lighted up briefly as light as day?"

Enclosed in this letter are cartoons that, while not terribly racy, are still impossible to imagine Dave sharing with a nicely raised girl like Eva a year earlier. In one a G.I. and a woman whose coloring and dress would appear to depict her as a North African European are discovered reclining under a palm tree by a sergeant who, with a leer, asks the G.I., "Wilt thou, Omar, report for KP?" In the margin Dave has written, "It's a lie! Haven't seen a white woman in months."

Another cartoon torn from *Yank* magazine shows a soldier on leave back home. He is sitting on a couch with a young American beauty in an impossibly low-cut evening gown. As the soldier grins and runs his finger under his shirt collar, the girl asks eagerly, "Now that you're home on furlough, what would you *really* like to do?" In the margin, Dave has written, "OH BOY!"

By May, Tunis is captured, and the Axis soldiers have been driven out of North Africa. Dave doesn't tell Eva about the battle for Hill 609, which he has participated in and which will soon bedevil his dreams, but describes the Americans parading through the city to the cheers of the people. The men, he writes, had "lumps in their throats" to realize they had brought freedom. "Whatever the cost, it's worth it."

In addition to hearing from Dave, Eva hears from his father, who provides a running commentary on what Dave's mood seems to be. Sometimes Mr. and Mrs. Johnson worry that he seems very troubled; other times they write that he now seems "more normal." Often they have not heard from him for some time and write to ask whether Eva has. Eva must be very busy with the harvest, they write; they know that it is nearly impossible to get help. Still, they are encouraged that "things look a lot better than they did at this time a year ago."

For his part, Dave hears so much from his folks about how much they love Eva that he's "jealous."

Eva was only seventeen when she and Dave began to date, and judging from the complaints in his letters from down on Snake River, it seems as if he was lot crazier about her than she him. But once the war is on and Dave is in such terrible danger, Eva does what women all over the world are doing: she turns what may have been a childish romance or even a casual acquaintance into a commitment.

At this time, as a woman named Dellie Hahne told Studs Terkel, there was immense pressure to marry a soldier. "That women married soldiers and sent them overseas happy was hammered at us," she remembers. "We had plays on the radio, short stories in magazines, and the movies, which were a tremendous influence in our lives." In these stories it did not take that much for a couple to decide they were meant for each other. "The central theme was the girl meets the soldier, and after a weekend of acquaintanceship they get married and overcome all difficulties."

The pressure was so immense that Hahne didn't even think to question it. So she married a man she "really didn't care" for, reasoning that she had to marry a soldier so she "might as well marry him."[4]

Eva too, it seems, understands what her role is now: she is the girl who is waiting at home for Dave. And this is who she dutifully tries to become. By August, Dave's responses show that Eva has been asking why he can't come home on furlough to get married. Other men have been home on leave. So many are getting married. Still in North Africa, he writes back, telling Eva of his excitement at seeing a Roman aqueduct and getting a glimpse of the "ancient world." He assures her that he hasn't stopped loving her but he's "changed a lot," and many of the "things you liked are gone." Still, he writes, he is sure that when he returns, she will "transform him back to normal life."

But not yet. He doesn't want to come home on leave until "the show is over." Eva, at home with her parents on the farm, will need to keep waiting.

༄ By autumn of 1943, Dave has taken part in the Allied invasion of Italy, describing the Italians he has met behind the lines as "helpful" and "emotional," sometimes offering the GIs lemons. He is smoking four packs a day, he mentions. All the guys are. Also, he can't send her the picture she has asked for. "Those of us in combat don't want our picture taken," he writes. He doesn't explain why this is so, and one can only speculate that their lives have become so hellish and they themselves so transformed that they know not to send evidence of their state to those at home.[5] In another letter from Italy, he "confesses" that he's become an engineer–tail gunner. He describes the beauty of the clouds and rainbows and also the "black roses" of anti-aircraft fire. He wants to keep "a finger in the war," he writes, his "trigger finger."

Still, he assures Eva, "as much as I love combat, I love you more."

It's hard to imagine that Eva is not frightened by what she reads. Dave's letters, with their references to the "beauty" of violence, are really quite alarming. Eva is surely struggling to comprehend the horrors he has been going through, and at the same time trying to hold in her head the picture of the boy she had known. This is her duty. It must have been difficult to grasp why he doesn't want to come home for a visit, and yes, why he can't see that, during her long wait, she needs a bit more reassurance that he really is her future.

But Dave refuses to come home.

1943 ⁓ "One Woman Can Shorten This War"

More than a year has passed since the pioneering Oregon survey of women's availability for war work. And by now no one, not even a girl as sheltered from the world as Eva, can be unaware of the immense change that has taken place in most women's lives since the war began.

The first steps have been tentative; no one could be sure how the idea of women doing war work would be received. But by now the magnitude of the manpower crisis is frightening, and the government has made it clear that there is only one solution: the country must, absolutely must, "employ women on a scale hitherto unknown."[1] One million women had to be added to the workforce by the end of 1942. And that is just the beginning. The expansion of war production is expected to bring in four million more women in 1943.[2] Some employers are still reluctant. But the Office of War Information has launched a massive PR campaign, making it clear that employers *will* change their minds because it is their patriotic duty to do so. The title of one War Department publication states the situation as unambiguously as possible: "You're Going to Employ Women."[3]

It isn't just employers who have to be convinced, however. Not surprisingly, some of America's men are slow to go along with the new idea. A 1943 Gallup poll showed that only 30 percent of husbands gave "unqualified support to the idea of their wives working in industrial war jobs."[4] Meanwhile, a *Ladies' Home Journal* poll revealed that 20 percent of working wives did not have their husbands' approval.[5] To counteract these attitudes, government propaganda urges men to encourage their wives and sweethearts to work. One recruiting poster shows a husband and wife standing in front of the flag. The wife states, "I'm proud ... my husband *wants* me to do my part."[6]

What may come as more of a surprise than the hesitation of men, however, is the fact that women themselves are not at all certain about venturing into previously all-male spheres. Having lived through an era during which it was considered particularly unseemly for women to work, many find it hard to believe they are really wanted.[7] As the government acknowledges, "getting these women into industry is a tremendous sales proposition."[8] And the women who are the focus of the sales pitch are an especially difficult group to persuade. They are not women who already work; the government wants these to stay where they are. Rather the campaign seeks to recruit women who have not worked outside the home before, who probably have never even considered it. Women like Eva.

To help make the sale, the Office of War Information organizes a propaganda blitz, making the recruitment of these stay-at-home women a priority campaign. Utilizing various agencies, the government goes to work with advertisers, magazine editors, and writers to produce ad copy, articles, and short stories that favorably portray women working in the war effort. While the propaganda strategies of the advertising industry are particularly "blatant," Maureen Honey writes, the writers, publishers, and editors in these campaigns are also fully on board.[9]

To provide tips to writers and editors on how these favorable portrayals could be created, the Magazine Bureau puts out a monthly Magazine War Guide. One such tip suggests an article on "what single women should dream about," which could include observations such as "the young woman does not regard marriage as her only career in wartime. She stays in business circulation," knowing that "her country needs her brains and skill." In magazine fiction, it is suggested, villains could be shown as "characters who selfishly thought only of their own troubles and failed to share their skills, resources, and energies with others."[10]

Soon attractive images of working women are everywhere. Material has been prepared for a variety of markets: romance magazines, confession magazines, rural newspapers, even church newsletters.[11] And, of course, stories about the new women workers are seen in most mass market magazines.

A clear target of such a campaign would be mothers like Grace. She is, above all else, a careful, respectable woman: war or no war, never would she have gone along with the idea of her daughter associating with low people in dingy surroundings. Like others of the time, Grace probably has held the view that it is generally a lower sort of woman who goes out to jobs. And Norman Rockwell's drawing of a brawny Rosie the Riveter on the cover of the *Saturday Evening Post*—the denim-covered thighs immense; the forearms muscular as a welterweight's—would not have helped. Indeed, Grace would have been horrified: Who would allow their ladylike daughter to go near such a creature?[12]

But the government is working hard to sell a different image, and in the October *Ladies' Home Journal*, a magazine Grace relies upon her entire life, she would have learned that the new working women are not really burly, tough, and man-like. Nor do they bear any similarity to the mistreated and underpaid factory girls she may have heard about. Rather, the article declares, these young women are healthy and clean cut; they look more like college girls than factory workers.[13]

A new book out—written by a young woman reporter who went into a factory undercover—reinforces this point: "A factory girl in real life . . . buys many of her clothes in the better stores, pays more for her permanent than you do, wears leg make-up and play shoes as glamorous as any you see in *Harper's Bazaar*."[14]

But there's more to war work than factories. A book called *Wartime Jobs for Girls* describes all the "fascinating" and important jobs that even teenagers, years younger than Eva, can do. Girls are needed almost everywhere in such positions as telegraph operators, train attendants, office workers, and department store clerks.

Given the attitudes of the past, there is, not surprisingly, concern about what all this will mean for the future. Already the question has been raised: Will women return to their traditional roles? Or will working women constitute "a threat to the cohesion and sanity of social life"?[15] But in these publications for young women— publications that are clearly part of the government campaign to get women into the workplace—the caveat that they will return home is muted if present at all. Rather, the girls, many of whom have known Depression era privation, are told that their war work "may be the beginning of a highly successful and satisfying career in a field that in postwar days is certain to expand."[16]

That the new workplaces are appropriate for nice girls—that they are even glamorous and fun—is clearly an important part of the message the government wants delivered. But another, more urgent theme would be even harder for women like Grace and Eva to ignore: men will die without the proper equipment. Women owe it to their brothers and sweethearts to keep the war plants churning out ships, airplanes, and tanks.

No, it is clear what any decent woman must do. And the ads and articles go beyond exhortation: they show women responding. One cosmetics ad pictures a young woman in a nightdress, sitting on her bed. It's a cozy, girl's room with frilly curtains and a glowing bedside lamp. Here all is peace and calm; nothing seems to have changed. But on her night table is the photo of a young soldier, her sweetheart perhaps, or her brother. As she does up her hair, her expression is thoughtful. We understand that she's making up her mind to leave the comfort of her home and do her part, maybe first thing in the morning. The caption, no doubt, reflects her thoughts: "One woman can shorten this war!"[17]

Eva's patriotic duty seems clear. Why should she be different from every other girl in the country? But if she remains home, she truly *will* be different. Though she probably does not realize it, most of the unmarried women in the country at this time are already working in the war effort.[18] Too, she is approaching her twenty-first birthday. She has waited at home for three years. She has got to feel—and Grace may have come to agree—that she needs something more in her life than the increasingly unsettling letters from the front lines.

So in September of 1943, Eva writes Dave that she might try to join the WAACS or to do some other war work. He writes back angrily. He is "very browned off" at the idea. The women's services are absolutely out; he has seen in North Africa what that "does for a woman." And he doesn't want her in some dirty factory either. Eva does not need to do war work, Dave insists even more fervently in a second letter. Rather, here is what she needs to do, not only for his peace of mind but also, it seems, if she wants to count on him coming back to her. "Eva, just stay where you are. Do what you have been doing and then tell me about it. Darling, this is the greatest thing you could do to keep me in the mood that when all this is finished, I'll have something clean, wholesome, and worthwhile to return to. Something that missed direct contact of war."

This letter is sent to Wing Valley as always, but by the time it arrives, Eva is no longer there. Grace forwards the letter to war-boom Portland, where Eva, despite Dave's wishes, has gotten a job in a VA hospital and will at last come into "direct contact" with the war.

Sometime in the early winter of December 1956, Virgil "Vick" Vickers packs his bags and leaves the house on Alberta Street in northeast Portland, where he has been living. It is a modest neighborhood but pleasant enough; many of the houses have covered front porches where one can sit and watch the gentle, incessant rain.

However enjoyable life may have been in Portland, though, the time has come for Vick to leave, and we know that he gets into his new red Ford and heads for Boise. We know too that the ironed-out, multilane, interstate freeway system won't be finished for another ten years and that to get from Portland to Boise Vick has to head east on old Highway 30. Today, if you are in a hurry to make this trip, you can put yourself in a hypnotic trance, stop for gas and coffee a couple of times, and, averaging about seventy-five miles an hour, hit Boise seven hours later. But in 1956, Vick has a much more involved journey ahead of him. For one thing, the old highway is only two lanes, slow and twisty, traipsing through every main street of every little town along the way. Then too, in the winter, the road can be treacherous, particularly when you reach Cabbage Hill, a stretch that takes you precipitously up into the Blue Mountains east of Pendleton. Because many of the east-bound drivers have just emerged from the mild rain and warm temperatures of Portland and are hitting the snowy mountains for the first time, they sometimes don't realize quickly enough that driving conditions have changed. You can see some nasty wrecks, as drivers lose control and spin sideways into oncoming traffic.

Whichever way you are going, the Blue Mountains have always commanded respect. To the immigrants struggling west on the Oregon Trail they represented a last fearsome ordeal, a final barrier standing between them and the mild, green promised land of the Willamette Valley. But Vick probably isn't thinking about exhausted families wrangling their wagons through the snowy passes. For one thing, unlike Eva, he's not a descendent of pioneers who came to Oregon by wagon train; he has no grandfather to imagine passing this way. For another thing, he's probably somewhat preoccupied with getting out of the state, just in case things back in Portland might be moving a little more rapidly than usual.

Even though he's in a hurry, however, I doubt that he makes it to Boise in one haul. So I would imagine he probably has to make a stop, maybe in Pendleton, the logical halfway point. Too, he's probably heard Pendleton is a fun little town, livelier than other burgs along the way, thanks primarily to the Pendleton Roundup. Then as now, the Roundup is famous in the Northwest and brings in a lot of visitors. As a result, the town feels somewhat festive year round, its tavern walls covered with old black-and-white photographs of bucking broncs and cowboys in wide chaps and beat-up hats.

Not that Vick is the type of guy to care about rodeos or other old-timey stuff. But he likes a town with a bit of nightlife, and Pendleton might be okay for a stopover. Only one night, though, and don't go getting ideas. Vick would not want to spend very long in a spot like this.

In fact, it's somewhat out of character for him to head this far out into the sticks. Not only is it a couple of days' drive to Boise through mostly empty country, but even when he gets there he isn't going to find the bustle of the bigger coastal cities Portland, Seattle, L.A — that he seems to enjoy. The 1930s art deco hotel notwithstanding, Boise's nightlife is known primarily for its nonexistence. Writing about the town in the midfifties, for example, an East Coast author can barely conceal his exasperation at Boise's dullness. "Compared to Portland . . . Boise was the stuffiest, deadest town in the Northwest—and Portland is no super hot spot. Most of Boise's sidewalks were asleep by seven at night. . . . There was no legalized peep show, no movies, no swinging night clubs. . . . Boise was no place to let off steam."

Vick surely had other options. From Portland, he could easily have headed north to Seattle or south to California, where he knows several areas quite well. But there are complications in California, and maybe he's tired of the rain in the Northwest. And so, whatever is drawing Vick to Boise, he arrives in mid-December and, as I see in Eva's notes, rents a room in the home of Mrs. Elsie Denton on Idaho

Street. It's another modest neighborhood, the one- and two-story houses separated by narrow alleys. Today, some of the houses are a bit scruffy, and the patches of lawn can tend toward weediness. The little blue house where Vick finds a room is small, obviously not built for boarders. Mrs. Denton would've had to have Vick sleeping in the bedroom next to hers and undoubtedly they share a bathroom.

I don't always trust the information Eva thinks she has about Vick. But the Idaho Street address makes sense when I visit Boise and start driving around. I see that the little blue house is around the corner from the Torch Café, where, as Vick's bank book shows, he cashed all those five- and ten-dollar checks when he first hit town.

By coincidence, I know the Torch Café quite well as I once wait-ressed there for a couple of weeks on the 7 P.M. to 3 A.M. shift. This was during my traveling hippie period, twenty years after Vick had been a regular there. Still, the place I knew—seedy if not a total dive—didn't look as if it had undergone any recent changes. Out front was a big pink neon sign advertising the Torch as the "Home of the Original Finger Steaks." In the kitchen was the owner, a silent, end-lessly working Greek, who, when he wasn't slamming out platters of onion rings and deep-fried steak strips, was swabbing out the greasy kitchen that never really got clean. I remember we got a big rush around 10:30 or so, about the time respectable places were closing. It was couples mostly, cuddling and smooching. Already looped. Lousy tippers. Rowdy but within limits: a no-nonsense woman named Pam kept an eye on things from behind the bar, and those who crossed a certain line would be taking their finger steaks home in a bag.

Today the Torch looks about the same, though it seems to have given in to its true low-rent nature and turned into a strip club. When I drive by in the middle of the afternoon, a fat bouncer in a Hawai-ian shirt regards me from the doorway. Boise, I guess, has progressed when it comes to nightlife. But in 1956, hot, greasy finger steaks, forty-cent well drinks, and a place that served until three in the morning was probably about as racy as it got.

Vick seems to have felt comfortable enough in a joint like the Torch to use it as a hangout; but for work, he prefers the classier establishments. From the paystubs he left behind, I see that it didn't take him long to get on at the Hotel Boise, only nine blocks from the Torch but miles away on the social scale. It is here, in that only-slightly-fading art deco palace, that Eva and Vick will meet.

ও We don't know if Vick is thinking about marriage as he hits town. If he isn't, it would seem that he's just about the only person in America who is not. For since the end of the war, marriage has become an obsession and the source of a surprising amount of cultural handwringing. The movies, of course, depict the desperation of single women, and at a time when the number of single people has shrunk to an all-time low, when people are marrying younger and younger, and when women over twenty-five are considered old maids, the movies appear to reflect a reality. By 1959, almost half of all brides were entering marriage before the age of nineteen.[1]

As Vick arrives in Boise in late December 1956, the topic of marriage is the focus of a glossy, double issue of *Life* magazine, just hitting the stands.[2] The issue, devoted to the American woman, may have caught Vick's eye, if only for the many lavish photo layouts of classy American beauties perched atop thoroughbreds or driving convertibles. Among the photographs and the full-color advertisements for no-iron dress shirts and dishwashers, however, are dozens of articles, all bearing the same stern warning: women must marry and have children. Then, once safely married, they must not let anything distract them from a life focused exclusively on home and family.[3]

The articles do not explore the source of the implied danger; if women are actually threatening to flee the bliss of homemaking, that is not discussed here. But some ill-defined malaise among women is the subtext of all the articles. In one of the pieces, a former Smith College English professor highlights the problem by repeating the question asked of her by an English visitor:

> Whatever is the matter with your American women? Everywhere I went I got the distinct impression that far too many of them are discontented, restive, and even complaining. They seem to me to have just [about] everything that every woman wants . . . beauty and brains, husbands who . . . adore them . . . , more freedom of every sort than any other women in the world . . . [including] opportunities for creative and constructive work.[4]

So why the discontent?

Here, only a decade after the end of World War II, memories are still very much alive, and the next issue of *Life* will commence a three-part series on Pearl Harbor. Surprisingly, however, none of the writers included in this immense issue on women's problems speculates on the possible relationship between the mysterious dissatisfaction now being observed and the changes in American life that occurred during World War II. Nowhere is it pondered whether, having seen themselves managing responsibilities and independence previously thought beyond them, women may as a result be less than entirely content in the confines of home. But if the cause of the woman problem remains a mystery, the remedy is clear and repeated endlessly throughout the issue: women can find happiness *only* in marriage and family.

In one article, for example, a group of psychiatrists has been consulted on the problem. Most echo views found in the widely popularized book *Modern Woman: The Lost Sex.*[5] Brought out immediately after the war, the book asserts that women who seek fulfillment beyond the home inevitably make themselves neurotic. As a result they put their husbands, children, and family on the "brink of emotional disaster."[6] And, perhaps because it's Christmastime, the editors have included an article by a pastor, reminding readers that marriage was present in "the first paradise" and that this is the one "blessing" that God did not take away from the misbehaving first couple.

Though women and the requirement that they focus on the home is the main theme of the issue, it is also absolutely clear that men too must be married. As anthropologist Margaret Mead writes, in America today, no normal man or woman will willingly remain single. While it used to be said that a "woman's place" was "in the home . . . . [Now] everybody's place is in the home" and the "only truly acceptable pattern in American life is marriage." Mead doesn't explain why this is the case or why it is more the case than at other times in history. As an anthropologist, she simply presents these statements as facts: "Bachelors and spinsters are both disapproved of and discriminated against"; and "perennial bachelors are sighed over psychiatrically."[7]

What she probably means but doesn't want to spell out in

a family magazine is that in psychiatric theory of the time, the image of the irresponsible male blurred into the "shadowy figure of the homosexual." As Barbara Ehrenreich writes, "men who didn't marry" were considered either "not fully adult or not fully mascu-line," and it was one view that bachelors over thirty "should undergo psychotherapy."[8]

All the same, the culture does allow men a bit more playfulness on the question of marriage than is granted women, as Vick has surely picked up on. The over-thirty bachelor played by Frank Sinatra in *The Tender Trap*, for example, is not exactly shunned. Instead, hungry single women—all of them beauties—fight for the right to clean his apartment, monogram his shirts, walk his dog. Of course, these good times are only temporary. As the title suggests, Frank has no chance of remaining a bachelor through the end of the movie.

If Vick got a laugh out of Frank and all his women, he may also have gotten a chuckle from an article in *Cosmopolitan* that gives advice on how men can avoid one of the country's twenty million unattached female "predators." One strategy is to head south where men stay single longer. Another tip: choose a windy climate so as not to be felled by perfume. And the author reports on the cost of mar-riage: two can*not* live as cheaply as one. Here too, however, marriage is inevitable and the piece concludes with the author's confession: he has to sign off now to go change his daughter's diaper, play with his sons, and dry dishes for his wife, "the most terrific predatory female ... who ever graced this earth."[9]

❧ It's hard to know whether Vick, arriving in December of 1956, has vowed to avoid "predators" or whether he is looking for some-one whose dishes he can dry. But we do know that he's looking to set himself up here after his hasty exit from Portland. And after hanging around the Torch for awhile, he gets serious and applies for a chef's job at the still-swanky Boise Hotel, which, as it will turn out, is a very nice place to work. The kitchen is in the basement, with the meals dumbwaitered up to the top-floor restaurant. It's an elegant touch you won't find at an ordinary eatery, and one that allows the cooks to sweat and curse without being glimpsed by the customers or by the pretty waitresses and hostesses. Another nice touch is that the hotel has fitted up showers and lockers for the staff. Vick can just drop his dirty work clothes in a hamper and step into the shower; none of the smell and grease of the kitchen ever need accompany him to the gracious floors above.

As a chef, Vick would be one of the first to go off shift in the evening, leaving helpers to tackle the mess in the kitchen. If he hurries, he can be cleaned up, changed into slacks and a sports coat, and riding the elevator up to the main floor before Eva has closed down her cigar stand. And after the evening's work, Vick could well be out of cigarettes.

Seeing him chatting with Eva under the warm lights, his thick, dark hair still a little damp and gleaming with newly applied Brylcreem, no one, I'm quite sure, would have taken him for a native Idahoan. Maybe it's just his dark coloring in a region of blue-eyed dishwater blonds. Maybe it's a hint of urbanity in his dress, the just-right touches that the legislators in from Idaho Falls will never quite master: the gleaming shirt collar peeking the perfect third of an inch over the well-cut sports coat, the artfully casual pocket handkerchief. Maybe too—as he and Eva sit together over their first drink—something about the look in his eye sets him apart from the other men in the bar, something intense, not easily read.

Eva and Vick, single at thirty-five and forty-three, cannot help but be aware that they are distinct oddities in marriage-mad America. What's more, neither is living the life that everyone is supposed to want. Neither has more than a couple of hundred bucks in the bank, and both live in cheap rented rooms where there are no color TVs, dishwashers, or even a complete set of dishes. But when they meet in the glamorous lobby of the Hotel Boise, it must feel as if they have come in at the end of a classic fifties movie: after a lot of confusion and crazy mix-ups, even some real tragedy and grief, the sweet, lovely girl and the handsome, true-hearted guy find each other at last.

And Eva—who has been through so much—has got to be thinking, Finally.

Finally.

1943 ∞ Shipbuilding Boomtown, Portland

When, in late 1943, Eva gets on the train to Portland, she is taking part in what will be the greatest internal migration in American history.[1] Before the war is over, approximately twenty million Americans will have left home to take up war work and by 1945, more than fifteen million will be living somewhere other than where they were when the news of Pearl Harbor broke. And though major war production centers are located all around the country, the biggest pull is to the West Coast, where nearly half the wartime shipbuilding and airplane manufacture is taking place.[2]

What Eva finds when she arrives in Portland that November is a bursting-at-the-seams boomtown. The city has been completely transformed from three years earlier; and by the war's peak, the population will have grown from 300,000 to half a million, with 190,000 employed in area shipyards.[3] Most work in the three shipyards at the mouth of the Columbia, recently thrown up by the nation's leading shipbuilder, Henry Kaiser, a man whom the *New York Times* has called the Paul Bunyan of the Twentieth Century[4] and whom others called Sir Launchalot.[5] In these yards, hundreds of the emergency cargo vessels called Liberty Ships, as well as tankers and other vessels, will be built by crews on round-the-clock shifts, outfits that repeatedly break their own astonishing records for production time.

Of these workers, one quarter will be women.[6]

Crowded as it is in 1943, Portland expects even more people to arrive soon. Just as Eva hits town a front page article in the *Oregonian* reports that the "already teeming and humanity-jammed" city can expect "even more hectic days." While there is cautious optimism by late 1943 that the war in Europe will be won fairly soon, a long, bloody conflict with Japan is feared. So the demand for labor has in no way abated, and shipyards continue to send recruiters all over the country; sometimes they even charter trains to bring workers to the West Coast.[7] Portlanders, an article in the *Oregonian* reports, can expect thousands more to arrive as a result of the stepped-up war in the Pacific.[8]

By now the skepticism about women joining the industrial workforce seems to belong to a barely imaginable past. Now, the topsy-turvy nature of the times is mostly good for a laugh. In an *Oregonian* cartoon, for example, a burly short-order chef muses, "The boss will sure be in a fix when I'm called up! He might even have to get a woman to do the cooking!"[9]

In the newspapers and magazines too, the tone has shifted; the dire, sometimes near-mystical references to sacrifice and loss from earlier in the war are seldom seen. And now that women working is an everyday thing, it is permissible to show them having a pretty swell time. In a cigarette ad, for example, a perky shipyard worker with a pompadour hairdo, bright lipstick, and a fitted, plaid shirt holds a lit cigarette as she declares, "Camels have a grand flavor and they don't get my throat."

Even the new fashions suggest that it's okay to be a bit more light-hearted. Rationing has meant the end of the long, pleated skirts worn before the war, and now advertisements are showing trim new dress styles that barely cover the knee. Often the new longer leg ends in an open-toed pump. Compared to the clothes in the ads, the floppy dresses worn by older woman pictured on the society pages look hopelessly dowdy.

With so much going on, wartime Portland has got to be tremendously thrilling for a newcomer who is young and pretty and who has sat out three years of war on an isolated farm, waiting for a guy she's not sure she knows any more. And as if to celebrate Eva's arrival, dim-out restrictions have just been eased: in dark and rainy November, everyone is exhilarated to see the neon signs and movie marquees flash back on.

Grace has been busy contacting friends of friends in Portland, trying to find a place for Eva to stay. But Eva, who immediately goes to work in the kitchen of a VA hospital, seems to have no trouble finding housing in a government facility; and the shopping list she jots on the back of an envelope—"plain stationery, air mail stationery, soap dish, anklets, slip, face powder"—shows that she is busy getting up to speed in her new life.

The first letters Eva receives in Portland are from Grace. To my surprise, they contain none of the worry and anxiety that so characterized the woman I knew in later years. Rather, she has perfect faith in her sweet, good girl and is doing everything she can to see that Eva has what she needs for this adventure. Grace writes that she is mailing the mirror and clock Eva forgot to pack. Also she's sending Eva's ration book, though, if Eva doesn't need her ration of sugar, she might send the coupons back; Grace could use the extra when it comes time to put up fruit.

In these first letters, Grace's thoughts and instructions are a study of maternal care and also of the self-sufficient ways of country people.

I washed your white satin blouse. It wasn't very dirty but was a little circled under the arms and the cuffs were dingy. Those new slips came & I thought they looked too wide thru the middle so seamed out some, didn't know whether they would be short enough or not, so hemmed one up a bit and left the other so maybe one or the other will be so you can wear it at once. I sewed with a long stitch so it won't be hard to take out if necessary. Be careful about pressing your new dotted blouse, a hot iron will draw and ruin it. Write and let me know how your clothes arrive. Do you want that green spring dress finished? Your print dresses are getting old and may not last much longer; of course, you may find something ready-made down there, let me know.

Eva is also getting letters from her father, Wes, the son of Cornish tin miners who found their way to a gold mine in the mountains not far from Wing Valley. His letters are sweet and funny, addressed in a loopy, old-fashioned script to "my dear little Sweetheart." He provides a humorous counterweight to Grace's bustling concern. His report is mostly about what's going on outdoors: there's a new calf, there seems to be a new nest in the pear tree, and Eva's "lambies" keep asking for her.

If Wes's letters cover the doings of the animals, Grace's letters keep Eva up to date on news from the Valley's church community. This homogeneous little community is surprisingly vexing for Grace, a descendant of Huguenots and a stout Methodist, who does not hold a high opinion of other denominations. Catholics, she believes, go to Hell, as does anyone who marries a Catholic. This terrible fate befell

Belle, one of Grace's cousins and her best friend in the Valley. Belle's religion does not stop the friendship; nor does the friendship stop Grace's disapproval.

Few Catholics live in the Valley; but there are several other protestant congregations, and these too have practices that trouble Grace. She strongly disapproves, for example, of the United Christian Church's baptisms: showy immersions, rather than the dignified "sprinkling" that the Methodists practice. Even so, her life has always revolved around home and church. And now with her children away, she keeps busy attending as many church events around the Valley as possible. The previous Sunday, she recounts for Eva, she went on to the United Christian church after Methodist services but had a disappointment. "Sure wish we had gotten there a little earlier for we just missed a wedding that they had between Sunday School and church."

Something that appears to come as a shock to Eva, as it must have for many women war workers, is her sudden, astonishing ability to make money, good money, better money than many Depression-era families have ever seen. Only a few years earlier, Eva's brother Aub bucked bails all day for a dollar. Now even unskilled war workers are making ninety cents an hour.

Eva, as if unsettled by her new riches, sends most of her first paycheck home in the form of war bonds. Everyone is being urged to buy bonds. Also, she writes, she wants to repay her folks "for all they've done." Naturally, they immediately reply that she doesn't owe them a thing. Wes writes,

> Mom said the reason you was sending the bonds was that you was going to pay back something you think you owe. Don't do it. We are satisfied by having a big lovely sweet girl. That is our pay for all the terrible heartaches, troubles, and money [Wes habitually uses a light underline to signal humorous remarks] and all the things that goes into fetching up kids. Now the next bond you buy you had better have your name put on cause you are going to need it when the kids start coming and not a bone in the pantry.

Still, with her next check Eva sends Wes ten dollars to buy a new hat. But Grace has told him, "You don't have to spend $10 on a hat, get a belt too." Wes writes Eva for instructions. When somebody wants to buy him a "ten gal hat," he hates to say no. But "in order to keep the old Farm running smoothly I will surely have to buy a belt to match the hat. What say you?"

Within a month Eva writes the folks that she has gotten a promotion and a "chevron" on her sleeve. Grace writes back to say how proud they are and passes on the comment someone has made at church: "That girl has ability!"

Eva is also getting letters from her brother, Aub, who is still stationed in Texas. Aub, who has been in the service for several years, probably has a better idea of what is going on in wartime Portland than Wes and Grace. But he seems to understand that everyone needs to do war work now. He is sure Eva will be fine and is glad for her to have some fun. "So you are planning a pretty busy social life," he writes. "Guess it will seem pretty lively after the Valley, and I think it will be great for you."

Like Eva, Aub was raised in a home where cards and dancing were frowned on, where no woman smoked, and where any form of liquor was viewed with an equal mixture of hatred and terror. This last was due partly to religious principle, partly to the whispered legend that drink played a role in the downfall of Grace's prominent pioneer father. Now, in what seems to be a response to a question from Eva—and perhaps in the attempt to set a good example for his little sis—Aub writes that, no, he doesn't "care much for drinking and smoking," no more than he ever did.

As Eva settles in, her social life is indeed busy. She is receiving seven letters a day from different men, she writes Grace, and has recently been given gifts of chocolates and flowers. Grace cannot help but be proud that her pretty daughter is a success. "Our little girl always manages with the fellows, don't she. Or rather they always come without any managing." In the next letter Grace comments on more triumphs. "Well, Honey, I think it was very nice for you to be invited out to that home for dinner. You always seem to have luck in this soldier business, so of course you would get the 1st Lt. Sometime when you don't have anything to do, you can tell me what you had to eat."

A few days later Eva writes that she has gone to a Methodist church, which Grace is glad to hear though she still can't quite imagine Eva alone in the big city. "Sometimes wonder how you find your way & if you should even go to church alone." Well, it seems Eva had an escort, even to church. In the next letter Grace writes, "You said you were with the Englishman that afternoon. How come he is in Portland? Was he a patient at the hospital?"

Grace has been trying to "remember the names of the different fellows you mention but I believe I'll just give it up for there is always a different one. Where did you meet Joe?" And for the first time a hint of concern about Eva's new life creeps in. "I am glad you are having a nice time, but do be careful not to be out until you won't get enough rest. I'm glad you are being careful about who you go out with."

Like many other women of the time, Grace and Eva have not experienced life beyond the confines of their home and small community. They were, of course, precisely the sort of women whose attitudes toward work had to be changed if the manpower challenge was to be met. But while Grace and Eva have been persuaded that it is time for Eva to help in the war effort, little has prepared them to understand the situation she will face in war-boom Portland. At home, for example, her parents knew all the boys, probably knew their parents and their grandparents. Even so, the fellows, if they wanted to take Eva to a dance or a picnic, would, as a matter of course, present themselves at her home, hair slicked down, to be inspected by her mother and subtly warned by her father.

Now, of course, there are no parents or any other adults to vet the fellows vying to take Eva out every night. Now, too, it is a fine line that young women are expected to walk, between traditional morals and the widely understood patriotic obligation to help the boys have a good time before they ship out, some to their deaths. It is a complicated situation and one that has come to the attention of the advice columnist in the *Oregonian*. She warns the young women filling the city. "Don't let the men get the idea they can't trust the girls they left behind. Keep the faith with them, girls. Have a good time without regrets. Stepping around to parties isn't what you live for, is it?"[10]

Though Grace is a bit worried about how much Eva goes out, her concerns seem to be more for Eva's health and safety than that her activities could jeopardize the engagement to Dave Johnson. There's a war on. The young people are under a lot of strain and need to have a good time. Dave too, as I suppose Grace may be worldly enough to understand, has no doubt had other girls during the years he's been away, perhaps even girls who are more than dancing partners. Indeed, this topic has been taken up, carefully, in Grace's trusted *Ladies' Home Journal.* The good American boy, readers are assured, never confuses the girls he might "'liberate' in Italy or France, with the real girl waiting back home."[11] As is repeated constantly, many things will be different "for the duration."

As for Dave, his letters from Italy continue to arrive in Wing Valley, to be forwarded to Eva in Portland. The war in Italy is ugly, Dave reports. The Germans are killing prisoners and making sniper nests of farmhouses. He writes, "We call the Germans 'Krauts' now. 'Jerry' sounds too much like a friend."

"Remember me?" he asks. "I'm the guy in love with a girl he hasn't seen in four years."

I don't know if Eva has shrunk from telling Dave that she has disobeyed him by leaving the farm, that she cannot fulfill his need for her to remain the one thing "untouched by war." Perhaps she's been too busy. Perhaps their letters have crossed. But by the end of February he has heard from her, and an icily casual letter from "somewhere in Italy" arrives at her residence in Portland. He writes, "Life has been rather uneventful of late. I've had a bad cold—there has been little flying for me because of that but I continue to enjoy myself no matter what the circumstances may be."

By now, he writes, she has probably received his previous letter in which he mentioned love and such:

I do manage this type of affair from time to time. I mailed it to your home, not knowing that you had moved to Portland. Your telling about visiting the fellows around Portland was interesting, but to be honest about the whole thing—I hardly recognize any of the names.

Then,

Frankly Eva, I wish that you would try to forget me. I think that would be much better for you. After all, I do like to run around and chase my excitement around the world. I think that is damned good advice myself and it may save you heart break later on.

Casually, he mentions that he's volunteering for a near-suicidal, low-level bombing unit. The implication seems clear. Without her waiting at home, he has nothing in particular to live for. This letter is followed by an urgent one from Dave's parents, who, to their dismay, have also been informed that the engagement is off. Dave, they urge Eva to understand, is not himself at present. They've tried to help, tried to explain to him that at home now everyone feels it is a duty to do war work. Eva is only doing what every patriotic American girl is doing: helping win the war and bring Dave and the other boys home. The only result of their intervention: now he's furious at them too.

It won't be until June that Dave is heard from again, this time writing to Grace from Corsica. Even before I read the letter, I can tell something is very wrong: his handwriting slashes so crazily to the right that the letters are almost lying on their sides.

What he must tell Grace is that he's cracking up. He has begun to relive all the horrible experiences, the bombing of Bath, the bloody battle for Hill 609 in Tunisia, other things he doesn't want to mention even now. He sleeps only when they give him pills or if—and he knows how this will shock Grace—he drinks himself unconscious. He hasn't been grounded yet, but he is to appear before an examining board and knows it will pronounce that he has had a "mental and physical breakdown."

He begs Grace not to tell any one. He doesn't write his own parents because "what they don't know won't hurt them." He doesn't write to Eva because she is "too loyal." But he had to tell someone, someone who is "near" to him. He also wants Grace to understand that he still loves Eva and that he has "never done anything to make her ashamed." But he can't come back to Eva this way, he writes, and he doesn't know if he'll ever be well again.

In February of 1957 Grace got a letter from Eva saying that she was engaged to be married. It was a man she had met only recently through work; she loved him terribly and he loved her. Neither of them could wait to marry, so they had planned a ceremony for the next month. The marriage would take place, of course, in a Methodist church, with a reception to follow in the Hotel Boise. In addition to Grace, Aub and his wife had been invited. And Eva wanted me to be the flower girl; if Grace would like to make my dress, Eva would send the material. She was thinking of a rose-colored taffeta.

I don't remember whether Grace was happy or worried. Probably she was worried; but then, as it seemed to me, she was always worried about something. I, of course, was thrilled that I would be the flower girl in a rose-colored dress. In my excitement, it probably didn't occur to me that this would mean the end of my visits to the bachelor-girl apartment and my evenings at the cigar stand.

Naturally Vick had to be brought home to meet Grace before they married, and since the wedding was to be so soon, they were planning to drive over the following Sunday for dinner. This threw Grace into a tizzy of preparation, even though she was going to serve the same fried chicken, mashed potatoes, white gravy, coleslaw, lemon cream pie dinner that she always made for company. When the day came, she was in such a fizz about getting everything just right, the table set with her wedding china and her good silver, that— shockingly—she didn't go to church.

Aub and his wife had driven over from Baker, where Aub was running a feedlot. Now they were sitting calmly in Grace's living room, demonstrating how relaxed *they* were. I, the flower girl, was invited too, and I too tried to act nonchalant. But Grace didn't even try, clicking back and forth from the dining room to the kitchen in her stack-heel church shoes, fussing over the table and the gravy and how everything looked, irritated at all of us for no reason that was clear.

Finally they drove up. A tall, dark man got out of the car, but, as we all gaped in puzzlement, Eva remained inside. Without acknowledging us watching from the doorway, Vick solemnly walked around the front of the car to open Eva's door and to help her step out. I remember pondering this. It seemed stupid for Eva to just sit there and wait for him to walk around and open her door. I'd seen plenty of grown couples get out of cars, and the women always opened the door and got out by themselves. Still I was fascinated. I wondered if this was what they did in cities, whether someday *I* would sit in a car and wait for *my* fiancé to walk around and open the door.

Another thing I remember is what Vick was wearing, city clothes of a sort we seldom saw: a yellow knit sport shirt, light tan pants, light beige socks with little clocks embroidered at the ankle bone. Such dress was unheard of in the Valley, where for an occasion like this a man wore new, clean jeans, a nice plaid shirt, his good cowboy boots, and his best belt, possibly with a sterling silver belt buckle in the shape of a horseshoe.

Unheard of, but again it rang a bell. We'd had TV for a couple of years by now, and Vick must have struck me as a living example of the type of modern men we saw in the shows and the commercials. Being of the new modern type, I knew, was important. People wanted to be modern, especially those who had been away from the Valley and seen things during the war. Even my parents wanted to be modern, and they tried to update our forty-year-old farmhouse by getting rid of the front porch, where people used to sit in rocking chairs of an evening. Now the house had a bland, flat front. And they tore out the 1912 bay window and put in a kitchen-breakfast room. Now we had something more like a 1950s "ranch" style house.

Of course, Grace's house still had the porch, the cozy little rooms, and the old-fashioned windows. But Grace was old. She was prewar.

Despite Vick's city clothes, Eva looking as if she might swoon any minute, and the excitement of the wedding that I would be part of, I remember that I was not especially bowled over by Vick. This seems surprising, given what I now know about the devotion he could inspire. And though I was only a little girl, I was already crazy about dark guys for some reason. One of my aunts was married to a black-haired man, and he just sent me. I'm not sure why Vick didn't.

He was nice enough to me, I'm sure, but, looking back, I don't think he must have been especially funny or playful. And I was a kid who was used to being noticed by adults. In the Valley, where families had all known each other for generations, we were all on familiar terms. Women who saw you in the store would ask how you liked baton lessons. Men who came by to talk to your dad would find something to kid you about, usually some boyfriend they were guessing you had.

I don't remember any of that from Vick. Maybe where he came from customs were different. Maybe he had eyes only for Eva. Maybe he didn't want to expend his charm for no good reason. But there *was* one thing about Vick that made an impression. He told us that he had a little daughter that he missed very much. I remember seeing her picture, so he must have been carrying it in his wallet. She was a girl a little older than me, around twelve, her hair in tight pigtails. Close to my own dad, I remember feeling sad that she couldn't see her father for some reason. I can't remember being told where the girl was, what her name was, or why Vick couldn't see her. Looking now at Eva's marriage license, I see that Vick put down that he was widowed; obviously the little daughter could not have been said to be with her mother.

I remember one other thing from that day: how Eva looked, thin as a model in fashionable fanny hugging slacks and a clingy sweater that stretched over the bullet points of a midfifties brassiere. Turning now to Grace's album, I realize how changed she was from the healthy-looking farm girl nestled among her sheep. Something had peeled off twenty pounds and turned Eva into a glamour girl, nearly unrecognizable as a daughter of the Valley.

In early 1944, Eva gets a letter from a girlfriend suggesting that she quit her "gruesome" job at the VA hospital and go to work at one of Portland's shipyards. "I've made a discovery while working there," the friend writes. "Women *are* given complete respect in language and in action. Not only are they respected but men feel no resentment at all—they seem to give them full respect as fellow workers and (though they won't admit it) they think it's fun to have women around to talk to." The friend doesn't know what kind of work Eva could do, but advises that even lowly stock room or janitor work "ain't so lowly at a buck nine an hour."

Eva could not, of course, have missed the fact that the three shipyards here, built by industrialist Henry Kaiser, are a very big deal.[1] Everyone has heard about President Roosevelt's recent visit to one of the yards, Oregon Ship, and has seen the photos of the president's tour. His open car was brought right into the plant, and a hatless, enthralled Roosevelt watched from the passenger seat as a new Liberty ship was launched.[2]

∽ The secret of the Kaiser yards' astonishing rate of production, as most Portlanders know by now, has been the incorporation of assembly-line techniques into shipbuilding.[3] Previously ships had been built from the hull up. When a hull was nearing completion, the deckhouses were added and "swarms of welders, electricians, pipe fitters moved in—getting in each other's way."[4] But now, instead of building the ship from bottom to top, one step at a time, different components are assembled separately and simultaneously, then hauled to the hull, and snapped into place by crews who work around the clock. If a piece such as a deckhouse is too heavy for the cranes to lift, as Kaiser explained to a *New York Times* reporter, workers simply cut it into four pieces, hoist it onto the nearly completed ship, and weld the pieces back together again.[5]

The welding itself is an innovation that not only speeds production but also allows Kaiser to draw from a much larger pool of potential workers. Welders, who can be trained in a specific task relatively quickly, replace journeymen riveters who require a lengthy apprenticeship. This simpler work and faster training has allowed Kaiser to take on the thousands of unskilled workers—many of them women—who have come west looking for war plant jobs.[6]

Thanks to these and other changes, Kaiser has been able to produce ships "at a pace undreamed of" before the war.[7] Though most of the workers never built or even saw a ship before coming here, they repeatedly break their own records for production time. As the war goes on, the average time to deliver a ship, which stood at 355 days in 1940, has been cut to 194 days in 1941. By 1942 the average delivery time is just sixty days.[8]

These ships, writes historian Doris Kearns Goodwin, "along with the outpouring of munitions from American factories," were largely responsible for the "improvement of the military situation" in 1943.[9] Later Winston Churchill will remember, "The foundation of all our hopes and schemes was the immense shipbuilding program in the United States."[10]

So no, nobody in Portland, or indeed anywhere in Oregon, could have missed the presence of the headline-grabbing shipyards and the thrilling role they are playing in winning the war. Nor could Eva have been unaware of the top wages being paid in the shipyards or oblivious to the newspaper and radio ads constantly calling out to women—"We need you!"—and assuring them that the job of winning the war is far from finished.[11] Now Eva's letters show she is indeed considering something that would have been unthinkable a year ago: going to work in a factory.

Shipyards had always been a white-male preserve, and when Roosevelt signed regulations requiring that African American men be hired, protests erupted, particularly in the South. But, as Frederick Lane writes, there was never any real question that black men would be admitted into the shipyards, at least in unskilled work. The introduction of women, however, presented a far more profound and intimate challenge.[12]

Before the war, remembered Dr. Forrest Rieke, who, as Kaiser's chief medical officer, tended physical and emotional problems, women simply did not enter the shipyards, even to keep the books or do other office work. And for many, the idea of women in the yards violated "traditional, deep convictions." While a number of the wartime workers were new to construction, others came from Kaiser dam and pipeline projects in the Southwest, where they had developed "strong convictions about what women's work was, what men's work was." It should be remembered, Rieke told an interviewer, that these men had labored in "hard, isolated areas, where the woman really was busy helping the family survive." In accordance with these beliefs, the career construction men had announced that "the minute a woman came in they were leaving."[13]

Such threats notwithstanding, the unthinkable happens one morning in May of 1942: the first two female welders show up for shipyard work. The men don't walk out, and by September, the dam has broken. Women are now all over the shipyard, and the *Bo's'n's Whistle*, which had previously mocked the very idea of women in the yards, now runs glowing features describing the fine job female workers are doing in a variety of tasks.

As the campaign to get women into all kinds of nontraditional jobs bears fruit, there is wide discussion of just what it will mean for the future. One predictable question: who will take care of the home—the marketing, cooking, and cleaning—if all the women are working in war plants? One predictable solution: have women do the housework when they get off shift. As one female welder ruefully remembers, after a long day at the factory, the responsibility of dinner and dishes fell to her. Meanwhile her brother-in-law, also a factory worker, would "stretch out and listen to jazz records."[14] The problem is compounded by the fact that household duties have become more time consuming. Rationing means standing in lines in the stores, and sometimes everything is closed when women get off shift. Further, with many laundries overwhelmed due to the lack of labor—in Portland it is reported that eighteen tons of unwashed linen has stacked up—sending the dirty clothes out is seldom an option.[15]

The question of how the housework and childcare will be managed is not the only concern. Many are troubled by a more fundamental question: Will women retain their femininity in such an environment? Will they remain attractive with grease under their fingernails and dust in their hair? To address this fear—as well as the real difficulty women have had finding appropriate work clothes in their sizes—Kaiser commissions a fashion designer to create attractive female work attire. A layout of drawings of the new styles in the *Whistle* shows long-legged women in sleek, shiny jumpsuits. The women in the drawings all seem to have twenty-two-inch waists and legs half again the normal length and, it must be said, bear little resemblance to the women I find in actual shipyard photographs.[16] Dressed for long days in Portland's damp chill, the real women are lumpy in thick pants and heavy jackets, their hair tied up in scarves.

Assuming that women, somehow, do somehow manage to dress attractively and to retain their feminine charm raises another question. How will they fend off shipyard "wolves"? The question is put to shipyard women by an inquiring *Whistle* reporter. The verdict: "Women get no more than they invite."[17] This response, though comforting in a way, speaks to another fear, less openly discussed, perhaps, but more unsettling. What if, in this unprecedented new situation, women lose their moral compass? What if they not only invite but excessively enjoy the attentions of their male coworkers and of the sailors who come through to pick up the ships?

As a Dartmouth sociologist describes the concern, the war seems to be producing a new kind of female, a "casual, fun-seeking girl," away from home for the first time. This girl, far from the oversight of "family and church," is likely to be "a bit lonely" and "want male companionship." Further, "quixotic references to 'patriotism'" often make these "young experimenters" feel justified in going further with men than they would have if there hadn't been a war on.[18] Others fear a sort of immorality that goes well beyond the yearnings of lonely young girls. "In the shipyards," Katherine Archibald writes, "rumor was continually busy with suspicions and reports of salacious activities in the obscurer parts of the ships or in some vaguely identified warehouse. . . . One persistent report concerned the activities of enterprising professionals for whom a shipyard job was said merely to provide an opportunity for pursuit of a yet more lucrative career.[19]

Perhaps as a result of such rumors, the *Bo's'n's Whistle* works to paint a different picture and begins to run numerous features on wholesome female workers. One cover story, "Shipyard Wife," describes a woman who is on the 7:49 bus every day to her job as a crane operator. Once a month she flies to California to visit her husband, who is stationed there. Then it is back to work, and we see her putting her hair in a bandana ("safety pays"), using her lunch bucket as a mirror. Her workday done, she stops off to buy bonds as she saves for the postwar home and the family she and her husband are dreaming of. [20]

∽ Whatever other people might get up to, there is surely no need to worry about the morals of a sweet, country girl like Eva. Her brother, Aub, has a different kind of warning when he hears she's considering going to work at Swan Island, a 260-acre outcropping in the Willamette River and site of the third of Kaiser's yards in the area. "If you take that job, I want you to stay clear of those women welders you were talking about. They are liable to hit you on the head with a blow torch or something."

And some girls *are* nervous about what they are getting into. A young woman named Marie Baker remembers that she had the impression that the women who worked in factories were tough. "I was scared to death, hoping nobody would hit me. . . . It didn't seem like nice people worked in factories. I don't know where I got that idea."[21]

Baker admits she was something of a "Caspar Milquetoast," but Eva, by now anyway, seems pretty fearless. So she goes out to Swan to assist in the production of oil tankers that will be sent to fuel the fleet in the Pacific.

By the time Eva arrives in mid-1944, the Swan Island yard has already turned out some sixty of the immense ships, and launchings are getting to be a pretty common thing. Each new ship is sent off with determined fanfare, and Eva could have experienced the excitement as flags flew and bands played. Wives of prominent men—and now, too, wives of shipyard workers—still christen each ship, and news cameramen capture the moment when the honoree of the day, eyes tight shut, manages to make the champagne bottle and the ship's hull connect.

Launches still rate radio coverage, and in audio recordings, I hear the announcer working to keep excitement up about the newly finished ship, the ships still to come, and the war that is yet to be won. The suspense is great, according to the announcer, as the lines holding the giant hull are cut one by one. Now the "boys in the yard are wagering about the exact moment" when the ship will start to slide down the way. "One is gone!" the announcer cries, as the first line is cut. "Two is gone! Cutting through three now! Mrs. Moore, get those magic words ready—a tense air of expectation!—There she goes! There she goes! And now—already!—men are swarming out to lay down a new hull!"[22]

December 22, 1944, is a day of special excitement. The shipyard has built an oil tanker in a record thirty-seven days, and in Eva's papers I find that week's *Bo's'n's Whistle* with its full page photo of the ship and screaming headline: "SWAN MAKES WORLD RECORD ON HULL 113."

If the great ships sliding down into the waters of the Willamette continue to thrill, less scintillating are the overcrowded converted school buses that have been painted an ugly brown and that shuttle back and forth between Swan Island and downtown Portland. Photographs show grimy men and women crammed into the bus, some standing, some eating sandwiches, some trying to catch a few winks of sleep.[23]

But Eva will not have to commute in the dirty old buses. Rather, she will live *on* Swan Island. Kaiser has been putting up barracks for many of its male workers since the beginning of the war, and Swan Island has become a little city providing for most of the workers' needs. Residents can take their meals at the immense cafeteria, get their mail, have their shoes repaired, and their laundry done. They can relax at a pool hall or an on-site movie theater.

With all this going on and so many living and working on the island, socializing comes easy. As one worker, Marie Gleason, remembered, "You'd walk in and you'd go past all these different buildings with different shops. And before everybody went to work, a lot of them would be standing outside. And they would stop and talk to you, the gateman and different ones asked your name. As the days went on, you met more and more. And lunch hour! Different ones would bring their lunches over, come and meet you and eat with you. You just met somebody all the time."[24]

By mid-1944, the news from Europe is encouraging. The Allies have landed in Normandy and the Italian invasion force that Dave had been part of has taken Rome. It seems likely that the war in Europe will be won fairly soon. But for workers on the West Coast, who have a particular connection to the sailors and merchant marines serving in the Pacific, many of whom have come through Portland to pick up ships, the war feels far from over. And in the yards, the around-the-clock pace continues: food and other services are available day and night, as are the entertainment programs that are frequently brought in. As seen in one midnight lunch, captured by a news photographer, hundreds of graveyard workers sit on the ground with sandwiches and thermoses, watching a song-and-dance act on an outdoor stage. Behind them is a magical scene of immense hulls and see-through scaffolding strung with lights.[25]

By summer, just in time for Eva's arrival, Swan Island offers another exciting feature: dormitories for women. A *Bo's'n's Whistle* photo layout shows modern-looking, two-story facilities that can house five hundred "girls." For a weekly rate of $4.90 and under the eye of a matron, the women share rooms that contain two twin beds, two small closets, two dressers, each with a mirror. Each floor has a large bathroom with communal sinks and showers. In addition there is "maid service just as any first class hotel," a feature that must have thrilled Depression-era farm girls like Eva.[26]

I don't know whether Eva looked into training for one of the higher-paying industrial jobs. I do know that when she arrived at Swan she would have been given a health exam, instituted to make sure women are given work assignments they can handle with safety. I suspect that Eva's poor eyesight would have kept her from skilled work like welding, but there are plenty of other jobs she could do. In fact, though "Rosie" got the publicity, most wartime women never touched a riveting gun or a welding torch. Rather, they were recruited to do hundreds of other jobs, from cooking in defense plants to working as bookkeepers and telephone operators.[27] And while there were certainly skilled jobs for women in the shipyards, here too the largest expansion of job opportunities for female workers was in unskilled categories. Women were placed in jobs as sweepers, laborers, painters' helpers, and tool checkers.[28] They took office and service jobs previously held by men. And now Eva gets one of these, becoming a cashier at the huge Swan Island cafeteria, part of what Kaiser's Dr. Rieke called "the biggest, best food service in the whole region."

All war plant workers must wear a photo ID, which, as one magazine article gushes, represents a new kind of wartime glamour: girls in Kaiser yards wear the ID "with more pride than if it were a five-thousand-dollar diamond brooch."[29]

It's propaganda, I know; still, there is evidence that many women love being part of the war effort and are having the time of their lives, enjoying the companionship of fellow workers, the thrill of doing something important for their country, and the "gratification of proving their mettle in jobs once thought beyond the powers of women." One housewife reports to the Office of War Information, "Some just love their jobs. I think they for the first time in their life feel important."[30]

It's no diamond brooch, but Eva keeps the badge; and all these years later I find it among her things. It's a substantial item fashioned of heavy metal, with a pin and clasp on the back, and it identifies her as Port Operations, Day Shift. A thick, yellowed plastic cover shields a photo of Eva, taken in front of a lineup-type background showing her to be five feet six inches tall. Her red hair is up in curls on top and wavy down the back, and her pretty young face is grave.

I don't have a photo of her on the job, but I do have a news photograph of a Swan Island mess hall seating several hundred workers. Nicely dressed girls with pretty hairdos circulate with water pitchers and coffee pots. Most of the men seem to be older, into their forties and fifties. They wear plaid jackets, and they keep their battered old hats on their heads as they eat. Though they would appear to be well fed (for 48 ½ cents they get soup, two entrees, vegetables, fruit, and dessert), to my eye, they still have Depression-era faces, haggard and a bit hollow-eyed. They don't really look like the type to chase a girl all over the shipyard. The young and the able and, I suppose, the more dangerously attractive are all in the service.[31]

Despite the dorms with a matron, many mothers worry about their daughters going to work in the war plants. Even if the girl isn't doing a man's job like welding, she is in a gritty male world, which many view as "terrible tough."[32] Some continue to be scandalized at the very idea. The mother of Inez Sauer, a busy young clubwoman before the war, declared that "no one in our family has ever worked in a factory," adding, "You don't know what kind of people you're going to associate with." Sauer's father was likewise horrified and forbade her from taking a war plant job. Sauer did it anyway, working on an assembly line to build the B-17 at a Boeing plant in Seattle.[33]

Grace undoubtedly has her concerns as well. But perhaps she reasons that a shipyard full of men in overalls isn't necessarily more dangerous than a VA hospital full of men in pajamas. Perhaps, too, she realizes that she has, to a large extent, already lost control of what Eva will do in Portland. Still Grace does not relent in her determination to trust that Eva remains her good, sweet girl. Certainly this is the message she continues to send in letters that are always proud and supportive. "That pay was sure O.K.," she writes after hearing of Eva's first Swan Island check. Any anxiety is muted. "Glad you have such a decent roommate for I was worried there wouldn't be any decent people around."

It does not seem that Grace has broken Dave's confidence and told Eva about his crackup in Italy, his sense that he can't come home to Eva in his present state, and his uncertainty about whether he'll ever be well. It's hard to imagine that Grace would have kept this critical news from Eva. On the other hand, Dave's crackup, coming immediately upon his hearing that Eva left home, could be construed as Eva's fault, a horrible, if unfair, burden for her to bear. Perhaps Grace hesitates to add this to all the other new things Eva is dealing with. All I know is that Dave isn't mentioned in Grace's letters and that Eva doesn't seem to be hearing from him.

But Grace has plenty to write about since, of course, Eva would still want to hear all the news from home. So Grace sends it all along: Grace and Wes went to Baker to get a hay buck. Grace painted the inside of the china closet. She dressed a chicken as there is a potluck dinner that evening at church. Wes adds a note telling Eva that all her precious "lambies" are fine. And he tells how the preacher missed the stage from Baker on Sunday morning, so "we had to put on church ourselves." Then he signs off as he must to go put on his "best bib and tucker" for the potluck dinner.

While Grace and Wes may have to get dressed up for a church supper once a month, Eva, as she now writes, is going out every night. Apparently she's taking the old brown bus into Portland in the evenings because she tells her parents that she has to worry about missing the last one back at midnight. Grace is still glad Eva is having a good time, but she doesn't know about going out *every* night. Eva will get worn out; she should think about her health.

↷ Within a few months, however, Eva will be up all night every night, as she has gotten promoted to a new job—nightshift cashier at a canteen for sailors who are in to pick up ships. By now people are getting used to seeing a woman behind the cash register. And after the drudgery of the VA hospital kitchen, this lively job must seem like a dream; now she truly is having a "swell" time. She writes, "Am so lucky to have such a job. I'm really crazy about it and I like Graveyard better all the time."

The canteen is busy, she says, with "City Folks and Day Shifters celebrating the weekend." That must sound okay to Grace, though the thought of Eva working all night probably raises motherly concern. But the next bit of news—Eva seems to be writing her letter at work—would give Grace even more pause. "We have several hundred sailors in here on the ships in the repair docks. So naturally they keep the cafeteria packed all night. Sure do have a lot of fun, turn down dozens of dates a night, and that's no kidding. Decided to keep track tonight and so far I've had 24 chances and the night's not over."

In another letter she mentions several men—"all perfect gentlemen" —including an ensign who took her to the opera *Carmen*. There's somebody called Shorty, a plant worker it seems, who comes by her station at midnight and spends the night while she works, "stretching his long self over three chairs." She and Shorty are having one of their "well-known fights." He keeps trying to persuade her to marry him, she mentions.

Somebody has a car, and Eva is having fun driving around, seeing the sights of Portland for the first time. If Grace and Wes have any gas coupons to spare, Eva could use them. Well, of course, a girl wants to go out and see things. Grace and Wes can certainly understand that. But there are men Eva doesn't mention in letters home. If they are gentlemen, they would not seem to be perfect ones. Somebody named Frank, for example, wounded and stuck in a hospital in California, writes that he's going crazy down there. One of the problems is that the only girls around are fifteen and sixteen, and it's "frowned on to mess with them."

Another letter comes from two men, Milt and Harry, who are just about to cross the international dateline and plan to celebrate by trying to "brew something up" out of raisins. They don't usually write letters, but together, they figure, they might just manage. Does she remember them, they wonder. If she wants to refresh her memory, she could look at some pictures she might still have, taken of them all at a penny arcade.

Then there's somebody named George, who is sending his apologies from another ship in the Pacific.

> Honey, I feel worse than a heel. I figured probably you would feel better if you never heard from me again but I could not hold back any longer. I think lots of you Eva and very sorry for being the heel I was. Won't you please forgive me. One of the fellows told me you said that you didn't want to hear from me again. And that you didn't need my love any longer. Is that true? Well honey, I would like to hear from you and I am very sorry, sugar. Excuse writing the ship is shaking. Yours, George.

Even though Grace is getting only part of the picture, she does begin to grow puzzled and increasingly concerned. Even a bit hurt. It's been six months, and Eva hasn't managed to make it home to visit. And now they aren't even getting letters that often. Finally Grace has to say something. She writes, "Was so glad to hear all about your work & that last big affair. I know you have had a lot of good experiences but I sometimes think you have been there about long enough. The little old Valley is getting rather vague in your mind it seems. Not much response to things I write about & I do know you are busy, Sweetheart but after all we all have 24 hours out of each day to do with as we like best."

In the next letter, Grace responds to something Eva has done, something that must be utterly shocking. Grace handles it as well as she can. "I expect you are pretty thrilled over your coat, but I surely think you went awful strong paying that much & am worried as to where you are keeping it. $425 could slip away pretty easy if you aren't careful with it." In a line inserted into the letter Grace remembers to add, "I know it's lovely."

I have to admit, *I'm* shocked. In today's dollars, Eva's coat would cost about $5,000. I comb the advertisements in the *Oregonian* trying to see how you could possibly spend that much on a coat in wartime Portland. The closest I come is a "tuxedo coat" of "sable blended muskrat" for $259.

Grace's letter commenting on the coat also includes a magazine article in which a woman shares her belief that she would have been happier in her life if she had been a better Christian. Grace—*way* too late it would seem—suggests that Eva join a church where there "would be a nice young people's group." And for the first time Grace allows herself to mention her own loneliness, how it's just her and Wes looking at each other across the table, how she misses her children. For the first time I glimpse in Grace's letters the woman I would come to know. She is worried about Eva. She is praying over Eva all the time.

I can see why Grace is scared. Maybe it has all been too much too soon. Maybe Eva *is* going way too fast. Still, I doubt if Eva has done anything approaching what is standard for today's college girl. The adrenalin of war notwithstanding, it is still a more innocent time. Though contraceptives are issued to male soldiers, they are not considered appropriate for unmarried women. At the beginning of the war there was some discussion of supplying contraceptives to service women, but the War Department decided against it, pointing out that "parents could hardly be expected" to give their daughters permission to join the WAACs "if medical kits of this character were issued."[34] In the Oregon shipyards, according to Dr. Rieke, birth control methods were not widely accepted, not well understood, and inspired little confidence.[35] And the consequences of unprotected sex were too awful to contemplate. As a woman named Dellie Hahne told Studs Terkel, "An illegitimate child was a horrendous handicap. It was almost the ruination of your life." As a result, she reported, there "was very little sleeping around. We'd go out in herds and stay up all night. We were still at the tail-end of a moral generation. Openly living together was not condoned."[36]

Eva's experience, I suspect, resembled that of Hahn's and of another young woman of the time, who, like Eva, was just having too much fun to get any sleep. "There were servicemen of all varieties roaming the streets all the time," she remembered. "There was never, never a shortage of young healthy bucks. We never thought of getting tired. Two, three hours of sleep was normal. I'd go down to the office every morning half dead but with a smile on my face and report for work. There was another girl there who was having a ball too, and we took turns going into the back room and taking a nap on the floor behind the desk."[37]

No, I doubt that Eva has become the thing that would have broken Grace's heart: sexually promiscuous. Rather, I suspect that something less obvious is changing Eva from the sweet, dutiful girl she has always been. For unlike the married women who work beside her on Swan Island, Eva has no home and children to anchor her. Unlike the older women, she's had no established life of her own, no settled understanding of what her path must be. Though the expression "for the duration" is constantly repeated, what does this mean to a young person who has never—on her own at least—experienced anything but the fast life of a war town? Could she fully grasp how abnormal this all is?

What I suspect is that in this life of freedom—and with the dizzying experience of making good money that is all hers—she finds herself much less certain about her future than she was a year or so ago. Is marrying a hometown boy and living the same life of home, family, and church her mother has lived really her only option?

Grace, who loves her daughter so deeply, seems to be picking this up. She is not alone; all over the country, as historian Henry Chafe writes, parents are waiting to see "if their daughters would come back home and settle down in a nearby community."[38] And like many others, Grace is starting to wonder. Could it be that this isn't just "for the duration"? Could it possibly be that Eva, as her mother has known her, is gone?

But then, thankfully—certainly from Grace's point of view—

something happens that could set everything right. I see the news penciled in an unfamiliar hand, probably that of a roommate, on the back of one of Eva's envelopes. "Hey you kid in the other bed. Don't you ever come home? The Matron said to tell you. Dave called. He's back."

1957 ℂ A Wedding, Boise

In February of 1957, several weeks before Eva and Vick are to be married, Vick writes a letter to Eva's brother, Aub. Of course, Eva has sent her brother and his wife an invitation to the wedding, but Vick too is writing now to say that he is hoping Aub will agree to be his best man. Though Vick has been in Boise only a few months, he wants Aub to know that he has been chosen over others Vick could've asked. "Don't think it was just an idle thought or that it was taken for granted. I really consider it a privilege. Of all the ones I know, you are the one I have wanted since our plans were made."

Vick, who is clearly working to make himself agreeable to Aub, goes on to mention the snow they've had in Boise and to express his hope that bad weather over in Oregon hasn't made it too tough for Aub to get his cattle fed. Vick writes that he is trying to do his "bit" for the beef industry. Whenever he serves up a steak, he "chuckles" to himself and thinks of Aub's fat steers.

Aub must have agreed to be best man because there he is in the wedding photographs, wearing a pale, baggy suit, bow tie, and the hangdog expression that farmers get when they have to dress up for a wedding or a funeral. And there I am, a round-faced eight-year-old in the rose-colored dress Grace has made. Other than the dress, I don't remember much about the wedding. I have a vague impression of the oddness of being in a church on a chilly late afternoon with hardly anyone there. But when I look at the black-and-white photographs of the wedding party, I find that I remember the colors. There's Grace, in a duster, as we called such long, light coats. She, of course, made it herself; I know that it is black but that the shiny fabric is shot through with gold thread.

And there's Eva in a lacy, "ballerina length" dress that I know to be a pale, pale blue.

The photo is being taken moments after the ceremony has concluded, but I'm the only one smiling. I am still excited, no doubt, about the important role I have just played and about the flower girl bouquet that I am getting to keep. The others—all momentarily lost in their own thoughts—stare solemnly. But by the time we get to the reception, things have loosened up considerably. Now the photographer has captured Vick and Eva in the Hotel Boise ballroom, standing in front of a huge framed aerial photograph of the city. They are cutting their cake and look to be having a great time. Eva's head is thrown back in uninhibited laughter as she reaches up to feed Vick a bite of cake. He smiles down into her eyes, hunching his shoulders and lightly clenching his fists as if to humorously demonstrate his effort not to just grab the cake and feed himself.

These two pictures, the one in the church and the one cutting the cake, could document almost any wedding. But a third photograph seems to hint of the puzzle I know this moment to be. Interestingly, it is the picture Eva chose to send to the society pages of the Boise and Baker papers. When the item appears in Boise, she will buy a dozen papers and clip out the picture along with the announcement of her wedding. Grace will get a number of copies of the item in the Baker papers. And among Eva's things I find a fat envelope, filled with dozens of the identical, yellowed clippings.

In this third photo, Vick and Eva are again shown in the hotel ballroom with the photograph of all Boise spread out behind them. Here they are making their first cut into the cake, Eva holding the knife and Vick covering her hand with his. Eva looks straight into the camera. She is thirty-five years old and has lived a chaotic life since she left the farm at twenty-two. In recent years she has been single and on her own at a time when such a condition is considered a tragic fate. She works at a low-paying job and—something to think about as the years slide by—one that is highly dependent on her classy looks. When she notices a new line in the mirror, she's got to wonder, how long will she be considered young enough for hostess-type work, the only occupation she knows? And when she's not young enough? What then?

But any such fears are gone now, and in this photograph she looks like a girl, aglow with love. She is smiling so widely that one eye is a little squinted. She is not thinking about posing glamorously. She is not watching her step. She has thrown herself into this body and soul. The man beside her must seem like a dream come true. Tall, dark, and well built in a sleek, black suit and narrow black bow tie, he could have stepped off the top of the wedding cake. As his right hand covers Eva's, his left is lifted slightly, as if he is proud to display the new wedding band.

I have spent a lot of time looking at this picture of Vick. I study him up close with a magnifying glass and zoom in with my computer; I tape him to the wall and, glimpsing him as I walk past, try to surprise myself into new understanding. In his eyes I do not see the simple abandonment of joy I find in Eva's. However, he is anything but blasé. He stares at the camera with bright-eyed intensity. I'm certain he's not faking. He is very, very excited.

At the same time, he knows what he's doing. He knows what he's done in the past and probably has a pretty good idea of what he will go ahead and do in the future. So what can he be thinking at this moment? In particular, what are his thoughts about the tremulously happy woman whose hand he covers with his own?

1944–1946 ∞ Swan Island Shipyard and Fort George Wright Convalescent Hospital

In the autumn of 1944, Eva's Wing Valley fiancé, Dave Johnson, is sent home from Italy. Though he has written, begging Grace not to tell anyone about his crackup, Grace now decides that it is time Eva knew. No doubt Grace understands that if Dave really wanted to end the engagement, he wouldn't have written to her in such heartrending detail. Nor would he have expressed his continued love for Eva or explained that he could not return to her in his broken condition.

For her part, Grace is undoubtedly thankful for Dave's return, praying that it will mean the end of Eva's adventure in the shipyards. So Grace prepares the way. She explains to Eva that the cold and dismissive breakup letter, in which Dave paints himself as a man who enjoys only "chasing excitement around the world," has a very different twin: his letter to Grace, describing his mental torment and his fear that he would never be well again. Grace writes her daughter, "I was quite sure you would want to know. Of course, we don't know what kind of condition he is in, but I imagine it is just nerves from being there so long. Anyway I wanted to let you know so I just did & I hope it doesn't cause any trouble & I guess it won't. Anyway when he gets home I think if you see each other you can do your own deciding better than any other way."

I don't know how Eva reacts to news of Dave's nervous breakdown. I do know that she has a few things on her mind other than Dave's return. For one, she has recently gotten the chance to be a "boss," with her own assistant; apparently she's advanced to some low-level management position in Kaiser's mammoth food service program. Grace does not know what to say about this. She is still proud of her daughter's achievements. But Eva needs to remember what her real future will be, and Grace wonders if it's good to be so involved with work that she can't "come home on quick notice," presumably when Dave returns.

When he finally gets back to his parents' home, Eva does manage to get a few days off work to travel there. The visit apparently goes well, for now the engagement is back on, and the future planned. Through relatives in Los Angeles and thanks to the communication training Dave has gotten in the Army, he has an offer to work as a film editor in the movie industry after the war. Grace surely regrets that Eva will be as far away as California. At the same time she has to be hugely relieved that, despite some anxious times, things will, after all, be turning out more or less as she had hoped.

But plans can't go forward just yet. Dave, though physically healthy, is still deemed by the Army to be very unwell, and he is sent to a convalescent hospital for psychiatric patients in eastern Washington, some four hundred miles from Portland, where Eva is now back on her job in the shipyard. Though he requires hospitalization, all seem to feel confident that Dave's problems will soon clear up, now that he is safely back home. Dave is more like his "old self" every day, his parents write. Grace too views the problem as one of simple nervousness. And Dave's grandmother, whom he visits in California, writes Eva that there is nothing really wrong with him; he's just exhausted. Despite the certainty that everyone seems to feel about Dave's condition, however, the cause and treatment of soldiers' mental and emotional problems are still poorly understood and highly controversial.

Grace, along with Dave's parents, would, of course, remember the World War I explanations for such emotional distress. One was that soldiers who claimed to suffer in this way were simply cowards and malingerers. Another theory was that the nearby explosion of shells caused mysterious, hidden damage to the brain or "shell shock." But the shell shock theory has been out of fashion for years. At a 1931 conference on military medicine held in The Hague, representatives from 140 nations agreed that there was no such thing as shell shock. Rather, as the newspapers report, the group declared that soldiers' emotional problems were the result of their own mental weakness, preexisting "neurotic conditions made acute by the shock of war."[1] One result of this finding was that when gearing up for World War II, the American military set not only physical but mental standards for inductees.[2]

Despite this screening, however, psychiatric problems begin to appear as early as the North African campaign of late 1942. Here Army psychiatrists are coming to understand that prolonged combat simply wears men out, both physically and psychically, a condition that is now being called "combat fatigue."[3] Now psychiatrists see that "the average soldier [reaches] his peak effectiveness in the first ninety days of combat and [is] so worn out after 180 days that he [is] rendered useless."[4]

This understanding does not, however, change the way men are deployed. One study notes that "no man is removed from combat duty unless he [has] become worthless. . . . The infantryman considers this a bitter injustice. . . . He can look forward only to death, mutilation, or psychiatric breakdown."[5] Not surprisingly, the truth about the toll being taken on men like Dave is not widely reported at home. And at this time, as Rick Atkinson writes, the conclusion that "modern combat could break any soldier" was not "acceptable to the U.S. Army."[6]

Furthermore, many in the military continue in the belief that "combat fatigue" is nothing more than cowardice under another name. This attitude is vividly portrayed in Leo Rosten's novel, *Captain Newman, M.D.*, set in a World War II convalescence hospital. Here a colonel views the patients as weaklings and slackers. "In every . . . theater of action," he rages, commanders are "begging for pilots, gunners, and navigators." Meanwhile, the psychiatrists are grounding and pampering "every odd-ball, every gold-brick, every feather-merchant and malingerer and yellow-belly."[7] While the real men are fighting and dying, these guys are sleeping in clean sheets, lounging in the sunroom and playing ping pong.

By late 1943, however, there is a bit more acceptance that combat-induced psychological trauma is real. Indeed, it is a development Grace would have read about in her October *Reader's Digest*. The article, written by the *Digest's* own war correspondent and based on interviews with military doctors in North Africa, explains that mental injuries are not only real, but they are "the most frightful kind of injury that war can inflict . . . a nightmare of mental fixations." Furthermore, it is a mistake to equate combat fatigue with cowardice, for these injuries strike all kinds of soldiers; "bravery or cowardice has little to do with it."[8] Rather, the men suffer from exhaustion caused by "constant hard fighting and lack of regular food and sleep." The recurring narrow escapes from death "keep a soldier's nerves keyed to the highest pitch." It is, the doctors report, a problem that builds up over time. The men, because they have a "general high sense of duty and responsibility" take it as long as they can. But sometimes they break down.[9]

There is good news, however. This condition is better understood now than during World War I. Back then, to cut down on possible malingering, sufferers were treated harshly, "isolated, allowed no visitors and no mail; they were given tedious, annoying work and bitter medicine."[10] Naturally very few recovered; "their war neuroses became fixed," and "they were shipped back to the States by the thousands, to become public charges."[11]

Now, the *Digest* reports, a more effective treatment is being used. Those with "combat fatigue" are being "given sedatives to help them sleep" and are "fed well [and] kept warm." Further, they are "purged of their nightmare story under . . . narcosis." A psychiatrist explains what has happened and talks "hearteningly to bolster their ego." These efforts produce good results. Recoveries are generally "made within four or five weeks, sometimes even within a few days." Such treatment is being given not only in base hospitals but also at the front "within sound of the guns, under frequent air raids."[12] And the article implies that soldiers treated at the front and kept in their own units are able to be cured and to return to service even more quickly. Not every man will return to combat, the article admits, but every man will continue to do good work and "no permanent mental disorder will make him a public charge after the war."[13]

Now almost a year after this report came out and with a problem of combat fatigue touching her own family, Grace may think back to the *Reader's Digest* article. Indeed, given her habit of keeping many years' worth of *Reader's Digest*s stacked neatly in her attic, she may well dig out the article to read again. If so, she surely feels that the explanation of combat fatigue corresponds precisely with what has happened to Dave: he has simply and understandably been worn out by the fighting and the terrible conditions.

As the article clearly states, these young men are being cured. They "will return to their families clear-eyed, and not tottering nervous wrecks."[14] With this information, it would be sensible to conclude that Dave will soon be fine. If it's only "fatigue," all he really needs is rest. But Grace may well have missed something, for it is only hinted of in the *Reader's Digest* article. The corollary to the claim of success in curing combat fatigue at the front or at base hospitals is that the military is making every effort *not* to send these soldiers home.

In their 1945 study, *War Neuroses*, Roy Grinker and John Spiegel explain the thinking behind this policy. To send a soldier home with a psychiatric illness, it was believed, was to doom him to an overwhelming and perhaps insurmountable sense of failure. This was thought to be a particular threat for the many men whose fathers served with distinction in World War I. As a result, only the most severe cases were "reluctantly" sent back to the States.[15] The fact that Dave is coming home, then, means that his case is extreme.

With everyone convinced that "all he needs is rest," it is highly doubtful that Eva is hearing much that is useful on how to understand and deal with Dave's condition. Even so, she will soon find that he expects her to singlehandedly solve all of his problems.

In one way, Dave seems to be doing well at the convalescent hospital. He has been promoted to sergeant and is teaching a class in radio technology. He enjoys teaching, he writes Eva, though one of his pupils is at a disadvantage: the guy has "half his brain blown away. Can't remember anything." Dave seems to be something of a celebrity at the hospital and is featured in the newsletter, *Minute Monograph*. The write-up that he sends Eva, which I find in her papers, features a caricature sketch of Dave with a lot of wavy dark hair and the same dimple in his chin. The article mentions his presence in the Blitz and in the North African campaign, as well as later air raids over Albania, Yugoslavia, and Italy. All of this, *Minute Monograph* notes, will give him a "backlog of anecdotes—grim and humorous—to last a lifetime." Dave has written on the bottom of the page, "There's going to be another story and a radio show. Some fun."

According to the *Monograph*, Dave now spends his time "relaxing with art, photography, and radio." But it is clear that he also spends a good portion of his time writing long, dense letters to Eva—one, sometimes two, a day. In them, Dave bears little resemblance to the cocky warrior of a year or so earlier, addicted to "chasing . . . [his] thrills around the world." Now, all he wants is Eva, idealizing her as the one person who can make him whole. He goes on for pages. "There isn't another person in the world who could possibly take your place. There isn't another person in the world who could fill the longing in my arms."

It isn't just physical longing. Dave believes that Eva can help him give up the thrill of combat, the adrenalin of war. With her, he will be able to appreciate "the pleasure and thrill of living a just and proper life." Eva has visited the hospital; and while she was there, she filled up the "hollowness" inside him. Since their last time together, he has been "sleeping like a baby" for the first time since falling apart in Italy.

Besides elaborating on his need for Eva, Dave's letters from the hospital are also full of instructions for steps she must now take. Most importantly, Eva should quit her job and come up to Spokane, where he has been assured she can find work. However, "there is one thing that will be settled when we're married—you'll only work as long as I'm in the service." But Eva writes that she can't leave Portland just now: she cannot be released from her shipyard work. Perhaps this really is the case: in the pages of the *Bo's'n's Whistle*, yard employees are constantly reminded that the war is far from over and are exhorted to stay on the job. In oral histories of the shipyard, I see that workers need a "clearance" to leave, though I also get the impression that these rules are not always enforced, especially for women.[16]

Dave, though, after years in the military, seems to accept that Eva is being held up by red tape, and he gets busy working on the problem, contacting his legal assistance officer, the Red Cross, and the U.S. Employment Service. Though frustrated by the delay, he is certain something can be arranged. It's a lot of work though, and he looks forward to the day when he will not have to manage Eva's affairs from four hundred miles away.

The problem of being released from work does not seem to be the only complication. Around this time, Eva gets a letter from her friend, Maxine, a thoughtful and articulate young woman who understands the confused feelings Eva has, now that her "future has come home."

"It's hard, isn't it," Maxine writes, "to get used to them after they've been away." And another factor is mentioned, a "tall, dark, and handsome gentleman from the South." The description fits the sailor Jimmy Wright, whose ship recently came through Swan Island and who is now stationed in San Francisco. Jimmy sounds all right to Maxine, but she warns, "Don't let your new dream close Dave out; it may be just a passing romance. What the heck is the new fellow doing now that Dave is home? I'll bet you have some trouble soon." She advises, "Eva, make sure you make it come out the way you want it. You have to know what you want."

Another girlfriend writes to admit that while she had "bawled" Eva out for hesitating about Dave, she's now hesitating herself. When she told her boyfriend that she wasn't ready to get married just yet, that she'd been thinking about going back to her shipyard job, he "broke down and cried. He sure begged me to not to go anywhere, only to him. But like you I just can't make up my mind."

In addition to the handsome gentleman from the South, the girl-friends' letters also mention long, tall Shorty, whom I now know to be a logger from the coast, in Portland for the big war plant money. "Still going with Shorty and liking it, aren't you?" writes a friend whose own fiancé has been reported missing in Germany. "I'm glad. I would hate for all the couples in the world to be separated."

In Eva's papers I find a few of Shorty's atrociously spelled, punctuation-free love notes. "Eva I went to the show the other night I didn't stay very long you werent their with me so I left I gess I have got it bad I gess I love you with all my sole your loving Shorty."

Even Aub down in Texas has heard about Eva's boyfriends and writes her incredulously. Dave, he says, must be more broad-minded than he is. "If I asked somebody to marry me and found they were 'going steady' with someone else when I was away, that would be it."

But Dave doesn't seem to know about either Jimmy or Shorty. Rather, he's busy discussing details of the future and still seems to believe the main problem is that Eva can't—then, as he comes to believe, won't—quit her job. At the end of November, the letters on the page slanting crazily again, he writes that he is going through hell without her. He can't sleep, can't eat, smokes way too much. Without her the skies are "threatening—they act as if they were going to burst right over my head and smother me in cold wet snow and fog."

Things are so bad, the medical officer wants to put him under narcosis again, but Dave is refusing the treatment. "I tried to tell them it was all because of you—they wouldn't believe that." And yes, he tells her—it sounds as if she has asked—his condition *is* Eva's fault. Her leaving the farm and going to work in Portland was "what made me break over there. It is now up to you to put me back together again."

Day after day the frantic letters keep coming. Dave can't bear to think of Eva working in the "hell hole" of the Swan Island plant. She's a "brat" for refusing to come to him. He is desperate for the taste of her lips, the smell of her perfume, her cloud of fragrant red hair. He *needs* her; only she can "paste" him together again.

I haven't been able to read all of these frenzied appeals; neither could Eva. A fair number of letters from Fort George Wright Convalescence Hospital have come to me and remain unopened.

Even though Dave is becoming increasingly manic, twenty-two-year-old Eva still does not seem to have anyone with whom she can explore the true complexities of her situation. Indeed, it appears that discussing a condition like Dave's is taboo, part of society's tacit agreement to downplay the fact that some men are profoundly traumatized. For while the magazines and papers now frequently discuss the "social problems of demobilization," the flood of information and advice for those at home does not differentiate between men whose experiences have been mostly "drudgery" and those who have been in combat. "Horrific" experiences, it is reported, are rare.

By 1944, though, the number of these extreme cases prompts the filming of a documentary by the Army Pictorial Service. In the movie called *Let There Be Light*, the Army line is that there is no shame in such conditions: "every man has his breaking point." Though some of the cases are heartrending, the film is still decidedly upbeat in a wartime propaganda sort of way, showing that, with proper care, these men can be cured.

Filmed from 1944 to 1946 in Mason General Hospital on Long Island with John Huston directing, the documentary shows real soldiers—most of them terribly young—who twitch and stutter and stare blankly. Some can't walk though nothing is physically wrong with their legs; some can't remember their names though nothing is physically wrong with their brains. These men, the movie explains, have reacted to the horrors they have seen in different ways, but all have a "sense of impending disaster" and feelings of "hopelessness." The injured men are being treated in several ways. Group sessions help "break through the sense of isolation." Therapists lead the soldiers in a discussion of their lives postwar. How will they deal with loved ones who can never understand their experience? How will they make the transition from military regimentation to civilian freedom?

Here too drugs may be administered, and the use of sodium pentothal, sometimes called "truth serum," is described in more detail than in the *Reader's Digest* story. In the film we see a psychiatrist administering the drug to a soldier with amnesia; once it has taken effect, the doctor hypnotizes the patient, taking him back to the traumatic moment when memory stopped.

Such patients, as Grinker and Spiegel write in *War Neuroses*, return over and over again to "one short, traumatic scene, living it through repeatedly, as if, like a needle traveling around a cracked record, they could not get past this point." The terror exhibited by a patient under narcosis, they write, is "electrifying to watch. The body becomes increasingly tense and rigid; the eyes widen and the pupils dilate, while the skin becomes covered with fine perspiration." However, under the influence of the drugs and with the help of a psychiatrist, "repressed emotions" can be released in "small enough" quantities that the weakened ego can "resume its appraising and rationalizing functions."[17] The psychiatrist in the Army film explains this effect in simpler terms. If the soldier can remember the repressed horrible experience, he can begin putting it in the past.

The use of sodium pentothal, called "flak juice" by the soldiers, is also seen in the novel *Captain Newman, M.D.*, where it is administered to a soldier named Little Jim. His symptoms are similar to those described in Dave's letter to Grace. Little Jim can't sleep, can't eat, and gets relief only by drinking himself into a stupor. He is hostile to the efforts of the psychiatrist, initially refusing the "flak juice" treatment because, he says, "That's for psychos. I ain't one of your goofballs." His explanation for his symptoms—"Some things ain't purty."

Finally, however, his suffering is so intense that he is persuaded to take the drug and the doctor guides him back to the traumatic moment when his plane was shot down. Though he survived, he was not able to rescue his friend, Big Jim. The information allows the psychiatrist to understand that Little Jim can't stop punishing himself for this failure. Little Jim, a highly decorated soldier who has often risked his life for others, is led to recognize that he is not at fault, that it had been impossible for him to save Big Jim. Now we see him mourn his loss in a more normal way, and the self-punitive behaviors begin to abate. Before long, Little Jim is rehabilitated and bounces jauntily back to the war, where he is immediately shot down and killed.

The Army documentary ends on a happier note. Here we see families and couples walking together on the grounds, and at the end of the movie we see the now-recovered soldiers boarding a bus to leave the hospital as pretty nurses wave goodbye.

Eva, if she'd had a chance to see the film, might have been better able to understand Dave's situation, and her own. For despite the rather stagy happy endings, the arresting footage of trembling, sleep-walking young soldiers makes it clear that "combat fatigue" is something more than exhaustion. Unfortunately, however, neither Eva nor her parents nor Dave's would have had a chance to see *Let There Be Light*. For after the film was made, the War Department had second thoughts and locked it away, refusing to allow its distribution until 1981. The reason given was concern that the film might violate the privacy of the hospitalized soldiers. It may also have been decided that the American public was not ready to see their returning heroes shaking and crying.

If little advice is forthcoming for those women whose men are coping with psychological trauma, there is no lack of counsel about the duty of women—all women—when their man comes home. The advice, often given by doctors and sociologists, develops two themes:

the first is that women must always remember the "enormity of his sacrifice"; the second is that women will play a "crucial role" in the "social aspects of demobilization." Indeed, as Susan Hartmann writes, the claim is now being made that women have "the biggest morale job in history" for the "personal side of reconstruction is woman's work."[18]

Role models in movies and in fiction reinforced this view. One heroine declares, "I'll simply and purely walk on eggshells when he comes home. If he wants me to be pale and grave and silent, I'll be it if it kills me. It's not my way, but I'll do it." Another fictional character explains that she puts up with her returning husband's harsh criticisms, remaining patient and quiet, "resolved not to quarrel with him."[19] The wife or sweetheart must, a *March of Time* film segment declares, "tolerate his outbursts." Above all, she must lavish him with affection and "expect no immediate return." If she steers this course, the "storms of readjustment" will soon pass.[20]

In most cases, this is probably true. But Dave, who entered the war a year earlier than most Americans and was baptized in combat as bombs rained down on Britain, has suffered far more than the average returning soldier. And while Eva isn't getting much useful information, it must be clear to her that, despite his frenzied appeals, whatever is wrong with him goes well beyond not having her in his arms.

So Eva is left to cope on her own with some extremely difficult questions: How serious is his illness and will he recover? Was it really "because of her" that he cracked in the first place? Is it really her responsibility to "put him back together"? Is that what she wants? After Dave has suffered so much, does it *matter* what she wants? Is it, as everyone is now saying, a woman's patriotic duty to be his "anchor," to renounce her independent life, marry him, and do whatever it takes to cure him? Is she a terrible person because she is hesitating? Is it wrong that she loves being successful at her job, having her own money, living on her own, and answering to no one? Is it wrong that she has enjoyed the company of other men in the four years since Dave, her first and only boyfriend, left her on the farm at seventeen? What does it mean that she thinks twice when Dave announces that, of course, no wife of his will work? Can she really go back to being who she was before the world turned so fascinatingly upside down?

These are questions that do not have to be answered, Eva decides, just yet, and despite Dave's entreaties and commands, she remains in Portland at her Swan Island job.

By April, 1958, all the letters Eva sent to Mexico from Boise have been returned unopened. Grace and Aub now know Vick is gone and know too of Eva's belief: Vick left because he was tormented by some trauma from the past, undoubtedly the result of his long years at war. Eva knows, she has told her family, of one incident during which Vick was trapped in a burning tank, his buddies all dead.

Trying to help, Aub too sends a letter to Vick at the Posada Aji-jic address. In a humorous letter reminiscent of Wes, Aub fills his brother-in-law in on the weather and mishaps in the feedlot. Then he gets to the point, writing that he is pretty sure the problem with Vick and Eva's marriage, whatever it is, can be worked out. Vick is a darn lucky man, Aub writes, to have a wife who loves him so much, and if people love each other, problems can be solved. Aub suggests, why not just give Eva a ring? Call her up right now. It would mean so much.

But this letter too has been returned unopened. And now, with Vick gone more than month, Eva has finally agreed to see her mother. Until now, Eva and Grace have spoken only once and then briefly. Of course, they wouldn't want to talk on Grace's home phone and risk being overheard by anyone listening in on the party line.

It wasn't that people in Wing Valley gossiped any more than those in other places or were any meaner about people's troubles. But with only three hundred some people in the valley, they all knew each other well, often back into three generations to the time the Valley was settled. Many are distantly related, as the early settlers sent word home, encouraging siblings and cousins to come West. If something went wrong in this little world—if a girl got pregnant; if a man gave his wife a black eye—well, this would become part of the family's identity in the Valley. Forever. Naturally, when something terrible happened, you tried not to let people find out.

So when the news first came, Grace took the unprecedented step of driving up to the phone booth that sat across from the store. But using the pay phone was almost as bad as talking on the party line. Though nobody could hear the conversation, everybody who drove past would gape at the strange spectacle of Grace standing inside the little glass box.

"Who's Grace talking to on the pay phone?" they would ask each other. "Wonder what's happened."

Since Aub was right here in the county and came to the Valley often and since nobody would imagine Grace having any business other than family and church, people could speculate. "Must be something about Eva."

If they are to talk things out, then, Grace and Eva need to meet. But Eva does not want Grace to come to Boise. Maybe she still has hope that, any moment, Vick will walk in the door with a story of—what— amnesia, maybe. Something. Some explanation. Because there *has* to be an explanation.

Of course, Eva can't come home. Seeing her there alone, knowing that Grace has been seen in the phone booth in agitated conversation, people in the Valley would put two and two together and figure something had gone wrong with Eva's marriage. Her *second* marriage, as they would all know. Then people would be sorry for Grace; they know how much she loves her daughter, and many remember Eva as the sweetest of girls. Only a few, knowing Grace's strong views on moral questions, would take satisfaction. Maybe this would teach some people not to be so all-fired righteous.

So Eva and Grace decide to meet at a halfway point between Wing Valley and Boise, at a park on a stretch of Snake River called Farewell Bend. I'm sure neither Grace nor Eva notice the irony of the name, so familiar is everyone with this place, named to mark the point where the covered wagon trains said goodbye to the comfort of flowing water and headed up through the high, dry desert of eastern Oregon.

Eva and Grace meet outdoors; like secret agents exchanging ominous information, they can't risk being overheard. Maybe too, as country people deep down, they just feel better at such a terrible time to be out under the sky. At any rate, Grace packs a picnic lunch and sets off. For some reason she takes me along. Maybe it's just too much to face alone. Maybe it's a relief to have me chattering about this and that. Of course, I haven't been told what's happened. I'm too young.

And besides, it's the deepest of secrets. No one other than Grace and Aub is to know.

⁓ I remember only a few things about this meeting. Mostly, I remember it was raw spring weather, cold with a whipping rain. I remember hoping they'd give up the picnic idea and that we could go into nearby Weiser for a hamburger deluxe and a pineapple shake. But at some point I realized this was no ordinary picnic. In fact, it wasn't a picnic at all. Eva and Grace sat in the car and I, despite the weather, had to get out and go play on a swing.

The main thing I remember is how Eva looked. Horrible. I can clearly see what she wore, maybe because it was so different from her usual sleek attire. I remember loose slacks and a baggy plaid jacket that hung on her as if on a skeleton. I remember that an ugly scarf tied up her hair. And I remember the strangeness of the green-tinted sunglasses that, despite the gray skies, she never took off.

Apparently I asked where Uncle Vick was; I find this mentioned in a letter. I can't remember either wondering or asking. I can't remember what I was told in reply. Not the truth. I'm sure of that.

1944 ∽ "The Taste of Independence," Swan Island

By late 1944, six million women who never worked outside the home have joined the labor force. Eva—despite Dave's insistence that she leave the "hell hole" of the shipyard—is still among them. The women now account for 35 percent of the civilian workers,[1] and their record in the shipyards is good. In one plant, Doris Kearns Goodwin writes, production rates shot up after women were hired; it was reported that "women were more patient with detail, more capable of handling repetitive jobs without losing interest, more eager to learn, less prone to hide their greenness, more willing to ask directions and take instruction."[2]

Despite the German surprise counteroffensive in the Ardennes, which reminds everyone that the war is far from over, the mood in the yards is decidedly more upbeat than two years earlier. For one thing, the tension that marked the first arrival of women workers seems to have evaporated. Now, "feminine" workers, as they are called, are everywhere, including on the front page of the *Whistle*, which frequently features a photograph of a pretty shipyard girl in bathing suit or shorts, often leaning against an anchor or some other massive shipyard implement. Frequent beauty contests are held as the many state associations within the yards select their own Miss Montana or Miss Kansas. One photo caption reads, "Here's evidence that a girl can work all day in the shipyard and still be glamorous."[3]

But the *Whistle's* coverage of women is not entirely focused on bathing suits and "glamour," and some women are shown in more natural activities. One group is photographed enjoying a rare sunny day, sprawled on a blanket amid lunch pails and thermoses. "Sun and Slacks," the caption reads, noting that the picnickers hail from duplicating, bomb control, and the paymaster's office.[4]

By now, what seems to be quite genuine appreciation of women's contribution is evident. In a June issue of the *Whistle*, for example, is a photograph of four women outfitters in tin hats. The caption reads,

"What these girls don't know about Swan tankers could be inscribed on the head of a pin without the aid of a magnifying glass."[5] Another item notes that "women do half of Swan welding. The eldest draws social security, the youngest is sixteen."[6]

And now the *Whistle* can report on what must have been a tense moment early in 1942 when a group of men looked up to discover that women "had boarded a ship and were hard at work." Enraged at this breach of their "all-male world," the men stormed out and chased the women away. But then the supervisor, a longtime Kaiser man, "marshaled his force of women" and led the group back onto the ship. Ever since, the *Whistle* writes, "the largely feminine Labor Erection—whose duties are to collect salvage and siphon water out of the boats—has had the situation well in hand."[7]

It is hard to know what a young woman like Eva would make of such a tale. Having arrived two years after the first women entered the yard and now just one among hundreds working and even living on Swan Island, the story of enraged men driving off women workers must seem like a peculiar bit of ancient history.

Another attitude that appears to be shifting—at least judging from the pages of the *Whistle*—is the notion that only women can do housework. In an "inquiring reporter" feature, workers are asked whether husbands of shipyard women should help at home. For farm girls like Eva, who've never seen a man wash a dish or make a bed, it must come as rather astonishing news that the answer is generally yes. One man states his belief that housework should be shared "fifty-fifty" though only if "the wife is working with the husband's consent." Another man has fewer caveats, replying, "Of course. And I'm a hell of a cook."[8]

The subject of shared housework is even considered good for a laugh, as a cartoon depicts a large, puzzled-looking man arriving in the yard, carrying a lunch pail and wearing a frilly apron. As those around him snicker, he says, "I just KNOW I forgot to do something."[9]

∽ Even though the shipyard is allowing itself to relax a bit on the subject of gender roles—the *Whistle* reports that the women chauffeurs maintain a bulletin board of "pinup boys"[10]—there is still plenty to worry about. Here, as elsewhere, people are wondering what's going to happen after the war. Foremost among the questions: will there be jobs? In the Portland area, approximately two hundred thousand men, women, and children depend on the shipyard for their livelihood, a number that is two-thirds of the area's entire pre-war population.[11] Further, two-thirds of shipyard workers have come from elsewhere. Will they be able to stay in Portland when the war work ends?

The question is taken up by the *Whistle*, whose reporting and editorializing walk a fine line between the need to keep workers on the job until the war is won and the need to begin preparing them for its aftermath.

On the optimistic side, a great deal of discussion focuses on projects that might provide future employment in the Portland area. A reserve fleet will be needed postwar, it is opined, requiring continued shipbuilding and repair. And as if to demonstrate belief in this vision, Swan Island begins planning for an immense new cafeteria system, a development that is followed closely in the pages of the *Whistle* and which Eva, who has proven herself in the field of food service, must be watching with interest. Remembering the early talk in books and articles about how girls' war work could lead to a "satisfying postwar career," Eva could well expect to continue and even advance in the sort of work she is doing now.

The plans for future employment in the Portland area go beyond shipyard work. It is reported that the wizard industrialist Henry Kaiser wants to keep a presence here and soon will announce that he is considering going into both steel production and automobile construction. Those in the West, he has said, need only "courage and vision" for the boom to continue.[12]

Even as bright employment prospects are discussed, however, there are also muted warnings that the area simply will not be able to absorb all of those who have come to work in war plants. Though many workers say they hope to stay in the Portland area, the *Whistle* warns, "city and state officials realize that actual circumstances after the war may alter the thinking of these people."[13]

For shipyard workers and area officials, along with others across the country, the anxiety about postwar employment is informed in large part by the experience of the thirties. One understandable line of reasoning is that just as the coming of war brought jobs, with the end of the war and the return of the servicemen, the terrible unemployment and poverty will return. It is a fear that is shared by some national prognosticators, who predict a coming period of dislocation that would "equal the Great Depression."[14]

Not surprisingly, one thought that is now beginning to form in many minds is that the women, recruited so avidly a few years earlier, will soon face an equally important responsibility: they must go back home so that available jobs will go to returning soldiers. As a male outfitting clerk tells the *Whistle*, "Women are doing a wonderful job." But after the war they should be supported by husbands since "the best way to avoid a depression is to get women to give up their jobs."[15] Another man agrees that women should return home, adding, "We'll sure miss them though."

It is not clear—not yet anyway—that women are ready to forget everything that has happened in the last several years and to refashion their lives according to the prewar belief that "woman's place is in the home." As the *Whistle* notes, "Here's something to think about for those who have assumed that women would naturally step down and give their jobs back to menfolks after the war: more than 53 percent of the women want to continue in industrial work."[16] And it's not just women in Portland who want to keep their jobs. Nationwide, there appears to be an even greater desire by women to continuing working after the war: a U.S. Department of Labor survey reports that 75 to 80 percent of women in war production want to continue working after victory is won.[17]

The women who want to continue working may not realize how rapidly attitudes are changing, but attentive readers post–D-day would have noticed a pronounced shift in the line being taken toward women workers in mainstream magazines. The fervent "We need you!" of 1942—and soon, "Women are doing a great job!"—is being replaced by a dismissive "soon we won't have to put up with women in the workplace anymore."

Time magazine, for example, runs an article a month after D-day entitled "Females in Factories." While conceding women's essential contribution to the war effort, the article simultaneously suggests that women workers are so much trouble that no one will put up with them under normal conditions. At the time more than three million women are employed in war factories, and the article admits that "in a factory job which does not require strength, a contented woman worker can turn out half again as much work as a man." The problem, though, is that it is nearly impossible to keep women contented. They expect "sympathy and special attention" and are "easily upset by problems at home." (This perhaps referring to the fact that many working women are still responsible for the cooking, cleaning, and rearing of children). At any rate, the women are "so prone . . . to complain, get sick, ache, stay home, quit, that many a factory supervisor will be glad when his women are paid off for good." For now, the article suggests one way to manage a female work force—transferring women to more suitable work; for example, "fat girls" can be given "a sedentary job."[18]

And this is certainly not the only wall upon which such handwriting is beginning to appear. In January of 1945, for example, a *Life* magazine editorial begins laying the theoretical groundwork for what will become a postwar certainty: the only fulfillment for women comes through a focus on home and marriage, not work outside the home.

Life, to be sure, also congratulates women on having done a good job during the war, though they have not done it in quite the hardy spirit exhibited by their "pioneer grandmothers." The article notes that women have even won some parity with men, which the editors do not begrudge; an Army nurse, for example, gets paid as much as other officers, and "the women earn it." But equal treatment of women during the war does not necessarily mean that women can expect the same after the war for, as the editorial asserts, under normal conditions, equality between the sexes is probably just not meant to be. "Scientists and philosophers have argued for generations about how much equality women are equipped for." While some claim that women "have no innate handicaps," others find that "woman's dependence and man's chivalry are rooted in nature."[19]

There aren't too many scientists and philosophers on Swan Island, though, where everyone seems to have lost interest in debating what women can and can't do. For Eva personally, opportunities are getting better all the time, as she gets a swell new assignment, one that takes her out into the Columbia aboard the huge tankers. Each ship must be given a shakedown cruise, and Kaiser has turned these into festive, promotional outings, as can be seen in the company film, *We Build Tankers*. Here we see a group of officers and politicians on deck, shaking hands and talking animatedly, as the ship pushes out into the river, flags and banners stiffening in the breeze.[20] Soon the dignitaries will go below where, if it's one of Eva's cruises, she will be their hostess at a celebratory luncheon. Among her papers I find a memento of one such outing. The all-American menu—steak, mashed potatoes, string beans, apple pie—has been typed out and clipped into a green construction paper folder with "Trip No. 7" noted in Eva's hand.

∽ While this is undoubtedly an exciting opportunity for Eva— another hint, perhaps, of career possibilities in the field of hospitality —her mother is not gladdened. Grace, of course, has never dreamed of working outside the home; when I knew her, she spoke disparagingly of women who went "to business" rather than staying home to tend their families. Yes, she understood that her daughter ought to do the patriotic thing, but now it's gone much too far. And though she was relieved when Dave came home, she is increasingly worried about Eva's behavior and state of mind. She, like Dave, can't understand why Eva doesn't want to quit her job, and she tries to remind her daughter of what's really important. "Makes me feel kind of bad when I see all the young girls around here married & seeming so glad & then thinking of you and what seems so very important to you now, but will burst like a bubble some day."

Eva's brother Aub, who has been suspicious of shipyard work from the beginning, is increasingly disapproving. I suspect he is also alarmed at the change that has taken place in his "little sis." Perhaps his views are shifting as the national message on women working begins to change. Now he too tells her enough is enough: she has spent enough time around sailors. And what's this he hears about sending money to help out one of her pals, some girl who is "working in a drive-in"? It sounds like Eva has met a lot of "riff-raff." Why can't she go home and rest? And why does she have to worry the folks so? Couldn't she drop them a line a little more often?

Even Wes comments in his humorous way: they'd been thinking about getting a hope chest for Eva, he writes, but now he hears "they've stopped making them since none of the girls can make up their minds."

Despite Eva's exciting new opportunities and her refusal to leave the shipyard, the engagement is still on. Dave writes to ask if she has the wedding dress and if he can see her in it. Or maybe they should skip the whole wedding business and just go to a justice of the peace right away? Oh, why *won't* she leave that filthy shipyard?

Finally, in December of 1944, Eva's moment of decision arrives. Dave gets word that he is to be transferred to Arizona and that he can take her with him. He assures her he won't be sent back into combat: "They say I've seen enough." Eva must quit her job. Now. And Dave, sounding calmer, writes, "Let's get married soon."

In Wing Valley, news that Dave is out of the hospital is met with renewed hope. Eva and Dave are expected home in Wing Valley for a joyful Christmas visit. But somehow, it doesn't happen.

"I got time off," Eva writes to a friend. "But I never made it to the train."

So Grace and Wes spend another holiday alone. Eva keeps her job at Swan Island. Dave—who everybody was so sure would be Eva's "future"—goes off to Arizona, and the letters between them stop.

1957 ∽ Honeymoon, Nevada and California

According to the write-up in the Boise newspaper, Vick and Eva take off on a honeymoon trip through Nevada, California, and Oregon. I envy Eva climbing into that big, blue '57 Merc and floating on out of Boise, out through the high, bright desert country of northern Nevada. In this part of the West, where settlements are far apart, people are in the habit of making frequent long drives through majestic country of sky, distant blue mountains, and tanned rolling foothills. The land is mostly empty of people and junk; and as a child of the region, you learn to go into a blissful trance as you roll along for hours and even days. I suppose, too, for those like Eva, who had experienced the gas and tire rationing of World War II, the making-do with beat-up old rigs, and the reliance on overcrowded public transport, the luxury of an open road, plenty of gas, and a big new car with triumphant tail fins must be just too delicious.

I know Vick loves the road. He had, I remember Eva telling us once, driven through all forty-eight states.

In preparation for the honeymoon trip, one of them—Eva, I'm guessing—bought a pack of postcards with the heading, "Travelin' Again," a few of which remain in her papers. The postcard, which can be used to update friends and family back home, shows a compass superimposed over a map of the United States. Below are little white boxes for the travelers to fill in. The boxes are labeled: "Today visited_____, dined at_____, plan to see_____, weather_____," and "miles traveled_____."

Eva is also collecting picture postcards from the places they visit, and it seems that one of their first stops is "Dick Graves' New Million Dollar Nugget Casino," as it styles itself, in Sparks, Nevada, just outside of Reno. I find nothing to indicate that Vick and Eva care about gambling. Probably Vick, who likes restaurants and nightspots, is intrigued by the ads for the Nugget's "five famous restaurants."

Maybe he takes a professional interest in one of the advertised specialties, "mahogany broiled steaks."

Eva and Vick move on to Carson City, where they stay at the Musselman Motel. The black-and-white postcard shows a row of old-fashioned tourist cabins of the sort I remember from the midfifties. The rooms, seen in one of the photos, have knotty-pine paneling and old-fashioned print curtains. Of course, Eva wouldn't send home a postcard showing a casino, but Grace would be happy to think of the newlyweds in the modestly charming Musselman.

In Las Vegas, though, they go flashy again, staying in one of the new two-tier motels, all done up in pink and turquoise and featuring, the postcard notes, "room phones, television, and radio, with a heated pool out front, just to the right of the parking lot." From Las Vegas they head over into California. They must have gotten all the way to San Francisco because Eva saves the drink menu from Skipper Kent's, where one of the specialties is "Love Potion. Fresh banana and rum. You're asking for it. No love insurance written on this one."

Everybody took snapshots in these days, and I remember Eva taking pictures of me and my ringlets the time we visited Boise. It's surprising then that though Eva has saved all sorts of other mementos, there don't seem to be any photos of her honeymoon.

When they return to Boise they are at home in the little basement apartment on Jefferson Street. They even make it into the 1958 Boise Business Directory with the listing "Vickers, Virgil (Eva) chef" and the Jefferson Street address. The previous year's directory didn't list Eva, even though she lived in the same apartment and was also employed in the restaurant business. It was understood, I guess, that the less said about a single woman the better. But now she is a respectable married woman and visible at last.

Despite their appearance in the business directory, it is not at all certain that an attractive couple like Vick and Eva will stick around a burg like Boise. And it may be that on their honeymoon trip through Nevada and California, they have looked into making a move. I know they have made at least one inquiry; in Eva's papers I find a letter to Vick from the manager of a hotel in San Francisco, offering Vick a job whenever he wants it. The man sends his best to Eva and adds that he is sure she too would have no trouble finding work.

But for now they appear to be happily at home in Boise, both working at the classiest place in town. And though they are now an "old married couple," Eva still gives Vick expensive and elaborate greeting cards at each holiday. While I never heard of Vick having any contact with the little daughter whose picture I once saw, Eva gives him a Father's Day card in June. "To my wonderful guy," she has written on the envelope. The card has drawings of hammers and saws on the cover, a tribute, perhaps, to Vick's handiness around the house. He gives her romantic cards as well. For her July birthday, he picks one that shows a white cottage covered in pink roses, the flowers heavy with glued-on glitter. He has signed it, "All my love always. Your Vick."

At Christmastime, she sends him another elaborate card, and in her things I see that she has saved some paper Santas she made to decorate the apartment. In late December she writes Grace, thanking her for the Christmas gifts, including socks knitted for Vick. He's crazy about them, Eva says, adding that work has been very busy, but they will all have to get together soon.

On Vick's birthday in January, exactly one month before the February night he will disappear, Eva sends him a last card. The cover announces, "A Birthday Confession: There's a Man in My Life!" The verse inside declares, "Because of you I'm happy / Because of you I know / The kind of love that deepens / As days all come and go."

Eva signs it, "To my wonderful husband with all my love."

In May of 1945, victory is declared in Europe; but in the Kaiser yards workers are urged to carry on as usual. If anything, as the *Bo's'n's Whistle* editorializes, victory in Europe means even *more* work for the Kaiser yards. An article headlined "West Coast on Spot" asserts that the need for ships to deliver the "Sunday punch" to Japan has become even more pressing.[1] In an interview, Henry Kaiser assures the country that his employees will stay on the job; and to underline the continued urgent need for workers, the *Whistle* announces a new recruiting drive.

All attention now turns to the Pacific and the long, hard fight that is expected there. On August 5, for example, an advertisement in the *Oregonian* explains why the "road to Tokyo" will be so tough: the Japanese still have four to five million fighting men, a "vast army of thirty-five million workers" on their island home, and war supplies that the "Japs have been gathering for years." But two days later, stunned headlines announce the destruction of Hiroshima and Truman's message to the Japanese: "Quit or Be Destroyed."

Oregonian coverage is a mix of astonished jubilation that such a blow has been struck, pride that plutonium for the atomic bomb was produced in the Pacific Northwest, and awe at what the existence of such a weapon could mean for the future. But also making the front page on this immense news day is a concern—what will happen to area jobs?

On this question, various officials express the hope that the shipyards will, somehow, manage to remain busy. It is noted that Edgar Kaiser, Henry's son, has "repeatedly told his thousands of employees" that the company would be finding more work for them postwar, and a report that has lauded "the high intelligence and ingenuity of Portland ship workers" is cited.

By August 10, the second bomb has fallen on Nagasaki. Japan, however, has still not accepted the need for an unconditional surrender.

And the *Bo's'n's Whistle* is still not ready to face the end of shipyard work, declaring, "Even if Japan should be bombed to extinction," the Japanese people may decide to fight a war "amounting to racial suicide in China, where they still have a tremendous fighting force." As if to emphasize that the new shipyard normal still reigns, the front page photo shows "bathing beauty boilermakers."

By August 15, however, word comes of complete Japanese surrender, and an aerial photo of Portland streets on the *Oregonian's* front page shows jubilant crowds in a snowstorm of confetti. Some of it is raining down from the Office of Price Administration, where workers have been joyfully ripping up books of rules and regulations.

Somewhere down there amid the screaming and the dancing, the kissing and the cork popping, I am sure, is Eva. But in addition to the joy, there has to be confusion. For it is suddenly clear that the takedown will be much swifter than has been suggested all through the summer. On the same front page that announces the end of the war, the *Oregonian* runs another headline: "Navy Cancels Kaiser Ships." And a few days later the *Whistle* too capitulates, admitting that shipyard work, as most have known it, is over. The sudden end of the war and cancellation of contracts, the newsletter reports, have "completely knocked out the planned program of gradually tapering off work toward the end of the year."[2]

In a kind of requiem, the *Whistle* runs a photo of women—all fully clothed—who stand together in a group. The caption reads, "No tears were shed by these Swan Island Plate Shop workers getting their quit slips, though many were undecided where to go from here."[3]

Eva writes home that she could lose her job at any time. She is probably right. As the job cuts begin, women are being let go at a rate of 75 percent higher than men.[4]

For some women, as Karen Anderson writes, it is a relief to quit a hard, dirty job. Some have worked only for patriotic reasons; others simply believe the woman's place is in the home or accept that their husbands wanted "a wife not a career woman."[5] But a good number, like Eva, have grown attached to the new way of life. Peggy Wolf, for example, a chauffeur in a war plant, told an interviewer, "Many women in here are plenty unhappy. . . . The taste of independence has spoiled 'em." And at an aircraft plant, it was reported that many women "came into the cafeteria and cried after receiving their discharges."[6]

Surely many women are sorry to see their jobs end. Only a year ago a government survey found that as many as 80 percent of women in the war plants wanted to keep working at a comparable rate of pay and at a similar job.[7] Now, however, with the war won, everything is different; and attention is focused on domestic bliss, which is, the newspapers and magazines "report," what everyone wants now and what women are going home to create. A piece in the *Christian Science Monitor*, for example, sets the scene: "Mrs. Jones will make the bed—the chore that bored us worst of all—and we'll find the house clean and lighted when we get home at night. The table will be set in shining array for supper! We'll forget this catch-as-catch-can, red-and-blue point three-shift way of living."[8]

This theme is also found in the *Bo's'n's Whistle*, which, for all its recent appreciation of women's shipyard work, is now able to state definitively what women will want after the war— domestic bliss. An article entitled "The Kitchen—Women's Big Post-war Goal," begins, "When the war is finally finished, most feminine shipyard workers want to put geraniums in the window of a cottage and care for their 'kids.'" The article features a drawing of a woman in overalls racing toward the front door of such a cottage, her lunch pail in hand, her tin hat flying off her head. In a second picture, she reappears in a polka-dot dress and frilly apron. She sings merrily—apparently in a duet with the bird outside her geranium-filled window—as she dries dishes. At her feet two toddlers pull each other's hair.[9]

At the *Ladies' Home Journal*, where the magazine's own poll has found that 79 percent of women said they enjoyed working more than staying home, it was nevertheless concluded that while women may believe that jobs "are more enjoyable," they still believe that "homes are more important."[10] And it won't be long before women's magazines and marriage manuals begin to warn that working outside the home has produced in some women a "failure to accept their femininity" resulting in "individual neurosis" and "social maladjustment."

Whatever their actual postwar "goals," Susan Hartmann writes, "women did leave the labor force as the war ended."[11] By 1946 the female labor force will have declined from its wartime peak of 19 million to 16.8 million. And women's share of the civilian labor force decreases from 35 percent to 28 percent. But these statistics do not give the whole picture. Though many women continue to work, most have been laid off from factories and other traditional male work places and have returned to conventional women's work.

Even the much-ballyhooed welders and riveters have found themselves unhirable. One experienced welder remembered with some bitterness, "During the war we were comrades; now we were competition." After the war, no one would consider hiring her as a welder; she could not even get work creating ornamental trimming on windows and doors. "We believed we were the new women," she remembered. "But we were really a joke."[12]

In the Portland area, where a high percentage of women had been hired for war work, opportunities for women are now few. Young, attractive women with "business" training could find work, albeit low paying, as file clerks and stenographers. Older and untrained women could work in the canneries, in poultry processing, and in the woolen mills; none of these dirty, tedious jobs, of course, provide the interest or even half the wages of war work.[13]

As for the big plans promoted by Henry Kaiser, none come to fruition; and by 1947 the company will have left the area. Furthermore, in Portland as elsewhere, women are being told frankly that they need not apply for most job openings, that "there's too many men that need work."[14] Many help-wanted ads reinforce this message, specifying the type of worker sought: "not over 45 years, male and white."[15]

There seems to be little outcry against the new state of affairs, though one protest comes from Margaret Hickey, head of the Women's Advisory Committee to the War Manpower Commission. She questions whether a society is "democratic" if it "utilizes womanpower in a crisis and neglects it in peace." But though the country had ardently wooed women into the workplace, the courtship was now over. "Perhaps," Hickey observes, "intentions were never honorable."[16]

৵ Though Eva will manage to hang on at the shipyard for another six months, she understands what's happening: it's over. Maybe, she writes Grace, it is for the best. And suddenly she seems to question everything that has happened since she left Wing Valley two years earlier—who she has become, what she wants or, at least, should want. Could this be the first time she's stopped to examine the changes that have taken place in her life?

Well, why not? She's barely twenty-three and has been thrown into a whirlwind of uncertainty and change that has upended life for people all over the world. Now she writes to Grace with sudden— if somewhat contradictory—insight.

> It's not that Portland is bad or even Swan Island. The people are the same here as they are all over the world, good and bad. It's just that no girl should live away from home & work. Not that it makes bad girls out of all good ones. I haven't changed a bit that way & never would if I lived here 10 years.
>
> It's just that you live too fast, it's bad for a person, physically and mentally. You become mixed up, restless, unsure & dissatisfied with life, people & the whole world in general. You never can really be happy, because you never know what you want. And if you do, you're afraid to take it because you know it would mean giving up something else you like.

What she is trying to describe sounds a lot like the coming-of-age confusion many young people face as they struggle to understand who they are in the world and what they want in life. But Eva, like everyone else who reads magazines or newspapers, is being told with increasing fervor that this type of confusion is not proper for women. That in fact there *is* no confusion: home and marriage are the only correct choices. Even the only sane choice.

It will be eighteen years before Betty Friedan's *The Feminine Mystique* will challenge the prescription, powerfully promulgated in the later forties and fifties and accepted by most of American society, that women's lives were necessarily passive, revolving entirely around husband and children. Here in 1945, twenty-three-year-old Eva can hardly be expected to question the certainties of her time. Given the powerful messages about what women must be now, she sees, as she writes Grace, that the "most explanatory" term for what she has become is "selfish." "I'll admit that Portland, my work, this way of living & this type of reckless, carefree, independent life has me pretty well under its power. I love it & I love Portland and I'd hate to give it up. In fact, I can't seem to do it, even though I know it means so little compared to the real life I've always wanted. Then sometimes I wonder if I even know what or who I want."

Because of the war, as Eva almost seems to understand, she has had the misfortune of glimpsing what it is to live a life on your own terms, what it means to have choices. As a result, she can barely find in herself the obedient and dutiful girl she used to be. Whether she can locate that girl or not, it is clear that she no longer has an excuse for living a "carefree, independent" life, even if she could somehow find a way to do it. Now, if she's a decent person, she will demonstrate that work has not caused her to forget what a woman should be, and she will immediately join the record numbers who are getting married.

And, as she clearly understands, she needs to do it fast. Now in her letters home there is note of urgency on this score, even panic. She has to nail somebody down before the whole merry-go-round comes to a crashing halt, work disappears, the dorms close, and the men who'd been buzzing around in seemingly endless droves all go back to wherever they came from to marry their hometown girls.

Many of Eva's friends have already left Swan Island, and all their letters include an update on marriage plans. Some have accepted proposals or are agonizing about the choice. For some, the marriage is already a reality. One of her friends, now living in California, snatches a moment from "making dinner for my honey" to write glowingly of her new life: she has an adorable baby, a new car, and she and her husband are going into business for themselves. The friend reminisces about her wedding in the rain in Portland, how Eva "hailed a police car for a taxi." It's time for Eva to get married too, she writes. "Swan Island is no place for you."

Yes, *everyone* is getting married. Aub writes that he's engaged to a girl who lives in the town near where he's been stationed. Even Eva's seventeen-year-old cousin, Ginger, is planning to marry a serviceman on leave. ("If anybody tries to say she hasn't known him long and might change her mind, she sure storms," Grace writes.) Ginger herself writes Eva with the exciting news, explaining that it's the right thing to do because if she doesn't marry her guy, he will "feel bad, everybody else coming back from furloughs with brides."

Grace's sadness is barely veiled as she describes cleaning and decorating the Methodist church for Ginger's wedding. It's a labor of love she'd always dreamed of performing for Eva but "guess one's niece is next best." The wedding went off fine, though "it sort of got me when Ginger went thru the whole thing nearly precisely as you had planned for your wedding."

And now Grace, tactfully, recognizing that her daughter has become someone she doesn't entirely know, makes one last effort to help Eva get settled. Could Eva, perhaps, try to make it up with Dave. Perhaps he can be excused for some of the things he's done or said since "he has been so hurt coming back from what he was in for so long & then things going for him as it has."

Grace is willing to accept that Eva may not "feel that way about him" anymore. Only, she has seen a letter Eva wrote to her cousin Ginger, describing Dave as "about the finest fellow in the world that could make you happy." If you meant that, Grace writes, "and if it were me I would see to it even if I had to go & propose now, for it is surely your move. I would surely hate to see you throw away your life's happiness for a few months thrills. Of course you know more about him and what you want than I do, but I do so want to see you happy & I don't see how the life in a shipyard can make for much happiness."

Eva obviously has been terribly conflicted, not just about leaving her job and the freedom of her working life but about Dave himself. It is not hard to see why she would have hesitated to marry him. His letters from the hospital are a bizarre combination of panic, need, and outrage. He has been completely unable to grasp or grant that she has had the right to love her own adventures and freedom as he has loved his. And perhaps most ominous of all is his insistence that it was her fault that he broke down in Italy and that it is therefore her responsibility to "patch" him up.

By now, the problems faced by couples like Eva and Dave have resulted in a bit more public examination, and in the October 1945 *Ladies' Home Journal* is an article that Grace, at least, would have seen. Entitled "Meet Ed Savickas: His Chances of Complete Recovery Bring Hope to Thousands," the piece features another soldier who became "paralyzed by combat fatigue" after months on the front line in North Africa and Sicily. Like Dave, he couldn't eat or sleep; and now, home with his wife and small daughter, he is "still moody and restless, hates crowds and noise." And he can be hard to live with. Sometimes he'll ask his wife to make certain foods but then won't eat them; sometimes he'll walk out in the middle of a movie. A photo of the young family at the table shows the wife and daughter eating as Ed, a handsome young man in a white sports shirt, stares at a milk bottle, his hands by his sides. His wife, Stella, is clear that none of this is Ed's fault, noting that previously he was the most considerate of men. "If anyone is to blame," she states, "it's Hitler."

Ed, though, is progressing. He has a job where he sees the company doctor and, once a month, a psychiatrist. If he follows their instructions, his recovery is a "likely bet." For now he needs "pampering and loving," which Stella patiently provides. This, the article explains, is her first job. Her second is to see that, as he improves, "he becomes the master of the household, not the baby."[17]

Here is the model that Eva, who has come to feel her recent life has been "selfish," should follow. And amid all the confusion that her life has recently become, she probably remembers that Dave, after all, is from home, comes from a good family, and has her mother's stamp of approval. Maybe his recovery too is a "likely bet"; maybe whatever it was that made her want to marry him a few years ago will return. So Eva comes to believe—or at least accept—that Dave should be her future. She follows Grace's advice, writing him and proposing that they marry right away. But he doesn't write back; nor does Eva hear from his father. She knows that Mr. Johnson, at least, would have written if there had been any hope. Eva tells her mother, "I'm sure I've lost him."

Now, Eva's letters have an air of elegy. The barracks and mess halls at Swan Island's sister shipyard have closed, and on this evening another ship is leaving. "Always hate to see a ship and all the guys leave after we get acquainted. These guys have been here so long, almost two months."

The funereal mood of Eva's letter isn't only for the emptying shipyard, but for the girl she has been for the past two years, the girl who, now, even she herself must view with disapproval. "I have had my fill of this sort of life. How sorry I am it took so long for it to all get out of my system."

Though the whole thing sounds like a chore, she must now make preparations to leave Swan Island and get married. "Took all my clothes to the cleaners. Want to get my wisdom teeth pulled and a good electric iron and some other things for my hope chest. And a stinking photo made. Then I'll be ready to move on any time the opportunity arrives." And opportunities do arrive. One is presenting itself in the form of almost daily letters from the handsome Southerner, Jimmy Wright, a sailor who came through Portland and is now stationed in San Francisco. His letters are intelligent enough, quite witty. Like Dave he yearns to hold her in his arms and breathe in the fragrance of her hair, but he's a lot calmer about it. Beyond this, he doesn't have much to report: he spends his time trying to stay awake on watch in the San Francisco fog, breaking the monotony with frequent sprees on shore, where he admits to getting plastered.

He sounds sweet. He "cried" after he had to part from her last. Unlike Dave, he is not issuing instructions and detailing plans. Rather he seems glad to leave things up to Eva, fantasizing about how nice it would be if she had a little apartment in Portland. And yes— he appears to respond to her question—he's wants to get married, though his family is against it. "They think I'm still in knee pants."

His family may have a point; though I'm not sure Eva realizes it, Jimmy is only twenty, three years younger than she. And from his letters, it is clear that binge drinking is his favorite activity. Eva, despite living a somewhat fast life in Portland, is still a girl who grew up in a home where alcohol was believed to be the root of most evil, and her letters express concern on this score. In response, Jimmy reports that recently he has tried not to get plastered; as a result everybody wonders if he's sick. He *did* go out drinking but didn't drink very much. He was proud that he got home sober. In a phrase that is similar to one Eva has heard before, he writes, "I love whiskey but I love you more."

Eva keeps Jimmy on the string. After Dave, it must be a relief to have someone who can take life easy and have a good time, who isn't a mass of recrimination and need. Who isn't barking orders every minute. Still, I'm pretty sure Eva is concerned about Jimmy's weaknesses, his drinking and his cluelessness about what he will do postwar.

Before long, she has someone better to tell her mother about—

a man named Pete, who's "a lot like Dave," which I take to mean a man with drive and a direction in life. His father is an engineer, Eva writes, and his family is Presbyterian. And now he seems to be the prime candidate. When Pete arrives back in California from the Pacific in early 1946, he writes Eva, and he does indeed sound interested. However, he has found himself in a horrible tangle of red tape. He writes, "I can't get paid until I get discharged, and I can't get discharged until I get to Maryland. I've never been so messed up in my life. I expect I'll be here a week before I catch a troop train east. It doesn't look like I'll get to see you until after I get home, but darling I'll be back to get you as soon as I can."

Eva writes back on the flowery pink stationery she saves for special, telling him that she "cried for joy" when she heard he was back in the States. But the letter, sent to California, then forwarded to Maryland, is returned to her and comes to me unopened. She doesn't know how to reach him, and he is not, apparently, contacting her. And Pete slips through her fingers.

Now, as if to underline the fact that Dave too is lost, a letter addressed to Eva arrives in Wing Valley. Writing on Paramount Studios letterhead, Dave informs her that he has recently married. This fact, however, appears not to have made him less bitter or more stable. "There is no use to say the usual trite things that are usually said at times like these," he says, his handwriting slanting crazily to the right. "In fact it is probably better to let the subject carry on in its own way."

Dave's parents have also heard about the marriage, and they write Eva in shock and sadness. "It is very hard for us to tell you how we felt about Dave's actions. You know, of course, that we had hoped things would be entirely different and that you would, one day, be part of our plans. Right up to the present time, we feel that it can't all be true."

Though Shorty, Eva's boyfriend from the shipyard, still loves her with all his "sole," he appears to know he's not in the running. He sends a final letter, written with a blunt pencil on ripped scrap paper: "Darling I am going back to the woods where I came from I can make more money their then I can in Portland." He expresses his hope that she will choose the right one to marry, warning, "If you don't it can't be corrected very easy."

By the spring of 1946, Eva, twenty-four and an old maid by postwar standards, announces that she's engaged to the sailor Jimmy Wright. Everyone sends congratulations. Aub writes to say he's sure Jimmy is a "good old boy." And friends in California who've had Jimmy over to dinner tell Eva what a fun, swell guy he is and how crazy he is about her. Before dinner, he called Eva on the phone and afterward was too excited and in love to sit down and eat.

Jimmy, besides being tall, dark, handsome, and fun-loving, really does seem to be a nice kid. While Eva wraps up her affairs in Portland, Jimmy, now discharged from the Navy, goes to Wing Valley to await their wedding. He gets along with Eva's parents fine and looks for ways to help out. He doesn't mind getting up on a tractor or doing some of the milking, and he even helps Grace iron the heavy towels. He'll be a good husband, Grace writes hopefully.

But Eva *still* can't seem to leave Swan Island. Jimmy, marooned in Wing Valley, tries to be a good sport, writing, "They are going to have the church fixed up and redecorated so it will be in pretty good shape for our wedding, if we are ever fortunate enough to have one." As the weeks pass, however, his letters grow increasingly frustrated. He's desperately bored in the Valley. He would never have come out if he had known Eva would not be joining him right away. He likes her parents and all, but there's absolutely nothing to do here once the milking is done and supper is over. He appears to know enough not to go up to the tavern, something that Grace—well known in the Valley for her strong views on drinking—could not have borne. But he's been driven to the point of buying a bottle and hiding it in the barn.

Reading this, I have to stop for a moment and think of Grace, who is undoubtedly doing her best to believe all will be well. Who is, I am sure, lying awake nights, trying not to know that the strange sweetish smell that wafts through her house late at night is that of terrifying, evil, life-wrecking liquor.

After driving Jimmy and everyone else crazy for a few more weeks—no one understands why she won't come home—Eva finally arrives, and Grace finally gets the chance to prepare the church for her own daughter's wedding. Grace is relieved, I suppose—though I remember hearing about a terrible argument between Eva and Grace, so terrible that Eva would not let her mother sew her wedding dress, instead going to her aunt to have it made.

Jimmy, I feel sure, deals with all the tension in his own tried-and-true way.

Though both Eva and Grace have serious misgivings, it is too late. The engagement has been announced, Eva has to be married, and they have to go through with it. Eva becomes Mrs. Jimmy Wright. And Jimmy's drinking problem? Now and for the next decade it will be Eva's problem as well.

If there'd been no war, of course, none of this would be happening. Eva, still a malleable child, would have married Dave at eighteen and would be the mother of several children by now. If there'd been no war and women's war work, she would never have glimpsed any role beyond that of wife and mother. Dave would work and run their affairs, and Eva would keep the house and raise her children, doting on them just as Grace had doted on her. Probably Dave would boss her around too much; probably as time went on, she'd learn how to get back at him with the occasional caustic remark. They would have their troubles, their ups and downs. But there would be no need to doubt who they were or what rules they lived by.

Even given the war, it was, perhaps, not too late when Dave returned. If Eva had been able to let go of her compelling life in Portland to join him in Spokane, she could be married by now to someone respectable and relatively accomplished. Although Dave's condition was clearly much more severe than most people understood, there was reason to hope he could've gotten better over time. Maybe if Eva had fully recognized the maelstrom she was in, she would have known to cling, at all costs, to a known quantity. Then things might have turned out all right. Then Grace would be able to hold her head up in the Valley, knowing that her daughter was married to a respectable local man.

Eva probably should have played her cards better. But she was young, new to the world outside Wing Valley and to the intoxication of freedom. And for a while, she just didn't feel like playing it safe. The desire to live for herself as long as she could was too intense. Now, though, she has begun to pay what will be a very high price.

PART 2

Vick has been gone exactly one year when, in 1959, Eva receives a twelve-page letter from a woman she doesn't know. The woman's name is Odette, and she's a bookkeeper who lives in Ballard, a working-class section of Seattle. Also a farm girl, she, like Eva, went to the city during the war, getting a job as a riveter for the tank landing (LST) crafts. Like Eva, Odette saw her personal life upended in the aftermath of the war. Her husband died, leaving her to raise a daughter, Leisa, alone.

For years after her husband's death, Odette writes, she did not think of dating. She was busy trying to earn a living and to make a home for her daughter. If she's had free time, she's spent it putting in a lawn or tiling the basement. Fairly recently, however, her girlfriend got her to go out to some dances at the Elks Club, and Odette found she could have fun again. Then, about eight months ago, she met a man at one of these dances, and he fell desperately in love with her. He was so crazy about her that he was jealous if any other man asked her to dance. This was it, he told her. She was the one he had been searching for. And he started talking about marriage right away.

Odette didn't want to be in a rush. As she told the man, the only real happiness she had known in her life was during the twelve years she was married to her husband. Now she knew "what hell it was to lose someone you love so deeply," and she was afraid she couldn't survive another such loss. The man understood; he had had a very similar experience when his dear wife Marie had died after a horrible illness. He had also, in a sense, lost his seven-year-old daughter, Florence, who, all had agreed, would be better off living with Marie's parents in California.

So he knew exactly how Odette felt. He had suffered in just the same way. But now he loved Odette so much, and he knew he could make her happy. She *had* to marry him, and right away. If she didn't, he was afraid he would give in to the entreaties of Marie's family in California; they were pressuring him to marry one of Marie's cousins. He didn't love this woman, but she had a lot of money. If he couldn't have the one thing he wanted, Odette's love, well, he might as well marry the cousin and be rich at least.

The week before Christmas he gave Odette an engagement ring. He said he'd meant to give it to her on Christmas Eve. But he found he couldn't wait even a week "for the whole world to know what a happy and lucky man he was." Soon after Christmas, they were married. As they had both been widowed, Odette had wanted a "quiet affair," but he was so excited about having a fancy wedding that she didn't have the heart to say no. He hinted that he wanted a wedding ring too, and Odette bought him one, a lovely ring with three diamonds. Then they had a nice honeymoon in California, an area her husband knew well and where he could show his new wife all the sights.

After the long hard years alone, Odette was happy and grateful to have such a wonderful husband. "Every day," she writes Eva, he said "how much he loved me and how happy he was. *Every day.*" On her birthday, he gave her a card: "To the World's Best Wife—From One Who Knows." The lines inside read, "the more I see of you honey, the more I love you." Her new husband couldn't do enough to help her around the house. She had "worked too hard alone," he told her, and even before their second date, he began coming over to mow her lawn. Once a sergeant in the Army, he now issued strict orders: she was not to touch that lawn mower. After they were married, he began making improvements to the house Odette had struggled to keep up on her own. He put up shelves, built fruit cupboards, and rigged a spring on the garage door so Odette wouldn't have to wrestle it open each time she came home.

Odette clearly appreciated a nice home, and soon her husband, who had a good job as a chef at United Airlines, wanted her to have something better than the little house in Ballard, something in Seattle's upscale Broadmoor section. After searching for just the right thing, they found a house they loved, and in June they put down earnest money and applied for a loan. Odette wanted to wait on furnishings until the loan came through, but her husband felt sure they would get the financing. So, on Monday and Friday evenings they went shopping and within a few weeks had selected almost everything they would need.

One Sunday, they got back to the little house in Ballard on the late side. They had spent the afternoon and evening at the new house measuring all the windows. They'd had to get it done because the next night they were going downtown to shop for drapes. Before going to bed, they had a piece of Odette's homemade pumpkin pie with whipped cream, his favorite dessert. After spending hours up on stepladders with measuring tapes and yardsticks, they were tired but happy. As they enjoyed their pie and coffee, they discussed the new home, the new furniture and, as Odette writes to Eva, "even mentioned the baby" that was on the way.

At eleven Odette went to bed; she had to be up early for work. Her husband said he would like to watch TV for a little while because he didn't have work the next day. Still, it wasn't long before he came to bed. "He put his arms around me, kissed me good night several times, and said, 'I love you, darling.' Of course, I said the same to him which we did every night."

While Odette was getting ready for work the next morning, her husband was sitting in the living room having coffee. "He seemed a little moody, so I kissed him goodbye as usual but then came back to him and kissed him again. I kidded him about being a good boy while I was at work." Then Odette left, and her husband, before packing up his clothes and the wedding pictures, before getting in the car and leaving forever, took time to tidy up the kitchen, washing the pie plates and coffee cups that had been left in the sink from the night before. He dried the dishes, then rinsed out the dishtowel, and hung it carefully on the clothesline in back.

Like Eva, Odette has launched an intensive search to find Vick. Unlike Eva, who got sidetracked by a vision of Vick in Mexico, Odette has taken a more methodical approach, and it has yielded better results. By contacting the motor vehicles divisions in Washington, Oregon, and California and requesting records in Vick's name, she's turned up quite a bit of information about her husband's activities. All of this she now shares with Eva.

To register the automobiles he bought at various times, Vick was required to give a place of residence. Though he always gave his real name, including, when requested, his middle name, some of the addresses on the registration forms were fake, a hotel or a nonexistent street number. But sometimes Vick went ahead and put down a real address and phone number. When Odette called the phone number given for an address in Modesto, she reached the wife he had spoken of, Marie.

Not only was Marie—who married Vick in 1948— very much alive, she had never suffered a serious illness and didn't have a female cousin of marriageable age. She *did* have a seven-year-old daughter, Vick's daughter, though the girl's name was not Florence but Susan. Susan was born in June of 1952, four weeks after her father vanished from their lives. Unlike Eva and Odette, Marie heard from Vick once after he left. A few days after he had gone, Marie received a letter, which she has sent to Odette and Odette now forwards to Eva. I find the letter in Eva's papers. "Dearest wife," it begins in Vick's familiar scrawl. "I know when I leave for the Naval Hospital that my lungs are in bad shape as I had a test a few weeks ago & it showed blood, but it isn't TB I am sure."

Vick goes on to tell Marie that he has wired his brother in Canada for money. "I told my Brother I need some dough as I have some coming to me. It should be around $4,500, so if I am not back here by Friday night I have gone up to get it & in a week I'll be back. Then I will have to go a better climate." In the same sentence, he gives Marie instructions about running the Cream Cup, a cafe that her father, a Portuguese immigrant, had recently acquired for the young couple to operate. "Go to see Mr Gooding by the first of week & tell him the score and get a manager to run it. Get a Bookkeeper to keep the books up to date and that place will pay off now that the hot weather is here. I will see that you get the dough, & papers saying you own the Cream Cup so don't worry."

In the next line he concludes, "I'll look after Vick and you look after Jr. Bye for now." The letter is signed, "Love, Vick," though, uncharacteristically, he has botched the writing of his own name. He seems to have written "i" twice, each "i" with a dot, then a scribbled out the letter before the last "k," which looks more like an "r." From the letter, it looks as if Vick has a pretty clear plan though he's in somewhat of a hurry. He needs to leave and can't wait for the money that he believes is being sent. He may have to return home briefly to get it. Then he's leaving for good. But something prevents him from just spitting this out. Many softening agents have been added to the letter: he's sick and Marie can surely understand he needs to go to a hospital; at the same time she shouldn't worry that it's anything as bad as TB; he'll be back Friday night or at least next week; by taking a few simple steps she'll be fine with the restaurant and will probably make money.

Though he's leaving forever, he writes, "Bye for now." Though he's abandoning his unborn child, he pauses to consider how "Jr." will be cared for. Even the botched signature seems to indicate that he hesitates to say what he's actually saying. Weirdly, it seems that he doesn't want Marie to feel too bad. As a result of the mixed message, Marie couldn't make head or tale of the letter. It was only after Vick made no further contact—even after the baby had arrived—that she realized her husband wasn't coming back.

Of course, she knew right away that he had driven off in their brand-new, sea-green Mercury.

Though Vick and Marie's daughter is named Susan, there *is* a young girl named Florence, and in January of 1953, six months after Vick left Marie, twelve-year-old Florence sends a letter to Vick at the Modesto address, where Marie still lives. Florence is writing from Baltimore, begging him to come back to her and her mother. Following this, several more letters arrived in Marie's mailbox, "beautifully written love letters," as Marie describes them in a phone conversation with Odette, from Florence's mother, Tessa. Tessa seems to think that Vick has gone to California to sell a house he owned. She too expresses her yearning for Vick's return. She clearly has no inkling that Vick had been married or that her letters are arriving at the home of a wife he has deserted.

Marie sends Tessa's letters along to Odette, who forwards them to Eva, who adds them to the collection of papers that has come to me.

Tessa's letters are indeed "beautiful," written in an ornate, Catholic-school hand on stationery engraved with the name, Mrs. Tessa McKee Nesbitt and an address on North Charles Street, Baltimore. In her "Dearest Vick" letters, Tessa's tone is determinedly upbeat, never recriminatory or weepy. Nor are her letters, like Eva's, frantic with passion and self-blame. Rather Tessa, who does not appear to have been married to Vick, skillfully portrays herself as a woman happily getting herself into shape for the day her man—whom she "misses in a thousand ways"—returns. "I've done quite a bit since you left, caught up on my sleep, mended my clothes, had my hair arranged in a style I can handle more easily, switched to Chesterfields to cut down on my smoking. And now I'm working on my figure; the impossible takes a little longer! I always forget your exercises until I have half finished my own, so I make a note to use yours the next night."

Tessa misses Vick, and she misses the beautiful green Merc. "It was the only car that made an impression on me. It seemed to have a very friendly personality. It was always ready to do just what we wanted. It made the summer cooler, the winter warmer." (Before forwarding the letter to Odette, Marie draws a thick black line under this reference to her brand new car.)

Tessa appears to live with her mother and her aunt, in addition to her daughter, Florence. The women run a rooming house, which, I suppose, is how Vick found his way to them. Though Vick is gone, they still speak of him all the time. "Aunt May puts meals on the table and says, 'I know Vick would like this.' My bedroom door fell off the hinges last night so Mother wondered why it didn't happen when Vick was home." But it is Tessa who is in love, and in another letter, she reminisces about the moment when Vick told her he was leaving. "I knew you must have reasons for going you couldn't discuss. I knew you had been restless for a long time, figured you planned to join the Army or visit Canada. I wanted so to go with you—if I could only have felt you really wanted me."

Tessa—possibly because things never got as far as marriage— is more resigned to her loss than Eva, less devastated than Odette, less flabbergasted than Marie. Still, she writes, "I love you now and forever above all things—and this is true whether this must be the end—or whether things could be that wonderful."

When Marie writes back informing Tessa that her letters are coming to the home of Vick's wife, abandoned by him in the ninth month of pregnancy, Tessa is shocked and apologetic. She replies, begging Marie to understand that she had no idea. She offers to do anything she can to help Marie find him, and she gives what information she has. She tells Marie that Vick hit another car while driving the Mercury; and a man came to the door looking for Vick's California address, which Tessa would not give. The man asked if Vick left in a rush, but Tessa stonewalled, telling the man, "We've rented rooms for many years so we've learned not to try to figure out why people do things."

While Tessa's letters to Vick are completely upbeat, tempting him with a portrait of the loving woman that could still be his, what she writes to Marie expresses a deeper concern. She, along with her aunt and mother, felt that Vick had become depressed, so much so that they feared he was "too despondent to be left alone," and they have "searched for him through every channel." They had believed he was in California, though they'd also gotten a tip that he had "gone to St. Louis with a guest from the hotel."

Now Tessa knows that nothing he said was necessarily true. No dummy, she realizes the car was probably the reason Vick gave her the California address. "He knew he could not sell the car without your signature." Tessa, possibly, was to be the go-between. Marie's suffering, Tessa makes clear, takes precedence over her own; and in her letter to Marie she mentions herself only once: "I suppose, it will take me quite a while to take this in."

Marie and Tessa aren't the only women included in Odette's report to Eva. There's one wife more, Linda. It was she who lived in the Alberta Street house in Portland and with whom Vick bought the new red Ford that he would drive to Boise at the end of 1956. I don't have letters from Linda and don't know much about her. I know only what she told Odette, who located her through automobile records. Three days before Vick disappeared, he asked Linda to let him have her engagement ring. It didn't fit quite right, he said; he wanted to take it to the jewelers to have it adjusted. Linda gave him the ring.

✑ So here's the story, Odette writes Eva—Marie, Tessa, Linda, you, me.

Odette is now on the twelfth page of her letter, and she has to wrap it up. It's late, and she has to put up her hair and get to bed. Of course, she has to be at work early in the morning. She is crying as she writes, and the ink runs; she apologizes for making a mess on the page and also for writing a "book." But Odette, who needs Eva to understand what has happened—perhaps Eva is one of the few people in the world who really *can* understand—has a couple more things to tell. She wants to tell Eva about the baby. At first, Odette says, she couldn't believe that Vick would really leave, knowing his child was on the way. But after hearing how Vick left Marie with a baby due in a few weeks, she had to believe it. She realized too that she couldn't raise her daughter and a new baby alone.

"Do you have any idea," she writes, "what it's like to walk the streets all by yourself and hunt for a doctor who will perform this kind of operation? Finally I found one, but he wanted $750 and it had to be cash. I told him I couldn't possibly pay that much. This was on a Friday. After he examined me, he said I was almost three months pregnant, and I had to have it done by Tuesday at the very latest."

As Odette left his office and crossed the street, a car heading toward her was coming on fast, and Odette thought, "Maybe it will hit me and I won't have to go on living." But the car didn't hit her; and the next day she went to the doctor again, persuading him to give her the illegal operation for five hundred dollars.

"I will never understand," Odette writes, "why Vick wanted a baby."

The last thing Odette wants to tell Eva has to do with some snapshots her husband had. They were recent pictures of him on a trip, beside a swimming pool, on the deck of what looked like a ferry. When Odette asked about them, Vick told her that, yes, he had taken a trip recently, but he "didn't enjoy it much because he was so alone." After that the pictures disappeared.

"Eva," Odette writes. "Was that your honeymoon?"

Somehow, the cruelty of this hits me harder than anything else. It is one of the moments I can see Eva as if I were there—in the postage-stamp kitchen of the Jefferson Street apartment, the tear-stained pages spread out on the table, only a lighted Tareyton to keep her company. But perhaps, eventually, wasn't it a relief for Eva to see that what had happened to her was not, in a sense, her unique tragedy? Not somehow her fate?

Yes, the war years upended her life, got her off track, resulted in hasty, faulty decisions, and left her single and vulnerable in the marriage-mad fifties. Still. Who could have been expected to understand something like this? Who had ever heard of such a thing? Sure, there are men who are unfaithful, who have affairs, who fall for another woman. But how many of them go through one super-charged romance and marriage after another? How many tell a woman they'll love her forever right up until the day they walk out? And Eva wasn't the only one taken in. Look at Odette—clearly intelligent, careful, and competent. She went for it. Whatever it is.[1]

For me, Odette's letter—when my own shock wears off—puts things in a different light. And I am ashamed to notice that I had unconsciously done what most of society would have done, blamed Eva for what happened. Such things, after all, don't happen to nice women. But this time it did. To several nice women.

I wonder if, like me, Eva now tries to understand, tries to puzzle out from the bizarre pattern of his falsehoods what is making Vick tick. He uses his wife Marie's correct name, just says she's tragically dead. He acknowledges that he has a small daughter, just gives her the name of another girl, Tessa's daughter, Florence. I speculate now that the picture Vick showed me and Grace of the daughter he missed so much was really of Tessa's daughter. This would seem to fit his method of offering a little weenie of truth wrapped in a great doughy bun of falsehood. But why? Obviously he needs to give his life a context that would make sense to other people. Why doesn't he just flat out lie? Why does he give these partial truths?

For Eva, still married to Vick, still alone, it would seem that Odette's letter is a bitter but ultimately salutary pill, that this news will finally allow Eva to say to herself, whatever he was, he wasn't in love with me. He was never really my husband. And now it's time to move on. Clearly it is Odette's aim, in this long and detailed letter, to show Eva that this is what she must do. It is as if Odette, by sharing with Eva how surreal their mutual experience has been, is trying to help them both erase Vick from their hearts and lives.

A few months later, in December of 1959, Eva gets another letter from Odette. The two have spoken on the phone by now, and Eva has made notes on all the information Odette has gathered on Vick. Odette apologizes for not responding to Eva's letter sooner, but she's been struggling with the financial mess Vick left her in, and at the moment she is boiling mad. On top of everything else, she's had to pay $225 for the annulment that will come through in a couple of days. Odette can't wait to get her own name back and to resume her

Social Security widow's benefits. From now on Eva should write to her as Odette Olsen. "You know, Eva," she adds. "Your marriage is not legal either."

It's another lengthy late-night letter. But now there are no tearstains. After all she has learned and all she's been through, Odette is getting over Vick:

> I get furious when I think about how terribly much he has hurt me, not only financially but in other ways too. I've learned too much about his past and of course none of it is good. I think about you and the others he has hurt and get so disgusted that actually I've lost my feeling for him. I've kept telling myself over and over that he is with someone else now, so why should I grieve any more. From his past pattern he hasn't wasted a minute of his time since he has left me. That I am sure of.

Eva has apparently written to Odette—as she did to Vick himself—with the belief that he was suffering in some way, ill, struggling with immense inner turmoil as a result of past trauma and loss. But Odette doesn't buy it. "He never said anything to me about not being able to stay in one place for very long or that he wasn't proud of his past or anything like that." And, "he wasn't sick before he left me—as a matter of fact he was putting on weight and complained about being too heavy. He didn't have trouble sleeping either. He slept like a baby. I do think though and have reason to believe he did a lot more drinking than I realized. Of course he could drink an awful lot without showing it."

ⅆ Folded into this letter as it has come to me are a dozen sheets of the cheap tablet paper Eva uses for jotting notes. She too is working through the financial damage. On one sheet headed "Bad checks," Eva adds up the total for checks Vick bounced in a three-day period right before he left—$75. Most of the checks are made out to the Torch Café, where he apparently resumed old habits, but one twenty-dollar check is made out to a Texaco station: Vick needs gas to get out of town. In another column she notes that the car payment is due and that she has received a five-hundred-dollar loan from Grace. Here too a charge account bill for $26 owed to the Boise department store C. C. Anderson, where, right before leaving, Vick bought three new suits.

I choke up a little to see that as she struggles to manage her expenses, Eva includes this item: "Diane baton $3." This would be the fabulous battery-powered baton, flashing blue at one end and red at the other that she sent on my birthday that year.

Compared to Odette, I suppose, Eva got off easy. However, the experience seems to have caused her to worry about her financial position and to wonder what the future may hold. I see that she has written to the Social Security Administration to make inquiries about benefits. The response must have offered some small solace; she has worked forty quarters, which entitles her to minimum retirement benefits. The computer printout shows her 1958 income to be $1,690, up two dollars from her 1957 total. This is down from the $2,250 she earned in 1956. As a married woman, perhaps, she felt she should not work quite as much.

But Eva is not thinking only about her finances. Also noted on the lined paper are details about the other wives she has been given by Odette: addresses and phone numbers for Marie in California, Tessa in Baltimore, and Linda in Portland, as well as ages for the daughters, Susan and Florence. Also in this set of notes Eva has jotted, "George and Clark, brother or brother and cousin" and "Ontario, Canada." But in other notes is an address for George "in care of Westinghouse Electric, Lima Peru." For Clark, Eva has an address on Magnolia Street in Tampa, Florida.

From this it is clear that Eva is still trying to locate Vick, and I see that she has written the Florida Public Utilities Commission requesting information on any George or Clark Vickers in the state. A polite letter in response apologizes for the length of time it has taken to locate the information from the department of motor vehicles. No records for a Clark Vickers were found, but there are sixteen George Vickerses for whom there are automobile records in Florida. The utilities commission has supplied addresses and in some cases date of birth. Eva has crossed off four of the men who are in their sixties, jotting "too old." She has tried to get telephone numbers for the rest. Five have no telephone listings, and some of the names turn out to be the same person at a new address. But she has gotten four numbers and has called them all, jotting "no brother" or "no brother Virgil" by the names.

Somewhat ominously, given what is to come, I also see in this packet of notes that Eva has calculated how long Vick actually spent with each wife. As I will come to believe, she is building a case that her own marriage was different from the others.

Joining the Search

I am impressed by the information that the wives were able to piece together, even though they were conducting their investigation in a day before internet or email, a time when the ability to Xerox a letter or a picture was in its infancy, and—for someone on Eva's budget— even a long distance phone call was a big deal.

While Eva and the other wives have learned a great deal about *what* has happened, I don't see them even beginning to understanding *why*. For them, Vick's motives remain entirely incomprehensible, as do the passionate courtships, the happy-ever-after weddings, and his sweet—if brief—embrace of domestic bliss. Perhaps most puzzling of all is the quality of love and empathy he so richly expressed, completely disarming one attractive, sensible woman after another, making her believe that the man of her dreams has finally come along.

Today, of course, we can reach into people's lives past and present in a way Eva and the others couldn't have imagined. With internet search engines, we can get address and phone information on just about anybody. Using government, genealogical, military, and a variety of other websites, we can locate records and facsimiles of documents and pictures. Long distance phone calls aren't the big deal they used to be, and a quick call to a county courthouse can produce key vital statistics. Historical societies and librarians all over the country are also willing to take a call or an email and are usually glad to help out, looking into old newspapers and directories and sending along a fax or photograph.

With the new tools available, as well as some old-fashioned ones, I decide I will finish what the wives started. Master of deceit though Vick may be, I will find him, and I'll learn what is making him tick.

To start, I go through Eva's papers again to see whether, as I learn more about what I'm looking for, she left any clues that I had previously overlooked. And indeed, I see several critical pieces of information that I didn't notice on my first pass through. For one thing, I see that I have a blurry carbon copy of several of Vick's W-2 forms from the Hotel Boise. When I examine these with my newly purchased magnifying glass, Vick's social security number becomes distinct. I also realize that I probably know his year of birth. If he was forty-three, as shown on Eva's March 1957 wedding license, he was born in 1914.

In addition, I have a military ID number on the postcard sent to Vick in Washington, D.C., by the Veterans Administration when, after leaving Marie, he had his VA records moved from the San Francisco office to the one in D.C. For some reason, he carried this card with him to Boise and then left it behind. I have to give him this much credit: he wasn't too worried about covering his tracks.

To begin the search, I set myself up with accounts in several people-finder and genealogy search sites, and I start trying to figure out how they work. In my first session, I learn that with a social security number, I can plug Vick into the online Social Security Death Index (SSDI), operated by the Social Security Administration. This, I realize, must be my first step. Surely he's dead. What are the chances that a guy like him, a heavy smoker, is still alive well into his nineties? If he's on the SSDI, I'll get date of birth, death, and city of last residence. If I can find out where and when he died, I might be able to find somebody who knew him at the end. As I enter his number I've got goose bumps. The key to the whole mystery might be right here.

No Virgil Bailey Vickers turns up. How can that be? Is this index for real? But Grace is there. And there's my dad. Could Vick still be alive?

Quickly I learn that the first three Social Security numbers identify the state where the card was issued. I'm shocked to see that Vick, whom I'd taken for a city boy from California, is really from Kansas. I sit late into the night with my laptop, searching obsessively for Vick on all the sites I can find. For the first time in my life I understand the women I've seen in casinos, sitting all day in front of the slot machines with a coffee can full of quarters. Like any gambler, I've had one little hit—Kansas—and now I'm completely hooked. Now I *know* the next clue is there; it's waiting for me if I just keep playing.

I search this way and that. I follow searching advice offered on the sites and spell Vick's name different ways. I reverse it. I search with and without the middle name, middle initial. I search sites that give addresses, phone numbers, and names of family members. I search marriage records, divorce records, military records, criminal records, census records. I see that on several of the genealogy sites I can look into high school yearbooks that have been scanned. I can access family tree information that individuals have put up; I can see pictures of peoples' relatives and their relatives' tombstones. I can call up newspaper articles with the words "Virgil Vickers" in them.

I search for hours.

And I *do* get more hits. When I enter Virgil Vickers into a people-search website, his name comes up. There he is. Virgil Vickers. In fact, more than a hundred Virgil Vickerses are shown to be living in the United States. For some, ages are given, though I am again skeptical. Two gentlemen are shown to be one hundred and twenty years old, while another is a relatively youthful one hundred and eleven. But though the name "Virgil" has gone out of style, all of those listed aren't old. Some are in their thirties and forties.

For some there are middle initials, though I find no Virgil B; I realize my strategy must be to follow up on all those in the right age range whose middle initials do not rule them out. I zero in on a Virgil Vickers in the Sacramento area. I Google the address. It's a nursing home.

It's got to be him. Didn't Odette write how they visited back in the Sacramento area after she married him? Maybe he liked California and always circled back; maybe he settled down there in his old age. I get out my atlas and see that the town where the nursing home is located is only fifty or so miles from Modesto, where Vick lived with Marie and where Susan was born. Maybe he had regrets in his old age and wanted to be near the daughter he abandoned. Surely it's too much of a coincidence that a man of the same name, the right age, would be in a nursing home here.

A frantic hour later, searching the relatives that are given for the man, I see that *they* are related to a Virgil K. So it's Virgil K. in the nursing home? But maybe somebody made a mistake entering the data; I'm seeing plenty of obvious typos on these sites. I call the nursing home number; they have to have somebody on duty late at night. As I dial, I am shaking. I should probably wait until I'm a little calmer, but I can't. So I dial, trying to plan what I'll say. Hello, I'm calling for Mr. Virgil B. Vickers. Virgil B., six feet tall, dark eyes? Born 1914 in Kansas? Yes? And when are your visiting hours? No, that's all right. I want to surprise him.

But the number given for the nursing home is disconnected, and there's no new listing. There's no such place. Not any more. I breathe again and realize that I have learned a lesson about false positives—or possible positives that can't be proven.

It's growing late and my searching has become a bit random. Googling, I come across a Virgil Vickers who is native American and who in 1940 claimed to prove from scars on his stomach that he was the reincarnation of his own deceased self. (Too young.) Then there's a Virgil B. Vickers, a developer, who's in trouble with a Nevada zoning commission. (The middle name, I discover after forty-five minutes or so, is Barnes, and he's ten years younger.) I find five men of the same name enlisting to serve in World War II. (None the right age or hailing from Kansas.)

I pause over a Virgil Vickers who died in Canada in 2004. I like the idea of Canada. Maybe Vick got married so many times in the U.S., he had to start over in Canada. I search some more, and up pops a picture of the actual tombstone. The epitaph, though, is in French, and this Mr. Vickers was born twenty years later than Vick.

Losing track of what, exactly, I'm looking for, I check out two Virgil Vickerses on Facebook. One has put up a picture of his car and includes in his list of interests paintball fighting. His remarks are prefaced by the word "dude." The other, twenty-five with a cute mustache, is presently unemployed, though he graduated from a university in India.

Still, by the time my index finger will no longer bend, I have learned a lot about this kind of searching: most of the news is daunting. Though a somewhat unusual name like Virgil is better than John or Michael, alliteration is bad. A lot of people appear to have gotten the same idea for a cool name. Also, just because something comes up—like the California nursing home—doesn't mean it still exists. I learn that I can get hundreds if not thousands of hits for Virgil Vickers on dozens of sites. I'd better find a way of determining what is worth tracking down and what isn't. If I don't, I could literally spend a lifetime on this. If I can't learn how to weed out the false leads, I would probably be better off spending my days playing the slots in Atlantic City.

However, by the time I finally go up to bed, I do have something concrete other than the facts that Social Security isn't showing Vick dead and that he's from Kansas. Searching the 1930 federal census, I find a sixteen-year-old Virgil Vickers, the only child of Wilbur and Lucy Vickers, living in a rented house in tiny Peabody, Kansas. Because I don't yet understand what I'm looking at, almost everything I think I learn that night is wrong: that he also lived with a German family (adopted!), that he *died* at sixteen (stolen identity!).

As it will turn out, I do have the right person, the right town, and the right parents. The slick guy with the clocks on his socks and the taste for big new cars started out as a Depression farm kid. Just like Eva.

The next day I get a letter off to the Social Security Administration, trying to find out if the fact that Vick doesn't show up on the Administration's index really means I'm looking for a man who's alive somewhere. While I'm waiting, I decide I will see what I can find on the wives. Back on the websites, I have immediate luck on Linda, the wife in Portland, who came right before Eva. Luckily for me, Vick and Linda crossed the Columbia River to get married on the Washington side. Because Washington State has many of its vital records digitized, I am quickly able to find a facsimile of the actual license for the marriage between Virgil B. Vickers and thirty-one-year-old Linda Greerson, giving their place of residence as Alberta Street in Portland.

It's my first marriage license. But it won't be long before I will become something of an expert on such documents. I will learn that they are quite varied, each requiring different information. One thing, though, is uniform, at least on licenses issued in Oregon, Washington, and Idaho. All declare that the couple is being joined in "LAWFUL WEDLOCK." I like the capital letters. They are a nice touch, intended, I guess, to give potential bigamists pause. I don't know how generally effective this warning has been. I do know that it's just about the only effort anyone in an official capacity appears to have made to ensure that marriages will be, in fact, legal.

On Linda and Vick's Clark County, Washington, license, the bride- and groom-to-be are required to fill in their dates of birth; and here's another little piece of information on Vick that will turn out to be correct. D.O.B.: January 6, 1914. Then I get lucky again. Also on the Washington State vital records site I find a facsimile of the marriage license taken out by Virgil B. Vickers and Odette Olsen in Seattle, King County, a few months after Vick left Eva. King County wants to know where the bride and groom were born; Vick puts down Newton, Kansas.

With these two marriage licenses in hand, I go back and find Eva's. It is folded carefully in an envelope provided by the Boise Methodist Church, with "Save" written in large letters. Here, the applicants have been asked to give their marital status; and while Eva checks "divorced," Vick checks "widowed." Of course, both Eva and Odette had heard of the tragic loss of his wife, Marie.

As I become more acquainted with Vick's pattern of deception, I notice that he lies flamboyantly, and, as it seems, pointlessly, about previous relationships, but reports vital statistics truthfully. Now with place and date of birth in hand, I contact Harvey County, Kansas, and obtain a copy of Vick's birth certificate. Virgil Benjamin Vickers was born in Newton, Kansas, on January 6, 1914, at 9:45 p.m. The child is white and legitimate, and his birth was attended by a doctor rather than a midwife. Far from being an only child, he is the sixth child of Wilbur, a farmer, and Lucy, maiden name Grant, a housewife.

ᘯ While the marriage certificates have provided information about Vick, the most valuable information of all will surely come from any surviving wives. But the information I have on the wives is, at first, of little help in locating them. Though I have Linda's date of birth in 1925, no place of birth is given. All I have to go on is the Alberta Street address where she and Vick lived. When I find that a Linda Vickers with the same date of birth married a Mr. Smith in Washington state, I give up on her for the time being. There are so many Linda Smiths that my people finder site refuses to report them.

I have better luck locating Odette; I find an Odette Olsen of the right age living in north Seattle, the only person of that name in the city. I have a phone number, but I don't want to call out of the blue. I don't want her to think I'm trying to sell something or running some scam. Also, I'm worrying about how people will feel, being pulled back into all this. So I work hard over a letter, trying to explain who I am and why I am dredging up the past in this way. I write that I was Eva's friend, and I've just got to know what happened.

I enclose a Xerox of Eva's wedding announcement with the photo of her and Vick. I circle my name where I am mentioned as flower girl so that she can see I'm really who I say I am. I also send a copy of the photo of Eva's wedding party lined up in the church and draw an arrow to myself, labeling it "me." Odette may be old now, but I know from her articulate and ultimately hardheaded letters that she's no dope. I don't really expect her to help me because I used to be a cute eight-year-old, only a few years younger than her own daughter, Leisa. Still, I figure it can't hurt.

As I'm putting the finishing touches on the letter, however, attaching the self-addressed stamped envelope, the Xerox of the clipping, and the wedding picture, I happen to drop by Google, and up pops an obituary for Odette.

Yes, it is the brave, passionate, hardworking Odette, dead at eighty-six, survived by one daughter, Leisa. The sweet obituary—written, I assume, by her daughter—describes her as "a talented seamstress, avid gardener, and exceptional cookie maker." I read that Odette was preceded in death by "two husbands," Leisa's father, Harry, who died in 1952, and a man named Robert Paul, who died in 1994. Vick, unsurprisingly, is not mentioned. And here, in the obituary, is the name of Leisa's husband, Morley Stenner. The name is not terribly common, and it doesn't take long to find the address and phone number for Morley and Leisa. They live in Santa Ana, California.

Again, I don't want to blow my chances by calling Leisa cold. So I labor over another letter, introducing myself and explaining that once I began to find out about this story, I just had to go deeper. I tell her that I feel I have come to know Odette through her letters, which I will be glad to return. I hope this doesn't sound—I hope that it isn't—vaguely extortionist. I promise Leisa, which, of course, is not her real name, that I will never reveal the identity of her mother or her or any of the other women or children involved. Again I enclose the wedding clipping that has my name and the picture with the arrow pointing to me, the flower girl.

I ask Leisa to call me or slip a note into an enclosed envelope, and I'll call her. I stay away from email. Maybe because my fingers hurt. Maybe because I feel the need to provide more solid proof of who I am. Maybe too I want to be a little like the women who poured their hearts out to each other in long, earnest letters. I leave one thing out of my letter: I don't mention the agonized passages where Odette tells of the abortion. I realize that at twelve, Leisa may not have known everything her mother was going through. If it seems she doesn't know, I ponder whether it would be my duty to "lose" those pages.

Though I am pretty sure that I have the right address for Odette's daughter, I send the letter by registered mail. I want to know that she's really there and whether my letter got into her hands. A few days later I come home and see a message on my answering machine. It's Leisa, calling from Santa Ana. She's gotten my letter.

"It looks like we have a lot to talk about," she says.

Odette and Leisa

I call Leisa back. She is smart and funny and generous; I feel as if I've known her forever. I throw away my list of questions, pour a glass of wine, and we start to talk.

Odette has not been gone for long, and her daughter is glad to reminisce. Her mother was of Norwegian descent—"scandahoovian" Leisa jokes—and grew up on a farm outside Seattle. Four years older than Eva, Odette was already working as a hired girl on another farm when the war started. Soon she married Leisa's father, Harry, a saw-mill worker, whom Leisa remembers as "outgoing, always smiling." It was a good marriage, she says.

When the war came, Harry, who had lost the movement of his left arm in a sawmill accident, was classified 4-F and went to work as a bartender. Then Odette, like Eva, went to the shipyards, where she got a job drilling holes in the sides of landing craft, the holes to be filled by gun supports. Making her own little piece of history, Odette's photo is on the front page of the *Seattle Post-Intelligencer* in 1945. She is one of the women being let go from the shipyards shortly after D-day.

Unlike Eva, Odette didn't mind leaving her job in the shipyard. She was happily married, and Leisa was on the way. The family moved to California, and Odette was glad to stay home to raise her daughter. But when Leisa was six, Harry unexpectedly and tragically died while undergoing a minor operation. For Leisa, things went blank after her father's passing; mostly she remembers her mother packing all of their things in barrels supplied by a moving company so that they could move back up to the more familiar Northwest.

Odette found the little bungalow in Ballard for the two of them, and once settled, she got a job in a downtown Seattle stationery store. There, while raising a daughter alone and despite the lack of formal training, she rose from a clerical position to that of bookkeeper. Even though the work was hard and the hours long, Odette kept her looks. She was always, Leisa says, "very well turned-out."

It was only then, having built a modest but solid life for herself and her daughter, that Odette, a widow of thirty-nine, met Vick. At first Leisa didn't think Vick was "that terrific." He was a great dancer, she remembers, as was her mother. And he had nice hair. But Leisa thought he looked "kind of greasy, like he used too much Brylcreem." And he struck her as "not that well spoken," careless with his grammar. Maybe, as a twelve-year-old, Leisa was unimpressed by adults generally. Maybe Vick's carefully constructed charm offensive just didn't work on kids. Maybe in hindsight, the picture of Vick has shifted. Then again, maybe Leisa was picking up something, as she says, "smarmy" about Vick that was somehow invisible to the women he had in his sights.

Later on, though, Leisa began to feel okay about Vick. He was, she remembers, "good to Mother and nice to me." He "seemed sincere." He particularly won Leisa's approval by bringing home good things from his chef's job at United Airlines, unknown delicacies like filet mignon and lobster tail. Leisa remembers too the excitement of the family's intended move, how they had already put down earnest money on a house in upscale Broadmoor.

I already know how much Odette loved Vick, how she treasured his ability to understand her loneliness and loss, having, as he said, experienced the same himself. I can see too how wonderful it must have been to have a companion again, a man in the house, another income, and someone to help shoulder the daily load of life. How wonderful to no longer be a misfit in a culture that viewed single women with suspicion. And, after so long alone, how delicious to be adored by a charming and handsome man.

I understand all that. Still, seeing again how bright and capable Odette was, I have to ask Leisa the question that perhaps puzzles me more than any other. It's a question about the one thing, as it seems to me, you can't fake. Was he intelligent?

"Of *course* he was intelligent," Leisa snaps. "Or Mother wouldn't have given him the time of day." Leisa is equally emphatic that Odette was not to be blamed for marrying Vick. They went together for quite a while. Vick had the good job with United. "Everything checked out." Listening to Leisa, I think of Eva who, for a long while, had no one she could even tell that Vick had gone. Odette was lucky to have had a daughter and defender like Leisa.

On the day Vick left, Leisa remembers, Odette was downtown at work, and she herself was out picking Seattle's famous strawberries. Odette got home first, and when Leisa arrived, her mother told her Vick was gone. "She was devastated, stunned."

That same afternoon Odette told her daughter that she was pregnant. Leisa, who wanted a brother or sister, argued for keeping it. She said she would help raise it. But in this time before reliable day care, Odette, who had no immediate family in Seattle, would have needed more help than a twelve-year-old could provide. Especially since Vick had cleaned out the bank account.

In the end, Lisa says, "pragmatism won out. It was the right thing to do." Still, as I read aloud Odette's letter and the passage about walking the streets alone, searching for a backstreet abortionist, I can hear Leisa's quiet sobbing on the other end of the line.

Marie and Susan, Modesto

After my talk with Leisa, I turn my attention to Marie, about whom I know a fair amount, based on what Odette reported to Eva. When Marie and Vick were married, the notes show, he was in the Army; and during the first two years of Marie's marriage, she traveled with him to postings at Fort Lewis near Seattle and Fort Knox in Kentucky. When the Korean War began, Vick went overseas while Marie waited at home with her parents in California. He left the military in 1951 and returned to Modesto, where, like everyone else, he and Marie started a family. Vick, of course, disappeared the next summer with Marie eight months pregnant. In Eva's neat hand is an address in Modesto for Mrs. Marie Douglas, who, I assume has remarried.

And now on a people-search site I find Marie Douglas, right age, with an address and phone number in a small town outside Modesto. I compose another letter, put in the clipping of Eva's wedding and the picture of the wedding party with me as flower girl. But a few days later the letter is returned with an attached note saying that it has been "refused." I go to the post office and ask the clerk what it means. I'm figuring she no longer lives at the address and whoever is there sent the letter back.

"No, it means she *is* there. She saw it and won't accept it." He looks at me wearily. "That's what 'refused' means."

I have Marie's phone number, but again I am too scared to pick up the phone. She's terribly important to me now. She might be the only one of the wives alive. I'm afraid I will say the wrong thing, she'll hang up, and I'll lose her forever. I try to think of the best way to approach her. Whatever I do, I should remember that Marie is in her eighties; I should hurry. I decide to send the same letter, this time by regular mail. Again I enclose the clippings and the self-addressed envelope. I tell her that the first letter was from me, that I had sent it registered only to be sure I had the right person.

I don't hear back. After a week I take a deep breath and dial Marie's number. An answering machine picks up, and I hear the canned, annoyed-sounding male voice that seems to be favored by older women. I leave my message: I'm the person who wrote about Virgil Vickers. I hope I am not dredging up too many painful memories. I'm sorry about the registered letter. I just wanted to make sure that I had reached the right person.

Since I don't know how far she'll want to go, I've decided to break the ice with one, nonpersonal question. I say that I'm trying to find out about Vick's war record. Eva believed this had something to do with why he left her, I say. Because of the refused letter and the working phone number, I'm sure she is there, maybe even listening as my message is recording.

I'm right. In a few minutes the phone rings. I see that it is the number I have just dialed. I pick up the receiver.

"Mrs. Douglas?" I ask.

"Marie," she says. "He's no good. What'd he do in the war? Not much." This is an expensive call, she adds. I ask if I may call her back. "It's your dime," she says, adding, "He's no good. He's just a rover."

Marie is sharp. From the beginning she gets what I'm doing, and though she doesn't have a good thing to say about Vick, she doesn't mind helping me to find out more. It's been a long time, though, and Marie remembers some things better than others. The first thing that comes to mind is the letter Vick sent a few days after he'd gone, the one that she sent on to Odette and that I found among Eva's things. It's the letter that starts, "My Dear Wife." This is something Marie remembers clearly; and if it's possible to quote and spit at the same time, Marie does it now. "I'll look after Vick and you look after Junior. Bye for now."

She remembers that it took a long time to realize he was really gone. Of course, she knew right away that he had driven off in their Mercury. All these years later, it still rankles. "Bright green! Brand new!"

Vick also hit the bank account where Marie had deposited the money she saved from her paycheck while he was in Korea. But he didn't clean her out entirely. He took only half of her money, perhaps in consideration of the fact that he was soon to be a father.

Another clear memory: the "beautifully written love letters" that came from Tessa, the woman in Baltimore whose rooming house

Vick found his way to after leaving California. Marie wants me to understand that she never held anything against Tessa. She could tell from the letters that the woman had no idea Vick had abandoned a wife and child in California and that she was shocked and horrified when she found out.

After our first conversation, Marie calls me up regularly. We'll talk for a minute, and then I'll hang up and call her back. She tells me new things she's thought of. She's remembering now that Vick got in trouble with the law one time. It was in Washington, she thinks. Something to do with the Space Needle up there. He was in jail maybe. At least she thought that's what she'd heard. I have to wonder, was Vick really in jail or did Marie just *wish* he was?

I ask her how the two of them met, and Marie remembers this fine. It was at a dance in Modesto in 1948; she was twenty-three. Vick had just come down from Vancouver, he told her. He'd been in the War. With the Canadians, Marie thinks. Yes, she remembers that he was with the Canadians in Italy. She remembers that he talked about how the Italian girls were pretty. Right after the war he went into the sawmill business with his brother. Or so he said. When he and his brother had some kind of falling out, Vick came down to California. By the time he met Marie, he had already enlisted in the U.S. Army.

Marie remembers how taken he was with her from the moment they met and how jealous he was; he didn't want anybody else even looking at her. Soon they were married, and Marie traveled with him to his stateside military postings. She is not quite sure what his duties were. He wasn't a cook, she's sure of that. It was something to do with equipment.

One other thing Marie wonders: "Did he ever tell you that his father had a coat of arms? He was kind of persistent about looking it up."

The new bride wanted to know her husband's relatives. When he mentioned something about having a sister, Marie said she would like to correspond. But Vick never came up with an address and later told her he'd had word his sister had died. He was sorry to miss the funeral, he said, but he didn't have time to go.

Marie, of course, wanted children, and a few months after her husband had shipped for Korea, she learned she was pregnant. When she miscarried, she wrote him, breaking the bad news. Vick wrote back to say how sorry he was that they had lost their baby. Remembering this sweet concern from the man who would later walk out leaving her hugely pregnant, Marie gives a snort.

When Vick returned from Korea, he began managing the Cream Cup, the restaurant her father had bought for them to run. It seemed like a good fit. Vick was friendly and popular, a great host. Everybody liked him. Later, when they heard what he had done, nobody could believe it. Vick and Marie seemed to have it all, the perfect fifties dream. Vick did, though, do something odd at the restaurant, as Marie remembers: right away he hired two women to run it. Marie was surprised. She had thought her husband would be running the restaurant day to day. But he told her he wasn't well enough.

Hearing this, I remember that in Boise he regularly visited an internist. The doctor's name and fifteen dollar fee are entered in Vick's Boise bank book. I ask Marie if she thinks Vick was really ill. But Marie isn't about to give the man *anything*, including the possibility that he was unwell. He did cough a lot, she says. She told him it was because of too many cigarettes.

I try to find out from Marie if Vick's daughter, Susan, now in her fifties, might want to talk to me. Maybe she would like to see some of the things I've dug up, such as the 1930 census report that gives information about her grandparents. For my part, I *really* want to meet Susan. Maybe she'll remember hearing things that Marie has forgotten. Maybe too, as Vick's daughter, she'll have access to information that I am barred from. Marie says she doubts her daughter would be too interested. "If he didn't want to see her, she didn't want to see him," Marie declares. I'm not entirely certain whose point of view this is. And later Marie does allow that Susan "would have liked to have met him." When I say I'll be in California in a few months, Marie says we can all have lunch. It will be Marie's treat. I've been paying for all these phone calls; she's buying lunch, and that's settled.

∞ On a sunny August day, I go to the restaurant Marie has chosen in a strip mall outside Modesto. It's a bright place with big windows. Large placards advertise lunch specials, and business is good. Waiting for Marie, I'm nervous and scared. Who am I, again, to be opening closet doors and letting all the skeletons out? What would Eva say if she could see me right now? For that matter, what are Marie and Susan saying about me as they drive to our meeting? "I want to be polite," I can imagine Marie telling her daughter. "But why is she digging all this old stuff up?"

Then here they are, and here is Marie, a small woman getting out of a large car. She is old but trim, her hair a becoming shade of nut brown, her features still well defined. Her lemon slacks and cream colored sweater set suit her perfectly. "Well turned-out," I think, remembering Leisa's description of her mother, Odette.

Remembering Eva.

And there, helping Marie out of the car, is a tall, younger woman. When she turns toward me, I see the deep dark eyes, something rangy in the shoulders. It's familiar in a way I hadn't at all expected. It's Vick.

I take a deep breath and start babbling: how appreciative I am; how kind they are; it must seem odd, I've appeared out of the blue; sorry about the registered letter, must have been confusing, alarming even perhaps!

"Quite a chatterbox," Marie observes to her daughter, as we follow one another into the restaurant. After we are seated, Marie says we should order the chef's salad. We all order the chef's salad.

Susan is in the restaurant business, married with two sons. Marie also has two sons—a high school teacher and a policeman—from her second marriage. She and Mr. Douglas, now deceased, bought a house next door to Marie's parents. For the thirty years of their marriage, Mr. Douglas ran a dry-cleaning business. Susan is attentive, but says little, and I have no idea how she's feeling about the whole thing.

I have already sent Marie copies of photos taken at Eva's wedding and a copy of the 1930 census showing sixteen-year-old Vick living on the farm in Kansas, the last child left at home. Now Marie and Susan have some things for me. First is a snapshot taken at a swimming pool. There's Vick in flowered trunks climbing out of the pool, wet, tanned, broad-shouldered, grinning happily. And then there's a photograph of Marie and Vick on their wedding day in 1948. They are outdoors, standing together on a broad walkway, framed by lacy shadows from the surrounding trees. Marie is very smart in a draped, two-piece white dress, dark gloves, intricate open-work high-heel shoes, and an immense white corsage. She has abundant dark hair and good legs.

I'm not surprised to see another nice-looking bride. But I'm a little surprised by Vick. Though he appeared to be the perfect groom in Eva's pictures, I see now that by the time he met her, he'd gone a bit downhill. Here, at thirty-four, nine years younger than when he married Eva, he is movie-star good-looking as he poses casually beside his bride, one hand in the pocket of his dapper pinstripe suit, a white handkerchief with four little peaks rising from his breast pocket. He's probably twenty pounds lighter than in the Boise picture, and his face is thinner. His cheeks have a sexy crease as he smiles. Even his hair is better than in Eva's picture, more natural looking. Maybe he *did* start to use too much Brylcreem.

It makes me a little sad: Eva didn't even have Vick at his prime.

And something else strikes me: his mood in the 1948 wedding photo seems different, calm and relaxed. Here I don't see the intense excitement of Eva's wedding pictures. Could it be that he hasn't yet started his bigamy career in earnest, that at this point he's just a normal, good-looking guy, joining the postwar wedding boom by marrying a pretty girl from a nice family?

I ask Marie if she has any idea what made Vick do what he did. I remind her that Eva thought wartime trauma may have played a role. Marie doesn't know. She does remember that he used to "kind of mumble in his sleep." Does she think it was something to do with the war? She shrugs again. That was the only reason anybody could come up with, she says. Back then.

Marie pays the check, and it's time for us to go. Susan and I follow her out of the restaurant.

"I had an aunt who never married," Susan tells me. "I always thought this was why." And, with Marie still walking in front of us, Susan adds something else, "I thought that registered letter had something to do with my dad."

Tessa, the Baltimore woman who sent love letters to Vick at Marie's Modesto address, doesn't seem to have been married to Vick; still, she and her daughter Florence, twelve at the time, would certainly be able to help fill in the story. But I can't find anything that would allow me to locate either of them. I decide to go down to Baltimore to see if anything will come to me as I stand in front of Tessa's house on North Charles Street.

Before that, though, I stop at the Baltimore Historical Society, where I learn from city directories that throughout the 1950s Tessa was a clerk for the Baltimore school district. I also see that Tessa's Aunt May is listed as family "head" of the house that is also occupied by Tessa, her mother, daughter, and assorted lodgers. Though Tessa presents herself as a married woman—her stationery is engraved "Mrs. Tessa McKee Nesbitt"—Mr. Nesbitt did not seem to be around. Tessa was still very much in the bosom of her family.

By now it's chilly November, and a brisk wind blows as I walk along North Charles to the three-story, bay-windowed row house where Tessa fell in love with Vick. The still-gracious old house is flanked on one side by a wide, cobblestone alleyway, and it must have been here that Vick parked the brand-new, sea-green Mercury that Marie was still paying on and that Tessa, in her letters, remembers so fondly. Today, as in the 1950s, the area is a mix of residential and commercial. Then, a city directory shows, a typewriter repair shop and a photography studio were on Tessa's block. Now there are fast-food places and chain drug stores. It's a workaday kind of place, nothing flashy. I wonder what Vick was doing out here.

Standing in front of Tessa's house, I'm remembering something—a letter that was in the shoebox Vick left with Eva, addressed to him in Boise from a man in Washington, D.C. I remember the man mentioned a time when the two of them worked together in the kitchen of the famous Mayflower Hotel in D.C. He's heard that Vick is now in Boise and has written, hoping there might be a job for him out West.

Thinking about the Mayflower, I'm remembering something else, the speculation in one of Tessa's letters that Vick may have left Baltimore "with a guest from the hotel." But out in Baltimore we're a long way from the Mayflower.

To see whether Vick could really have commuted from West Charles Street into D.C., I take the MARC train back into the city and, since there was no Metro in 1953, I walk to the hotel on Connecticut Avenue. It's a long, chilly way. But when I step inside the Mayflower and stand looking down the vaulted, chandeliered, block-long promenade, I suddenly grasp something about Vick I haven't quite seen before: besides loving to get married, he loved prominent establishments.

I remember how Vick found his way to the Hotel Boise, that thrilling architectural triumph resembling a "French luxury liner." I'm thinking too about the United Airlines kitchen where Vick worked when he was married to Odette. At that time, air travel was still considered an exciting luxury.

Certainly the Mayflower would fit the bill as a prominent and glamorous institution; for most of Vick's life, the Mayflower was in the news as *the* location of political and diplomatic events in Washington, D.C. As an eleven-year-old farm boy, getting dispatches from the world beyond Kansas on the family radio, Vick could have heard that President Coolidge was inaugurated here in 1925 and that in 1927 a thousand people attended a breakfast celebrating Charles Lindbergh's flight. Here too during the 1930s President Roosevelt had his birthday galas, raising money for polio research. During World War II, de Gaulle and Churchill were sometimes in residence, and stars like Marlene Dietrich appeared at benefits.[1]

Would Vick really have been in the Mayflower's league? In the fifties, the kitchen appears to have been a very big deal. The hotel took pride in having its own butcher and doing all baking on-site. World-class European chefs presided over a hundred cooks. While other fancy restaurants made do with two kitchen shifts, the Mayflower was proud to claim three. It's a high-power place. Still, Keith McKinsey, manager and hotel historian, tells me that someone with Vick's experience could have gotten on, a prep job at least. After all, they had those three shifts to fill.

This, I realize, was surely Vick's M.O. He would hear about these exciting and famous establishments on the news or maybe read about them in one of his men's magazines. He'd see images of handsome men like himself in stunning surroundings and say, That ought to be me! While he seems never to have had the money to be a guest at the Boise or the Mayflower or to fly on jets, maybe he could get in through the kitchen door. Now I consider again Marie's vague memory that Vick had been in jail and that his capture had something to do with the Space Needle. Did he try to get on there? Certainly the Needle, with its rotating, flying-saucer–shaped restaurant built for the 1962 Seattle World's Fair, would offer the sort of prominence and glamour that Vick seemed to love. A job there would really be top of the world.

Here under the chandeliers of the Mayflower, I remember something else from Vick's shoebox—the card from the Veterans Administration, notifying him that his records had been transferred, undoubtedly at his request, from San Francisco to Washington, D.C. Checking notes on my laptop, I see the card was sent to Vick at an address on Seventeenth and P, only a four-block walk away. Checking the date, I see that the card was sent in March 1953, a month or so after Vick left Tessa in Baltimore and her love letters to him begin to arrive at the home of Marie in California.

Though Tessa thought Vick had gone back to California, it appears that he didn't leave the area at all but moved closer to his job, into an apartment in the red stone townhouse that still stands on P Street. It appears, further, that he did not live there alone, at least not for long. For on May 1, 1953, Vick and a young woman named Kathleen Rittenhouse took out a marriage license in Alexandria, Virginia. It is noted on the license—which I find in an online search of vital records in the D.C. area—that the wedding was to take place that same day.

Kathleen, a twenty-five-year-old divorcée, gives her occupation as clerk and is probably one of the army of low-level government workers. Vick lists himself as a once-married widower and gives his occupation as cook. In response to the form's questions, he provides details about himself that I know to be correct: his birthplace in Newton, Kansas, and his parents Wilbur and Lucy. Other than the claim that he's a widower, there's only one little white lie. Vick, who is thirty-nine and marrying a twenty-five-year-old woman, puts himself down as thirty-five.

Not counting Tessa, who wasn't married to Vick, Kathleen brings the count of Vick's wives to five.

As I get to know the wives, a pattern is emerging. Vick was not looking to marry party girls, rich widows, or daughters of prominent men. Rather he was looking for nice, good-looking women with solid working-class backgrounds. Several had felt the disappointment of an ill-fated wartime marriage or the grief of widowhood. With the possible exception of Marie, all bore the stigma attached to unmarried women in the fifties. And even she, twenty-three and still single in 1948, was something of an "old maid" by the standards of the time. But they all held their heads up and were capable of soldiering on, working decent jobs, supporting themselves and sometimes children. Though they had come from modest backgrounds, they were trim and stylish, "well turned-out."

And they had something else in common. They all demonstrated a great capacity for love and loyalty. Marie as a young bride in Modesto saved every penny for the time when her husband returned and their life together could begin. Eva in Boise was sure Vick's departure had to do with his suffering and her own shortcomings; she appeared not even to consider the possibility that he had done something callous or cruel. Odette in Seattle was drawn to Vick in part because of her empathy for the losses she believed he had suffered. When she found out what he had done, she had to work to stamp out the love she felt for him.

Tessa in Baltimore, though similar to the other women in many ways—the working-class background, the love that will last "beyond all things forever"—is interesting to consider as an outlier. It seems evident that she too was felled, to use Odette's phrase, by the "love he gave so generously." Even after he was gone, she wrote of her willingness to go with him "anywhere any time." Still, she and Vick appear not to have married. Why not? Was it that Tessa, however hungry for a man, did not, like the other women, struggle alone but rather lived with three generations of female relatives? Is this why Vick didn't rush her off her feet and into a hasty marriage? She just had too much ballast? Much more, surely, than Kathleen over in D.C., a twenty-five-year-old divorcée working a low-level government job.

What does seem clear from the wives I've gotten to know is that Vick was able to spot women capable of great empathy and loyalty. But this only makes his actions more puzzling. How can a person know and value these qualities well enough to search them out repeatedly and then behave in a way that says "none of it is worth anything"?

Why?

So. Why did he do it?

As I've worked on this story, I have gotten interesting suggestions for what might have been making Vick tick.

"Was he oversexed?" I am asked. (Usually by men.)

Well. Nobody has said so. But nice women in the 1950s would probably not mention such things, certainly not in letters. Still, there is not the slightest hint anywhere that he had an exceptionally powerful sex drive or that extra-terrific sex was a piece of the package he offered. And if sex *was* his main thing, surely there would have been a more expeditious way to have it with lots of women. Wouldn't it have made more sense to take up with the party girls in different towns, rather than women who had to get up for work every day?

Or, if he had a taste for respectable women, wouldn't merely hinting of or promising marriage have sufficed in most cases? Surely, even in the fifties, Vick could've had sex with these relatively mature women without having to go through the high-powered courtship and the big wedding. Surely a good-looking, smooth-talking man would not have to bother with mowing lawns, measuring for drapes, or being taken to meet Mother.

No, I think it was about more than sex. And from what I have learned about bigamists generally, sexual abnormality usually isn't part of the picture. A British study, for example, finds that when the overall criminal careers of convicted bigamists are examined, evidence of aberrant sexual behavior is rare. What this group *does* go in for is "white collar crime," especially fraud and forgery, crimes that require the same skills necessary for successful bigamy: misrepresentation, deception, and betrayal.[1] Could it be, then, that Vick simply found himself stifled in marriage? For while fifties society insisted that one must be married to be fully adult and while most men accepted this prescription, there were those who sought to avoid the "trap."

James Jones, in the early fifties novel *From Here to Eternity*, portrays women as "bait," used primarily to trick men into a life of drudgery and humdrum. It's true that the men in the book, like those in the 1953 movie of the same name, value not only sex but also emotional connections with women. But there is no question that these soldiers—men like Vick who enlisted before the beginning of World War II—will ever transfer the love and loyalty they feel for the Army to a wife. When one soldier's "shack job" suggests that they marry, he explodes. "Why the hell do you think I got in the Army? Because I didn't want to sweat my heart and pride out . . . all my life and have a raft of snot-nosed brats . . . .What the hell do you dames want? To take the heart out of a man and tie it up in barbed wire and give it to your mother for Mother's Day?"[2]

Of course, most men did marry,[3] and for some, the requirements of the modern, bureaucratically controlled workplace were a source of misery. Indeed, the emasculating nature of conformity is a concern that is widely discussed postwar.[4] Even the pristine and glossy suburbs where the perfect fifties families lived were sometimes viewed as a problem for men. For though society insisted that men be the breadwinners and that women not challenge them in the workplace, it was still feared that women who waited at home would entrap and control men in settings that were "soft, manipulative, seductive, feminine, and weak," depriving men of "traditional male vigor and authority."[5]

Some of this angst can be seen in the 1955 film *Rebel Without a Cause*, where the James Dean character's actual "cause" for rebellion seems to be the weakness of his father, played by Jim Backus, a man in an bib apron, unable to formulate advice or stand up to his steely wife.[6] In *The Man in the Gray Flannel Suit* the Gregory Peck character is driven by his wife to climb the corporate ladder and bring home a bigger paycheck. And as early as 1948, Dick Powell plays a bored insurance man in *Pitfall*. His question, "Whatever happened to the man who was going to sail around the world," is crisply answered by his wife: "He has a family to support."

If the Powell character was never going to sail around the world, he undoubtedly was not going to take advantage of another option available to men who were tired of the confines of marriage and job and become a Beatnik. Still, the Beats—like the Army men in the

James Jones novel—reveal that a vein of male resistance to married life runs deep and that it has not been entirely eradicated by fifties marriage propaganda.

For the Beats joyfully and defiantly refused any responsibility to women, children, or a conventional occupation. If Jones's Private Prewitt sees marriage as "barbed wire" around the heart, Jack Kerouac writes in *Dharma Bums*, "Pretty girls make graves."[7] And just as Prewitt walks out on the woman he has been living with when she threatens to become a responsibility, Dean Moriarty, in Kerouac's 1957 *On the Road*, walks out on a wife and baby daughter. Both scenes make me think of Vick's exits and perhaps give insight into his thinking. For, as Moriarty is on his way out the door, he gives no thought of his wife or the children he has fathered. Rather he thinks only of the freedom that awaits him. "Bitterness, recriminations, advice, morality, sadness—everything was behind him, and ahead of him was the ragged and ecstatic joy of pure being."[8]

Another fifties view of male freedom—one that, on the surface at least, would be much more agreeable to suave, well-dressed Vick than that espoused by the scruffy Beatniks—could be found in *Playboy* magazine. Here men were urged to remain "free" so that they could indulge in luxurious pleasures like hi-fi recordings, travel, and expensive liquor without considering the needs of a family. For *Playboy* there was nothing "queer" about remaining single. Indeed the magazine loved women as "guests to a den of cocktails and jazz"; it simply hated wives. Furthermore, *Playboy* derided the pathetic married man. "Take a good look at the sorry, regimented husbands trudging down every woman-dominated street in this woman-dominated land. Check what they're doing when you're out on the town with a different dish every night."

And what of men who say they are happy in marriage? "Naturally. Do you expect them to admit they made the biggest mistake of their lives?"[9]

Could it be that Vick, who, after all, spent the first decade of his adult life in the all-male environment of the Army, is especially attuned to this alternative cultural message: a man has the right to be free, have his pleasures, to live outside the boundaries of women and their needs. And while, according to *Playboy*, most men won't admit that marriage was the "biggest mistake of their lives," perhaps Vick, when the romance cools off, is a little more ready to face this fact.

Perhaps. If Vick had walked out of one marriage or even two, we might speculate that he had the courage to face up to a couple of "mistakes." But Vick demonstrates just the opposite, insisting, even at the end, how much in love he is, how *happy* to be married. Certainly, we hear no such sentiments from Private Prewitt or Dean Moriarty. Also, he marries over and over in a way that neither James Jones, the Beats, nor *Playboy* could have possibly condoned.

Okay, then. Was he just a chiseler?

It's true Vick often drove off in the couple's new car. It's also true that right before he left Boise, Vick bounced checks worth about seventy dollars. When he left Marie, he took half the savings account, several thousand dollars. And he cleaned out Odette's bank account. Eva, of course, had to struggle, to cover the bad checks he wrote. Marie certainly felt the loss of her savings, and Odette was furious at what Vick had cost her. Still, given the time Vick invested in the marriages, the amounts he took were exceedingly modest. And when I look at the carefully balanced checkbook that Vick kept during the year he was in Boise, I don't see a high roller. Rather, I see a Depression-era farm boy keeping track of very dime, carefully noting every check, even if it was only for two dollars.

But maybe I am considering con men in the wrong way, assuming they are all looking for big money. Maybe, as a 1955 *Saturday Evening Post* article suggests, Vick's Depression-era frugality was an excellent quality for a chiseler to possess. The article "A Way with Women" details how a man can live quite well and without much risk by running small scams on numerous women. And though the *Post* doesn't make the point, the subtext seems to be that in the midfifties, desperate, single women are sitting ducks for this kind of exploitation.[10]

It's a coincidence, probably, but I do notice that the article—which, of course, does not approve of the practices it describes in such detail—came out a few months before Vick married Linda in Portland and his career in high-speed bigamy began to take off. Too, I can't help but be struck by the similarity between the scams described in the article and some of the practices I know to have been Vick's. The article describes, for example, the ring scam. Simply tell the woman that you've decided the ring she's wearing isn't good enough and you want to take it to the jewelers to have the setting redone or to get a better diamond. She gives you the ring; you leave town.

Vick, as we know, ran something similar on Linda in Portland. Linda's engagement ring didn't fit properly, he said. He would take it to the jewelers to be adjusted. Then he left town in the new red Ford with the ring in his pocket. An added twist is that the engagement ring had been purchased by Linda herself; Vick was going to "pay her back" later when some money he was owed supposedly arrived.

In Odette's case, Vick appears to have bought her ring. But he also "hinted" several times that he would like a nice wedding ring too, so Odette bought him one, a "lovely ring with three diamonds," which he took with him when he left.

Then there is the equally simple—at least if you are dealing with a trusting, loving person—joint bank account scam. She puts in her savings, and you make a show of doing the same. But you don't actually put anything in, or maybe you put in a big check that is no good. Before any of this is discovered, you clean out the account—or in Eva's case bounce a lot of checks—and are gone.

According to the *Post* article, there are other benefits for the man who runs small-time swindles on numerous women. He can usually count on staying with his current lady for a while and getting free room and board. Then, when it is time to move on, her "relatively small contributions" in jewelry and cash will provide nice walking around money until the next opportunity presents itself. The beauty part for the man who is "modest" in his needs is that petty swindlers are almost never pursued across state lines by law enforcement. Rather, according to the article, it is the "greedy" men, those who try to take women for a lot of money, who come to the attention of the FBI and end up in jail. To avoid this fate, the article explains, scammers should follow two simple rules: don't cross a state line with more than $5,000 of stolen money or property; don't cash a worthless check in one state drawn on a bank in another.

The similarity between Vick's methods and the ones detailed here are striking—the modest amounts he made off with and his pattern of shifting from state to state when moving between women.

Okay, I'm convinced. Cautious little bankbook or no, he *was*—at least on his way out the door—a small-time swindler. But I'm also convinced that he was something more than that on his way *in*. If he hadn't been, I don't believe he could have inspired such devotion in so many rational women. Further, many of his actions don't seem necessary for a small-time scan. As the *Post* article shows, a man didn't have to go through the whole ordeal of marriage just to get each woman's "small contribution." Even if Vick felt marriage was needed, why not something modest? Why waste her money—assuming that's who was paying—on a wedding dress, fancy reception, and honeymoon? Why not clean her out while she still had it? Why put down money on a new house and furniture? Why express the desire for a baby?

I look again at the expression on Vick's face as he and Eva cut the cake at their wedding reception. This is a man who is very excited. I just don't believe all this emotion is caused by the knowledge that in a year or so he'll get to write seventy dollars in bad checks and drive away in a soon-to-be-hot car.

There's one more speculation on what was making Vick tick, the one held by Eva and, to a lesser extent, by Marie in California. In this theory, Vick's actions were the result of wartime trauma. Marie and those around her appear to have made this assumption simply because it was a known postwar problem, because Vick had been in the service, and because they couldn't come up with any other explanation. But for Eva, as she articulated it in the letters she sent off to Vick in Mexico, this belief was strong. Her theory: he was struggling with inner demons, not only the loss of "most of his family" but the aftermath of "years of war." In the wake of Vick's departure, unable to grasp how the loving man she knew could simply abandon her, Eva expressed her belief that Vick, due to posttraumatic suffering, was temporarily not himself.

Having come to understand Eva's relationship with Dave through the World War II letters, I can see why this explanation would have been compelling. She has seen it before, has once before been shunned by a man in the throes of combat-induced trauma. Surely, faced with Vick's incomprehensible abandonment, she remembers Dave and the letter from Italy, coldly ending their engagement. But he hadn't really meant it, writing Grace that he had broken with Eva only because he didn't know if he would ever recover his mental health and could not bear to let her see his present condition. Still later, as he began to recuperate, it became clear that the harsh breakup had been only a symptom of his deranged condition. In reality, Dave adored Eva and wanted her desperately.

If it had happened before, why couldn't something similar be happening again? Vick, suffering extreme and ongoing posttraumatic distress, perhaps even trying to protect Eva from the horrors of his condition, had fled. But that didn't have to mean he didn't love her, only that—like Dave—he was in too much pain to handle things in a normal way. If Eva was using what she knew of Dave's case to develop a theory of Vick's actions, it's possible that she was also using that experience to understand what her own behavior now should be.

In 1945, she couldn't or wouldn't do what Dave begged: come to the convalescent hospital, marry him, and, through her love, "knit up" his shattered mind. Rather she had clung to her other boyfriends and her "thrills" at the shipyard. She had been "selfish." She stalled so long that that her family was dismayed, and Dave finally broke it off, leaving Eva to what may have felt like the punishment of her dysfunctional marriage to the alcoholic Jimmy Wright.

I admit that when I first read Eva's frantic letters to Vick in Mexico, I thought them nearly unhinged. How could she portray herself, the one abandoned, as the person at fault, a "miserable failure as a wife"? But, now understanding her experience with Dave, I can see that this self portrait could be drawn from her sense that once before she had "failed" the man who loved and needed her.

Dave, once his mania subsided, remembered his love for Eva. Perhaps Vick would too. And perhaps Eva would get a second chance to prove herself loyal and loving, to put into practice the advice given women at the close of the war: don't ask too many questions; be patient and loving. When Vick came to himself—as her thinking may have gone—she would, this time, be faithfully waiting.

Then came Odette's reports of the other wives. Surely this put things in a different light. In Eva's notes, however, I think I see her working the new information into her original theory of why Vick had to leave. At first I was puzzled by the arithmetic she was doing on scratch paper, little problems of addition and subtraction. Then I realized that she was arriving at a number for each of the wives, indicating the months Vick spent with them. The marriages to Linda and Odette lasted only a few months. Marie's marriage was the longest, nearly four years. But from this Eva subtracted the time Vick was stationed in Japan and the months when he was at different military bases in the United States—almost the entirety of his marriage to Marie.

But with Eva there were no long periods spent apart, no moves from place to place, no military camaraderie to provide escape. Rather they were together all the time, at work and in the little apartment. Inseparable. And he stayed a year, far longer, as this reasoning appears to go, than with any of the others.

Possibly this is what she believes: Vick wanted her. He fought his demons to stay with her. She was the exception.

Though Eva was convinced that Vick's actions stemmed from years of wartime trauma, I am skeptical. By now I know Vick was expert at cooking up elaborate falsehoods that drew from, while sometimes reversing, real situations. There's the story, for example, about his beloved wife Marie, dead after a horrible illness, and the one about the little daughter he yearned for but was somehow prevented from seeing. There's the sad tale he told Odette about the snapshots of him on trip, a time when he had been so lonely and miserable he couldn't enjoy himself. As Odette later deduced, the photos were taken on his honeymoon with Eva. At this point, obviously, we can't accept anything Vick said about himself.

We do know, though, that he served in Korea; at least that's what Marie, his wife in California, believed. Just to make sure what he was telling Marie was true, I have, through the Freedom of Information Act, obtained a summary of Vick's service from the U.S. National Records and Archives, finding that he enlisted in 1947 and that he indeed did serve in Korea from the start of the war until 1951. So could something horrific have happened to Vick in Korea, something that prevented him from staying with Marie and with the other wives?

Knowing that I am following up on Eva's belief that wartime suffering influenced Vick's actions, Susan, his daughter in Modesto, sends along some things from Vick's time in Korea that she's kept all these years. First, there's a snapshot of Vick, taken in Japan in 1950, which he sent home to Susan's mother, Marie. In the photo, Vick, tall and trim, arms crossed, leans against the front of a truck. In the background are immense tank treads. He's in boots and muddy fatigues with the bill of his cap pushed back; I see that he's wearing sergeant's strips. Flanking him are a couple of baby-faced soldiers, ten or fifteen years his junior. They all look relaxed, like they're having a pretty okay time in postwar Japan. On the back of the picture Vick has written in his usual scrawl, "Two TK crewmen of my crew that work on the TK wrecker one is a driver & workman and the other a helper. We are out on maneuvers [here the letters are especially scribbly; I don't think Vick knows how to spell 'maneuver'] at the base of Mt. Fuji. Vick."

Susan has come up with something else from her father's Korean War years, four yellowed newspaper items, clipped by Marie a year before Susan was born. The stories are based on a press release that the Army has sent both to the Modesto paper and to the paper in Smithson, the small nearby town where Marie was living. I am expecting the articles to contain some generic stuff for hometown consumption, so I am shocked to find that Vick is being hailed by the Army as, of all things, an inventor. By the time I finish studying the clippings, my idea of Vick has undergone a significant change, for the articles Susan sends report that Vick has been recognized by the Army for an invention that is "being judged for patent rights." The press release, headlined "Commended for Ingenuity," lauds Sgt. Virgil B. Vickers, serving in the Seventy-ninth Heavy Tank Battalion of the Twenty-fifth Army Infantry Division, as the inventor of a tool that can be used for "removing double pin tracks on heavy tanks." The invention is simple, the article notes, but it is a great labor- and time-saver for the troops.

One of the clippings, datelined Osaka, features a two-column Army photo of Vick kneeling near a huge wheel, tinkering with some wires. Shown in profile, he is frowning thoughtfully. I can barely recognize this serious, intelligent-looking man as the same who will appear in Eva's wedding photo eight years later, his eyes glazed with excitement.

Though it is a surprise to hear of Vick's achievements, certainly nothing in any of this suggests that Vick suffered physical or psychic injury during the Korean war. Rather, he seems to have been having a good time in the U.S. military. In the records the Department of Defense makes available, I see he entered as a private but emerged as a sergeant first class. When he left the service, he did so with an honorable discharge. In addition he received several decorations and medals, including Army of Occupation (Japan), United Nations Service medal, Korean Service Medal with three bronze service stars, and the Good Conduct Medal. These awards are no big deal. Anyone who served in Korea received a Korean Service Medal. Still, the three bronze stars show that Vick took part in three campaigns.

And the Good Conduct Medal, awarded for "three years of faithful service" indicates that Vick was considered reliable and capable of commitment.

So could there be anything at all to Eva's belief that Vick suffered some sort of posttraumatic condition, the result of "years of war"? His Korean service seems to have been a cakewalk, after which he returned to his young wife in seemingly perfect condition.

I have no evidence—other than Marie's memory of Vick's remarks about Italian girls—to show that he served in World War II. U.S. Army records show him only in Korea. And, as I discovered on my first night of searching, none of the five Virgil Vickerses I found on a World War II enlistment site could have been him; none were the right age, and none came from Kansas.

If Vick didn't serve with American forces in World War II, the only other possibility could be that he, like Dave, joined up with the Canadians. And so, because the Canadian National Library and Archive in Ottawa will send military information only to next of kin, I ask Susan to write requesting anything they have on her father. When the records finally arrive, sent on to me by Susan, they are a gold mine: two dozen oversize pages, many filled with cramped handwriting, showing in minute detail Vick's activities during his years in the Canadian Army. They paint a remarkably intimate picture of who Vick was in his twenties and—not always the same thing—who he said he was.

The records show beyond doubt that Vick served as a volunteer in the Canadian Army. Like Dave Johnson, he traveled to Vancouver to enlist in the summer of 1940, less than a month after the Battle of Britain began. Bizarrely, they could easily have bumped into each other in a pub catering to Americans.

Unlike Dave, who switched to the U.S. Army when America entered the war, Vick stayed with the Canadians for five and a half years. Both, though, saw a year and a half more of World War II than most Americans, a fact that may have given Eva another reason to equate Vick's experience with Dave's.

Before being sworn in to the Canadian Army, as the records show, Vick undergoes an extensive intake interview. Here, as I will come to understand, he is telling the truth about half the time. He indicates that he is from Kansas, that he graduated from Peabody High School, that he's a Baptist. He states that during the thirties he attended a junior college in Dodge City, Kansas, meanwhile working as a cook. He also tells the interviewer that he was clerk and cook in his father's Newton, Kansas, hotel. In the last two years he worked as cook in a Seattle coffee shop.

He says that he is single with no children and no living parents. A brother, George, given as a farm laborer in Iowa, is listed as his only next of kin. In the "interests" box, the interviewer puts down tennis and golf, also noting that Vick has played fullback in the sport of "American rugby." It is also mentioned that Vick "reads considerably," both "good fiction and digests." The Canadians are interested in the farm background of those they enlist. In response to these questions Vick says that he was born on a farm, worked in wheat farming for three years, but that he has no interest in farming after the war.

He is fingerprinted and photographed—though the photo is not in the file—then taken into the Fifth Canadian Motorcycle Regiment, a World War I cavalry unit that has recently been mechanized to meet modern military requirements. As the war progresses, the group will be reorganized again as a tank unit and be designated the Ninth Canadian Armoured Regiment.[1] The unit does not immediately go overseas but spends two and a half years in Canada, where Vick, in addition to completing a course in cooking and serving eighteen months as a cook, qualifies as a tank "driver mechanic and gunner operator." In 1942 he is transferred to a tank outfit.

Vick waited in Canada for his war to start during roughly the same period Eva waited at home in Wing Valley, from 1940 to mid-1943, when as his group is preparing to go overseas, Vick is interviewed again. The interviewer's notes show him to be 5'11", 174 pounds, in very good health. Results of a battery of tests indicate he has "above average learning ability" and could be considered for officer's candidate school. "He appears to be an alert man, willing, and good army qualifications," the interviewer writes. "He is very keen to go overseas." When asked his reasons for signing up, Vick replies, "Adventure."

Finally Vick ships to England, where he'll spend three months before embarking for Italy; here his tanker regiment will participate in the northward advance. Vick will be in Italy for three years before shipping to Northern Europe, where his unit takes part in the liberation of the Netherlands. By the time he is honorably discharged back in British Columbia, he has a number of medals, the 1939–45 star, the Italy star, the France and Germany Star.

Vick, then, would appear to have been a success in the Canadian military as well, serving honorably, receiving valuable training, getting the "adventure" he had sought. I notice only one small glitch. While still in Canada, the record shows, Vick "deserted Army and reenlisted in another name." The Army does not appear to have been fooled for long, possibly referring to the fingerprint and photo on file. Vick was allowed to return to service using his real name but was "severely reprimanded" and his pay docked. It seems he made no such mistake again.

The highly detailed Canadian military records reveal no other problems. Though Canadian tank units saw combat in Italy, there is no record of Vick being wounded, and in his entire five and a half years with the Canadian Army he spends a total of two days in the hospital. It is clear that neither the American nor the Canadian Army gave Vick a medical discharge, as Eva had been led to believe.

When it comes time for Vick to be discharged, his one misstep occurring four years earlier is not held against him. Indeed, the discharging officer's view is favorable, even admiring. "Vickers is a tall, well-built man of 29. He is alert and cooperative. Impresses as being above average in intelligence." Vick tells the interviewer, who appears to have a role in deciding whether Vick will get "re-establishment credit," that he plans to "open a service station and lunch counter in Vernon, B.C., that he has already purchased the lot and will start building immediately." He will use the credit extended veterans to "purchase building material, supplies, etc."

The outlook, the interviewer writes, is good. In view of Vick's experience as a cook and as a driver mechanic in the Army, "there is every reason to believe that he will be successful in this proposed type of business and should experience no great difficulty in becoming re-established in civilian life."

It is only in reading this final interview that I learn of another asset Vick has in the Vernon, B.C., community. Since 1940 he has been married to a local girl, Ada, who was eighteen at the time of the marriage. The wedding took place three months after Vick arrived in Canada; throughout the war, Ada lived in Vancouver and in Victoria and waited for her husband. Now, in 1945, Vick tells the military interviewer that "his wife has experience in restaurant work" and "my brother-in-law and myself are going to be business partners."

The venture was apparently not a success, however, for by 1947 Vick had left Canada and enlisted in the U.S. Army at Port Townsend, Washington, a town near the Canadian border. By 1948, he is married to Marie. The story he tells her, that he had been in the lumber business with his brother in British Columbia, contains the few grains of truth with which Vick likes to flavor his lies. He has not, of course, mentioned to Marie that there was another a wife in Canada. As far as I can tell, none of the wives ever knew of Ada, who brings the running total to six.

Though nothing on the record hints in any way that Vick was traumatized during his military service, I can't quite give the theory up, if only because Eva believed it so passionately. Perhaps she—with her own previous experience of a man deranged by combat—was one of the few people to whom he could speak of what he had endured. Perhaps even if a man had not been wounded and did not end up in a psychiatric ward, he still could have seen things over years of war that left him profoundly shaken, prone to abnormal conduct.

To get a better idea of how the disorder we now call Post-Traumatic Stress Disorder (PTSD) looks, I ask Larry Weinberger, a Ph.D. in clinical psychiatry who works with contemporary veterans, to look over the evidence I have on Vick.

Vick, Weinberger says, doesn't fit the profile of PTSD. For one thing, as depicted in the wives' letters and in the memory of those who knew him, Vick was outgoing, capable of making friends effortlessly, and he was very much at ease in new situations. He was liked by people of all sorts, from Marie's shrewd, successful father in Modesto to the preteen daughters of Odette in Seattle and Tessa in Baltimore.

We can see something of how Vick approached people, Weinberger points out, in the letter he wrote to Aub, asking him to serve as best man in the upcoming wedding to Eva. The letter, Weinberger says, "is very effective, appropriate, and graceful. It shows an easy respect." And it is completely unlike the communications of those with PTSD, who are usually "emotionally withdrawn, not gregarious or socially successful."

Nor does Weinberger see in the letters a man who is out of control. He points out Vick's letter to Marie in Modesto, where, before revealing that he is leaving forever, he advises her on how to run the Cream Cup restaurant. Here Weinberger sees "a sense of planning, elaborate and rational. This is a well-organized individual. He's not acting on impulse." Not only is there rational planning, but there's "a high level of intelligence needed to pull off the things he did. Maybe he didn't have a formal education, but he is smart and able."

Looking at the letters of Tessa, Eva, and Odette, where the women discuss their experiences with Vick and their feelings for him, Weinberger puzzles over the man's "astonishing ability to cultivate relationships so quickly" and to convey such a powerful sense of love and caring. Again this does not fit the pattern of those with PTSD, who "talk about anger but not about love."

"It's so striking," Weinberger says as he looks over the wives' letters. "No one sounds angry. The women were not abused physically or emotionally. They were satisfied.

"It's not PTSD," he concludes. "Nothing fits the profile."

So what could it be? Weinberger ponders. Vick doesn't come across as malicious like the typical sociopath. Nor does he appear markedly grandiose or extremely narcissistic. He is not excessively controlling of the women. Nor does he seem to care about power: he gains good positions but doesn't try to advance. He throws everything away.

The strange thing, Weinberger says, is that the "risk/reward ratio doesn't add up. He lies so much and takes such big risks. People are chasing him down. But it's all for so little benefit. The financial rewards are minimal. There *is* a benefit for him. It's just something that's not apparent to us.

"What," he asks, "do you know about his childhood?"

The Vickers Family,
Kansas, 1910–1930

I've never been to Kansas and have to start with the map. The first thing I notice about Newton, the town where Vick was born in January 1914, is that it appears to be very nearly at the exact center of the continental United States.[1] Maybe because of this, it has always been a crossroads, bisected by cattle-drive trails, major highways, and rail lines, both east-west and north-south.

Now that I'm here, I realize that while Vick may have been a country boy, he wasn't country like Eva and me, growing up in the outback of eastern Oregon. In Wing Valley, ringed by arid foothills and high, snow-capped mountains, we were physically isolated from the outside world, an hour's drive from the county seat of Baker and half a day from Boise. But in Newton, even the most staid farm family must've been aware of constant coming and going by people different from themselves.

Newton has been like this since the earliest days, when, for one turbulent year in 1871, the railhead of the Atchinson, Topeka, and Santa Fe met up with the Chisholm Trail in Newton. Settlers were afflicted not only by an influx of drunken cowboys and crop-trampling Texas cattle but also by gamblers, bordello-operators, and other lawless frontier types drawn to the action. "Bloody Newton" could claim to be the "wickedest" town in the West until, to the relief of honest people, the railroad pushed on to Wichita.[2]

Although longhorns no longer rampaged through town at the time of Vick's birth, the railroad was still prominent. Newton was the dispatching headquarters for the Santa Fe line, and in the 1914 *Newton Journal*, the railroads supply a good deal of the local news as people drive onto the tracks when a train is coming, slip between the cars, get hit while walking along the rails.

In addition, there's a fair amount of editorial fretting about what sort of people the trains are bringing into town. One story details a push to make it a federal crime to trespass on the railroad right-of-ways. This law, it is believed, will cut down on "thefts, highway robberies, and even murders committed by hobos." And a front-page editorial urges vigilance against the sort of out-of-towner who showed up at the previous year's Old Settlers' picnic. On that occasion, "the sheriff was called to stop five gamblers." This, the paper fumes, is unacceptable "in a farming community that is in one of the best counties in Kansas or any other state."[3]

While the railroads presented challenges, they also offered exciting opportunities, as quarter-page advertisements reminded readers on a near-daily basis. The Santa Fe, for example, advertised special rates "for home seekers to points in various states." Other promotions for rail travel contained drawings of Asian women in native costume and invited readers to visit "Golden California," where they would see "quaint bits of oriental life." For the "winter tourist," why not make the $25.75 round trip to San Antonio to see cactuses and cowboys? And then there was scenic Canada. Interested persons were invited to attend a free illustrated lecture about Canadian rail travel at the Star Theater in Newton.

Under this barrage, even the most deeply rooted and monotony-tolerant folk must have paused on occasion to consider the ease with which a person could step onto a train right here in town and find himself, a day or two later, in an unknown place where identity and responsibility could simply melt away.

Reading the Newton papers, I wonder whether this duality could be a clue to Vick's contradictory behavior. In Newton, people clearly value a settled, hardworking life; still, you're never far from the sound of the trains, coming and going all day and all night. Were some of Vick's decisions influenced by this early exposure to the lure of exotic locations and the ease of departure?

So who were the Vickerses? Were they among the deep-rooted and settled? Or was there something about this farm family that made the sound of the train whistle especially difficult to resist? I have already learned that Vick was not an only child, as I had assumed on my first night of searching. Nor was he adopted; a birth certificate shows he was Lucy and Wilbur Vickers's sixth child. And by now I've tracked the family over a twenty-year period, getting a census snapshot of them every five years from 1910—four years before Vick was born—to 1930, when he was sixteen.[4]

I am not entirely surprised to learn from census information that Vick's father, Wilbur Vickers, did not have a hotel in Newton, Kansas, in 1937, as Vick told the Canadian military interviewers. The Vickerses did not even live in Newton at the time but in Peabody, a smaller town to the north. Rather, from U.S. and Kansas census forms I have learned that the family was always involved in farming and that they moved continually: in each of five census years they were living in a different place. In 1910 they were living in El Dorado in Butler County, Kansas, but by 1915, when Vick was an infant, they were living in Newton, the seat of Harvey County. In the years after that they lived in various farming communities in Harvey and Marion County, always on rented ground.

Because of my own background, it is hard for me to fathom what it must have meant for a farm family with six children to move so often. As a child in the 1950s, I lived on a farm that had been in my family for nearly a hundred years. Every day I looked out at a barn built by my great-grandfather; every night I listened to water running through a ditch that he and other men of the Valley dug to bring water down from the mountains. From my own life, I had drawn the conclusion that the essence of farm life was knowing every inch of your property intimately and staying in the same place forever.

So I feel safe in assuming that the Vickerses were in desperate circumstances to have been driven from place to place, their children never at home in one community or one school. The fact that they are shown on most of the census forms to be working rented land means that Vick's father was no more than a tenant farmer; the fact that he moved so frequently seems to show that he was not making a living in that lowly occupation.

Could this be a key to Vick's behavior? Could a childhood cheated by poverty and insecurity be the source of his love of fancy hotels and restaurants, his need to marry one solid, respectable, "well-turned-out" woman after another?

To a family already apparently struggling there came the Depression. While this section of Kansas was not as utterly devastated by dust storms as the western part of the state, times were still plenty hard. By 1931, when Vick was seventeen, farm-purchasing power in Harvey County was half of what it had been in 1929. Everybody had to live "tight," eliminating anything not absolutely necessary. Farmers had their phones taken out to save a few cents a month. And though this was not the center of the dust bowl, on some mornings you looked at your pillow and saw your head outlined in fine grit.[5]

Some didn't make it, and Earl Thompson's novel, *A Garden of Sand*, set in Depression-era Wichita, describes the struggle of dispossessed farm families living "on relief" in shanty towns at the outskirts of the city. Here the mothers spent their time picking the stones out of the "relief" beans, and every kid who went to school in "crumby relief bib-alls" and "cheap, tire-soled shoes" knew that his plight was as "publicly obvious as that of a prisoner of war."

In the world Thompson creates, shame and poverty lead straight to youthful nihilism. It was, he writes, "a season so desperate" that it produced "a bumper crop of young would-be desperados." Some of them robbed banks, viewing the money held there as "trapped communal property, for they had never known anyone *personally* who had ever had an account."

Others—and here I think of Vick—operated on a smaller scale and were wanted on some petty charge in a dozen states. Small forgeries were often a "consistent method of getting walking-around money"; no check was "written for over $100. Towns in which they had been before were towns they approached cautiously again."[6] Some of this rings true for Vick. Maybe he was formed in a time of poverty and desperation where the road always beckoned, where there was nothing much to believe in but doing whatever it took to keep breathing and keep moving. There could be something to this picture. But once I am in Kansas, I learn that it will need some serious retouching.

Driving around Newton, I still like my idea of the farm town at the crossroads, haunted day and night by the whistle of the trains. Today Interstate 135 cuts through Newton north-south, and Highway 50 goes east-west. Both the Union Pacific and the Burlington

Northern/Santa Fe railroads still pass through Newton, and tracks still dominate the town. These tracks, along with the activity of the fueling and switching yards, cause a lot of traffic delays. Indeed, trains are so apt to appear out of nowhere that the city of Newton website has a page entirely devoted to railroad safety. Drivers are warned to "expect a train at every highway-rail intersection."[7] And, I'm told, people in Newton never have to think of an excuse for why they are late for an appointment. They simply exclaim, "Train!"

    To learn something about the kind of family Vick came from, I visit the basement of the Harvey County courthouse, where property deeds are recorded. I explain what I have learned to the registrar of deeds: the Vickerses were poor, working rented land and moving frequently. But after searching through one of the immense old record books for a few minutes, the registrar looks up with surprise. "No," she says. "They were rich."

She has found a property record showing that in March of 1912, Vick's father, Wilbur, bought two hundred and forty acres of farmland just east of Newton, paying $33,600. For the time, the registrar says, it's a huge sum of money to put down on a piece of property—the equivalent of three quarters of a million in today's money.

Then why, if they were that well-off, did they later live on one rented piece of land after another? I drive out to where the Vickers's property in Newton would have been located and stand there puzzling. It's prime farmland, all right, flat and treeless.

To try to understand how a farm family got so rich—and then how they lost it—I drive the thirty miles southeast to El Dorado, where the family lived before coming to Newton. There—in another basement registry of deeds—I see that in 1910 Vick's parents began to buy up property in El Dorado. At the time a big oil strike was expected; when it came, the value of property would skyrocket. Wilbur is not listed in census data as a farmer. Rather, it seems clear, he is a land speculator.

To finance their land purchases in El Dorado, Wilbur and Lucy apparently sold out their rather substantial agricultural holdings in Indiana.[8] But why? Why leave a place where they had lived for the first twenty years of their marriage, where they had raised their children, and where Wilbur undoubtedly had family?

Did they hear about the prospects of oil, decide to go to Kansas and make a killing in land? After twenty years of marriage and five kids, was Wilbur—maybe Lucy too—experiencing a midlife crisis? Did they want to see someplace new? But if it was Wilbur and Lucy's aim to make a killing in the oil boom, it would seem that they blew it. By the time of the first strike in 1915, Wilbur and Lucy were gone. They'd sold out and moved on to Newton.

Once again, their movements are puzzling. Maybe they weren't trying to "time" the oil strike, but simply thought to buy and sell in what was, even before the first big discovery, a hot real estate market. Maybe, once they got to El Dorado, they decided they didn't like living in a hyped-up town with their five country-bred kids. Maybe they wanted to get out before things got even crazier. Or maybe something else went wrong, something personal, that made them pull up and leave. Whatever their reasoning, they were out of the El Dorado area by early 1912. Maybe they hadn't made a killing, but they did have the large sum of $33,000 to put down on the prime two-hundred-forty-acre property outside Newton.

It is here that Virgil, their sixth and last child, is born in January 1914. The baby arrives into a well-established family: his eldest sister, Clara, is twenty-four; and his brother Clark is twenty-one. In addition he has two teenaged sisters, Esther and Elinor, and a nine-year-old brother, George. Though Vick is a late and probably accidental arrival for forty-five-year-old Lucy and fifty-one-year-old Wilbur, we have evidence that he was welcomed, for on a late winter day of that year, arrangements are made to photograph the new baby. Someone has brought a straight-backed chair out from the house for Wilbur, prosperous-looking in a suit and tie and a light-colored stockman's hat. Behind him is a lone scraggly tree, flat winter fields to the horizon, and an immense sky. On one knee Wilbur holds the infant Virgil. The baby is tiny as a doll, dressed in a long white dress and frilly bonnet, its hands clenched in two little fists.

The picture, sent to me by one of Vick's great-nieces whom I have located online, seems to show that, after their adventure in El

Dorado, the family has now resumed the identity they had before leaving Indiana, that of a prosperous farm family with a big spread close to town. Then something went wrong. In early 1916, when baby Virgil was two, courthouse records show that Wilbur sold the Newton property. What's more, he took a beating, selling for $24,000, a loss of $9,000 or one third of the price he paid four years earlier.

～ On the second floor of the beautiful old Carnegie Library building, now the Harvey County Historical Society, local historians Pam Navrat and Tom Sandwell sit with me at a long table, trying to help make sense of what happened to the Vickerses. What's especially puzzling, Sandwell tells me, is the timing of Wilbur's sale. World War I was on, and the disruption of wheat farming in Russia meant that markets were excellent for Kansas farmers. "We were feeding Europe. In Kansas, 1916 was the golden age of wheat."

Looking again at the copies of the Newton land deeds from the courthouse, we notice that when Wilbur bought the property in 1912, it came with two mortgages totaling $9,000. The loss Wilbur took was exactly the amount of the two mortgages against the property. Maybe this debt had something to do with why he had to sell. Back then, Navrat says, you didn't pay the mortgage on a regular schedule over decades as most of us do now; rather you contracted to pay the whole amount on a certain date, a plan that today we call a "balloon" payment. Navrat notes that Wilbur's mortgages actually came due a couple of years earlier but must have been carried over. The banks would do that sometimes, she says, if you had good credit. Once—maybe not twice. "In those days, if you couldn't come up with the money, you lost your place."

Maybe Wilbur had a "bubble" mentality, Sandwell speculates. After his experiences in El Dorado, he may have assumed that land could always be resold for a profit. Or maybe Wilbur overexpanded and couldn't get his money out fast enough when the mortgage came due. If he had to sell to settle his debts, he may have been in no position to hold out for a better price.

Then, the family experienced another tragedy, this one concerning twenty-year-old Clark, the family's second child and oldest son.

Eva, I know, had heard of this brother, believing him and another brother, George, to be Vick's sole surviving kin. When Vick disappeared, Eva searched frantically for the two brothers. From her notes, I can see that she thought Clark was in Tampa, Florida, perhaps working for the railroad, and that she wrote for any records.

Again I am puzzled by Vick's strange pattern of lies. For while it's true that Vick had a brother George, who was alive in 1958, his brother Clark had been deceased for forty years, dying suddenly in 1917, as the *Newton* papers report, after a few days of illness. The cause, the paper reports, was spinal meningitis.

So, by the time Vick is three, Wilbur and Lucy have sustained several major blows. Though Wilbur sold the Newton property for the large sum of $24,000, he does not seem to have owned property again. Perhaps more debts had to be paid. Perhaps he could never squeeze enough out of the land to get the capital to buy again. For whatever reason, the family, once so firmly rooted, would move frequently throughout Vick's childhood, never to live on their own property again. These losses must have been devastating for Wilbur and Lucy. But what would it have meant to a little child?

I might be able to find out something about Vick's early years in school records, Navrat suggests. Kansas, she tells me, has kept attendance and grade rosters for all its one-room schoolhouses; I can find them over at the courthouse. Maybe these will give a snapshot of Vick as a child. Was he already behaving abnormally?

Back at the courthouse basement, I look up the records for District 46, and there is Vick, eleven years old, one of fourteen pupils in the school, ages six to eighteen. From the record, however, Vick seems to be perfectly normal, even above average. I'm a little surprised to see that his highest grade, 96, is in "orthography," the term used for spelling. He has a 92 in arithmetic and his lowest score, 90, is in language and grammar. Many of the children have scores in the 90s; maybe they are all above average. Or maybe they have an easy teacher—although six-year-old Hubert manages to consistently score in the low 70s.

At twelve, Vick has a new teacher who uses letter grades and who seems to be a bit tougher: few on the roster are getting As. Vick's highest grade is a B, and he has a number of Cs. He doesn't seem to have much interest in history, getting a C minus in both U.S. and Kansas history. Still, though he does not have the stellar grades of a girl named Estelle—almost all As—he is way ahead of poor Hubert, who now hovers in the D range.

In both years, Vick's attendance is average, not the best, not the worst. Certainly, nothing here marks Vick as a troubled child. Furthermore, I find evidence in the school records that Wilbur, despite his reverses, is viewed as a citizen in good standing. In 1927, he served as clerk of the school district, a position that required him to give an accounting of school expenses. In the folder for District 46 is an onionskin copy of a typed note sent to Wilbur by the superintendent of schools. The superintendent thanks him for his report, which is "so nicely made out and right in every detail."

Despite the troubles, then, Vick seems to have been a normal boy and Wilbur a good family man, respected in the community. At Wilbur's death of a stroke in 1938, his obituary notes that he is survived by his wife and five children, three brothers and two sisters, nine grandchildren, and "many friends here who mourn his loss."

I have one last thing to do while I'm in Kansas: drive north from Newton to visit the Riley County courthouse. Knowing Vick, I've checked the fat books of marriage records in the counties where I know he lived—Harvey and Marion—with nothing coming up. But on a genealogy website I have one clue that suggests a possible early marriage when Vick was still in this part of Kansas.

Sure enough, in the Riley County courthouse I find an affidavit for the March 1935 marriage between Virgil B. Vickers, 21, and Edna C. Foster, 18, daughter of carpenter William Foster.

Surely this is Vick's first marriage. But for my purposes, Edna puts the running total at seven.

It was a Saturday afternoon wedding, according to the *Manhattan Mercury and Nationalist* newspaper, and the new couple would be at home on Third Street. The bride, the article mentions, would continue to attend high school.[9] Her studies, however, would have been cut short. Even though four years later Vick would attest in Canadian Army intake papers that he had no dependents, Edna gave birth to a son eleven months after the marriage—the baby, William Wilbur, apparently named for both grandfathers. And, although Vick would tell the Canadians that in 1935 and 1936 he attended business college in Dodge City, Kansas, taking classes in subjects such as typing and arithmetic, he was actually in Idaho, perhaps having traveled west with his wife looking for work.

In Twin Falls, Idaho, he found something: a city directory shows him there with Edna, listing him as a cook at the Rogerson Coffee Shop. It was here their son was born in February of 1936. Vick's son, William, is deceased, but as I will learn from his widow, Jeanette, who still lives in Kansas, that little family was soon abandoned; and in 1938, Edna, back in Kansas, would be granted a divorce and custody of her son. In a complaint filed in Riley County District Court, she says that she has not seen her husband for over a year and does not know where he is. Nobody does, it seems. When Vick's father dies in that same year, the obituary gives Vick's place of residence as Texas. But Vick told the Canadians he was in Seattle from 1938 until his enlistment in August of 1940, working as a cook.

If Vick in his early twenties is already perfecting his skill at evasion and disappearance, Edna, though still very young herself, appears to have had her fill of travel, and she stays in Manhattan (The Little Apple), Kansas, for the rest of her life. In the following years, she will live with her parents, working in an insurance office and raising her son.

Though Vick had told Eva and Odette that he had a little daughter whom he missed terribly, showing the picture of a girl in pigtails, he never mentioned a son. But now I have seen his son, William Vickers; I find his picture in the 1954 Manhattan High School "Blue M" yearbook. Even before I read his name, I spot him. While he seems to have inherited a somewhat receding chin line from his mother, the upper half of his face is clearly Vick's, the dark eyes, broad brow, and straight nose. The eyebrows and hairline are identical. William, however, seems not to have turned out much like his father. Unlike the overachiever boys in the yearbook who go out for football, track, band, orchestra, debate, and student council, William's only activity is something that everybody participated in, something called "interest club."

Vick, on the other hand, continues to live a busy and complicated life. As William is graduating from high school, his father has already married and left Edna in Kansas, Ada in Canada, and Marie in California. Before William is old enough to buy a drink, Vick will have married and abandoned four more wives: Kathleen in D.C., Linda in Portland, Eva in Boise, and Odette in Seattle.

Though Vick remains an enigma, by 1960 all the wives—at least those who've left a paper trail—are moving on. Odette has her annulment, her name, and her widow's benefits. Linda marries a man in Aberdeen, Washington. Marie in Modesto marries a man with whom she will have two sons. And in Kansas, Edna finally takes the plunge again, marrying a man with whom she will live until his death.

All, that is, except Eva, who hasn't sought a divorce or an annulment. She is still Mrs. Vickers. She is waiting for something. But what? What makes her different from the others?

In the years after Vick left, Eva continued to live in the little Jefferson Street apartment. Now, however, she didn't visit Grace very often. And on her rare trips home, she acted as if she were still in her bachelor girl life, sleeping until eleven, sitting at the kitchen table in a shiny dressing gown, her hair up in a net. She was thin as a teenager, and her face without its eyebrows or makeup was so unearthly white that it seemed she *was* made up for something.

Older now and growing more critical of adults, I noticed how Eva took forever to do things, how she would fuss over the same little breakfast for an hour, crushing the two saccharin tablets in the bottom of the bowl, measuring out the All Bran, pouring on the milk, then waiting and watching as the cereal softened before finally, slowly, eating.[1] It was silly. A farm woman could have slammed out dinner for a hay crew in about the same time it took Eva to fix a bowl of All Bran.

Another thing I remember was that she didn't want to see people. I remember once she actually ran to hide when one of her high school friends pulled up in front of Grace's house. Poor Grace had to make up a story about Eva being in the bathtub or resting with a headache, neither of which would have kept a normal person from coming out to say hello. Eva, I grasped, knew she would appear too strange to her old friends, all settled, married women, all comfortably plump, the result of two or three children and two decades of good farm cooking.

Undoubtedly, though I was only eleven, I had imbibed society's message that a woman should not be single and childless. Certainly, too, I understood—if only from watching *I Love Lucy*—that a woman's attempts to have a career, whether in a chocolate factory or as a TV pitchwoman, were always going to end up as a joke. At any rate, I no longer thought that living in a tiny, bare apartment and working in a hotel was all that great. Though I never stopped loving Eva and though, under her doting gaze, I always became miraculously pretty and smart, even I came to understand that she was peculiar.

I don't remember that I ever puzzled over why she was that way. Of course, I understood World War II to have been the central event in most adults' lives. My parents had met in an officers' club swimming pool, my father a flier, my mother, a co-ed who would go on to get college credit for sewing her trousseau. And at the dinner table, talk was often of those heady years. I knew the war stories of Valley men: the one shot down in Belgium, the one who had been a prisoner of war in Germany. I knew that Eva's brother Aub never managed to get overseas despite his best efforts. I can even remember a German hired man we once had and the way he would repeatedly—and to me, incomprehensibly— insist, "Vee did not *know!*"

But on Eva's war, there was only silence. I never heard that Eva had worked in a shipyard, and I had little idea of the role women played during the war generally. Nor did I know that Oregon was a shipbuilding center and that women were aggressively recruited for the yards on the Columbia. Maybe, given the postwar rebuff of women who had momentarily stepped out of their traditional roles, this was understandable. Women in the war factories had been necessary. But now the whole episode was best forgotten.

Even Grace, for whom Eva was a chief topic of conversation, never mentioned those times. Never mentioned what happened to the boy from down on Snake River, how he had served on the front lines, and then how he suffered. Never discussed how Dave's experiences altered Eva's life. Nor did Grace mention Eva's time in wartime Portland, how overwhelming it must all have been. Never mused how, after the war, people had to get married so *fast*. Never discussed Jimmy, the shame of his drinking, the shame of divorce.

Eva herself never explained, never complained, never offered herself to be pitied. And when she got "fixed up," as our expression had it, to go back to Boise, she could have outshone anyone in the Valley, maybe the county. When she hugged me before stepping onto the Greyhound in Baker, she still had her stiff, pointy brassiere, her exotic aroma, and her conspiratorial wink.

Though Eva had taken no steps to get a divorce or an annulment from Vick, she had by 1960 begun to date, and sometimes now she would be driven over from Boise by a man named Bud, a pleasant, dark-haired, only slightly pudgy French Canadian, who had a counter job at the Boise Post Office. I remember that on one visit Bud taught me to count to ten in French. I also remember that—by our frugal standards—he spent a shocking amount of time in Grace's bathroom, indulging in long, late afternoon baths. He used up so much hot water that Grace's small heating unit couldn't catch up; to wash the supper dishes she had to heat water in the teakettle.

Despite this to my mind at least—effeminate habit, Bud seemed like a pretty okay guy, who was clearly crazy about Eva. She was thirty-eight now, and if the movies are any reflection of general attitudes, she was very lucky to find a decent man willing to marry her. As a thirty-eight-year-old widow is told, only somewhat jokingly, by a friend in *All That Heaven Allows*, eligible men of forty "won't settle for anyone over eighteen." And a thirty-three-year-old woman in *The Tender Trap* describes what's available at her age: "drunks, lunatics, and pretty boys looking for someone to support them."[2]

Rather than seizing the opportunity to marry nice, respectable Bud, however, Eva was stalling once again, much, I'm sure, to Grace's dismay. Though Grace and Eva never talked about the subject in my presence, I once overheard what I'm sure was an argument about whether Eva should marry Bud. I couldn't make it all out, but I do remember hearing Eva cry, "Boring!" And I heard Grace—her voice, for once, full of all the grief and humiliation Eva had put her through—hiss the word back: "*Boring!*"

Boring or not, though, Bud, it certainly appeared, was something Eva was thinking she should do. Then, in January of 1961, she surprised everyone by leaving Boise for Portland. At first it seemed that she had gone to get treatment for her chronic eye problems. This, I can see, was the assumption of a Boise friend, who dropped her a line. But once in Portland, Eva got an apartment and a hostess job at one of the big hotels, working her preferred night shift. And by spring she was receiving letters from Bud at her new address on Southwest Twelfth, a short walk from downtown. In his letters, Bud, who favors green ink and elaborate curlicues and who puts all names in quotation marks, puzzles over what has just happened. He too had thought Eva was making a brief trip to Portland to see an eye specialist.

Still, in his letters, Bud continues to plan for their future. He appears to believe that what stands in the way of their marriage is Eva's "legal matter," which I take to be the fact that she's still married to Vick. This, he feels, will be cleared up soon, and he writes that he is saving up for the "little white cottage with green shutters" they have talked about. As a result he has become "some what of a scotchman."

If he is not, perhaps, the brightest man in the world, Bud's letters are always loving, always full of faith and hope. "I don't want you to get deeply rooted in Portland, so therefore I can't help wondering what you are doing there either. How long are you planning on staying?

"You have my heart in your hand," he adds, "so please don't crush it."

Bud would write faithfully all through 1961, and that summer he visited Eva in Portland. When it was time for him to leave Portland, he dropped her off at work, then began the long drive to Boise. But, as he writes in his curly green script, at the outskirts of Portland, he turned around, thinking he would pick her up after her shift and see her for a few hours more. Then he reversed course again, telling himself. "It will be just as difficult to leave at a later time so I should drive on."

In another letter there has been some sort of spat, which has caused Bud "torture and anxiety." But now things seem to have been resolved, and he writes again of the day "in the near future when we can be together forever." He assures Eva that he knows she wasn't trying to hurt him. The problems, he writes, "all stem from our being apart when we should be together."

Like Bud, I don't understand why Eva made this move. It's true that her eye problems were highly complex, often requiring treatment by the type of specialist that could well not have been available in Boise.

Maybe she really did go for eye treatments and then surprised herself by deciding to stay in the invigorating city she had loved during the war. Maybe it was a relief to be someplace where everyone didn't know her story. Maybe it felt good to put more distance between herself and Grace's anxiety over how she was living her life. Maybe, too, she had finally given up hope that one day Vick would walk down the steps of the basement apartment on Jefferson Street.

Whatever her thinking, Eva, once in Portland, began to run a familiar pattern of ambivalence and delay. Bud's letters of yearning and puzzlement are a milder, saner, more mature version of Dave Johnson's daily missives from the convalescent hospital in Spokane urging, begging, and commanding Eva to marry him immediately. And Bud, though more patient and stolid, also resembles Jimmy Wright, who, increasingly confused and frustrated, found himself cooling his heels out on the farm, waiting for Eva to come home and get married.

What I suspect is that Eva, once again, knows that she really should marry. And she probably is rational enough to know, at this point, that she should settle for a nice, loving man with a steady job, even if it doesn't feel like magic. But she just can't bring herself to go through with it. She keeps Bud on the string but moves three hundred miles away. And, of course, she remains married to Vick.

About this time, too, she hears from her first husband, Jimmy, who has written asking if she or perhaps Grace has his Navy discharge papers, which he needs for employment purposes. He's up in Alaska now, working various jobs, panning for gold, and acting as a guide for hunters who come up from the Lower Forty-Eight. Now he's hoping to get a job driving a water truck. Eva sends the papers and a note; apparently she tells him that her marriage to Vick hasn't worked out. Jimmy writes back expressing sympathy; he had hoped that their divorce "would at least give one of us happiness, and it sure hasn't me." And now he dares to wonder if just maybe they might give it another try. "I have never believed our ways of life were so different. In fact for several years thought they were very congenial. Maybe you will decide to give me another chance."

Well. Could it be that as she ponders life in a little white cottage with good, dull Bud, she remembers the appeal of free-spirited Jimmy and speculates on the attractions of an Alaskan adventure? She writes him back, even sending him the picture he requested. This, he replies, he puts "on the ceiling over my bed and then every time I look up I can always think what a fool I was."

And Eva has asked a couple of questions: Has he found a "nice girl" by now? Has he stopped drinking?

In "the longest letter I've written in years" Jimmy responds to her questions with what feels like the brutal honesty of a guy who, at least, knows what he really is. "No, I haven't found some nice girl, mainly because I haven't looked for one. I never go out with nice girls any more. Haven't had a date with a decent girl for three years. I only look women up to satisfy my physical needs. As for love, I still save all mine for a memory I guess. One face always comes to my mind when I think of a wife or companion. You would be surprised at the conversations I carry on with her picture."

And the drinking? "No I haven't quit drinking. I'll quit for several months and then really go off the deep end when I get to town." The last time he came in to Anchorage, for example, he went on such a bender that it took his hunting partner eight days to find him. After this, there appear to be no further letters. Jimmy, however loving his heart and honest his self-analysis, exits the picture for good.

Mena and Janice, 1961

Whatever makes Eva move to Portland, I find no hint that she thinks she will find Vick there. Indeed, she's had no word of him since the last letter from Odette in late 1959. But then, in the spring of 1961, just as she is setting up in Portland, Eva gets another letter from a woman she doesn't know, Mena Z. Cimmiotti, of Glendale, California.

The letter begins, "Let me introduce myself. I am the 5th Mrs. Vickers."

"As you may have judged," Mena writes, "he left me too. I've been luckier than most, because he had a woman in trouble in Palm Springs, and she had her lawyer after him. That is why he became afraid and ran. We were married only two months."

The woman is writing to ask the date of Eva's marriage and annulment or divorce, so she can arrange her own annulment. Vick, Mena says, was still driving Eva's 1957 Merc when she met him. She adds, "I have a '61 Pontiac. Now knowing what I do, I guess he was after my car." Still, Mena doesn't seem to bear Vick ill will. "I am very sorry for him. I know he must be sick and wish I could help him but I'm afraid with all I am doing I shall never hear from him again."

The woman is guessing he's in Las Vegas; she doesn't think he could have gotten much farther as he didn't have much money. But she thinks he has probably left California, not only to escape another woman whom Vick had gotten "in trouble" but also the Palm Springs police who had a "warrant for bad checks."

This Mrs. Vickers (of course, she is actually the eighth, but she doesn't know about Edna in Kansas, Ada in Canada, or Kathleen in Washington, D.C.) has a maiden name that is excellent for searching, and I immediately find Mena Z. Cimmiotti on a Clark County, Nevada, marriage record. There she is marrying Virgil B. Vickers in Las Vegas, April 1961. In response to my request, Clark County sends me a facsimile of the marriage license to add to my collection. The license gives Mena's date of birth, 1918, and her place of residence, Glendale, California. Vick gives his address as Palm Springs.

In Las Vegas, applicants are asked to describe their marital history more fully than in other Western states. Maybe in the divorce capital it is understood that marriage is a messy business. Asked the reason for her 1947 divorce, Mena has put down "mental cruelty." For Vick, once again, the convenient designation is "widower."

Mena is a little different from the other wives. I like the matter-of-fact tone of her letter to Eva. And I like her clear-eyed speculation that Vick probably married her for her car. I like her for *having* her own brand new car. And I guess I am impressed that she has had the stamina to carry on alone all during the fifties. So I'm happy to see more of her. I find her on a 1953 passenger list of a ship bound from L.A. to Hawaii. She's even civic minded, the first wife I've found listed on a county voters' roll. There she is in 1950, on a Los Angeles County voters' list, living at a Palmer Avenue address in Glendale. Then, a librarian in the Glendale Public Library locates her in city directories from the 1960s: Mena Z. Cimmiotti, who lived on Palmer Avenue, worked as a proofreader for the *Los Angeles Times*.

Maybe some of this explains why Mena appears to have taken her marriage debacle somewhat in stride. Unlike Marie and Odette, she didn't have a baby on the way. Unlike Eva, Mena had a good job for a woman of the time, one that used her brain and didn't depend entirely on youthful good looks. She had a life—and a car—even without a man. And I'll bet she would have a thing or two to tell me about Vick.

I'm sad, then, to find her on the Social Security Death Index. Somewhat eerily, she died the same week that I dared, for the first time, to open Eva's box of papers.

Surely news of yet another wife—with even more women in the background—ought to finally prompt Eva to begin divorce or annulment proceedings. But that doesn't happen. And again I pause to ponder what she can be thinking. Is it possible that word of another brief marriage actually confirms her notion that Vick's marriage to her was the only one that was "real"?

Whatever questions Mena's letter raises, it seems to make one thing clear. Eva hasn't heard from Vick and can't have been operating on any suggestion that she might find him in Portland; he has his hands full in Southern California. It will turn out, however, that she has unwittingly moved closer to him. For in late 1961, Vick leaves the complexities of his life in the Southwest and heads back north. He is probably traveling by car and undoubtedly passes through Portland, though it does not appear he has any idea that Eva is there or that he stopped off. Rather, he makes his way back up to Seattle.

I'm not sure exactly when he hits town. But I know that he has arrived in the Seattle area by November 30th, for on that day, at 11:45 in the morning, Vick, who gives his place of residence as Federal Way, a bedroom community to the south of the city, and Janice Kavenaugh, who lives in the nearby suburb of Auburn, are married by a justice of the peace in Tacoma.[1]

The Bigamist, 1953–1962

Vick seems to be moving into high gear now, the intervals between marriages shrinking to a matter of months. I can't help but be impressed at his nerve. Doesn't he worry about being caught?

But as I come to understand how bigamy plays in the popular culture of the fifties and early sixties, I can see why Vick might not have been too concerned. For while bigamy is indeed a crime, it is one that society does not take very seriously. In fact, it is often treated as a joke. One reflection of this is a series of stories that ran in major magazines in the midfifties, featuring the adventures of a fictional cowboy named "Bigamy Jones." Jones is a man who "got married whenever he felt like it. He usually felt like it."[1]

Reading one of the stories, I notice that Jones's method for courting women resembles Vick's own. First he detects exactly what a woman is looking for in a man; then he becomes whatever that may be. For example, Bigamy Jones sets his sights on a woman who, he deduces, is the "nursey type." Accordingly, he pretends to be sick and eats "lye soap to bring on a fever." After that she is his. He gloats, "I got her figured out for sure. She likes a real complaining man." Another way in which Jones is like Vick: he knows how to make things happen fast for he "never bothered about any bills of divorcement."

A less lighthearted but still sympathetic portrait is found in the 1953 movie *The Bigamist*, in which Edmond O'Brien—playing a dark-haired, married businessman, who looks a good deal like Vick —meets a waitress played by Ida Lupino. She's a stoical but sad figure, whose boyfriend, stationed in postwar Germany, has dumped her for a *fräulein*. O'Brien is traveling on business; he and Lupino are both lonely, and their acquaintance becomes an affair. When it turns out she's pregnant, she's prepared to go it alone. O'Brien, however, does the "right thing" and marries her.

It's clear that we are expected to empathize, at least to some extent, with the O'Brien character. Wife number one, played by Joan Fontaine, is attractive, but she's a career woman. Probably this is why, the movie hints, she is unable to get pregnant. And then, how could O'Brien just ditch poor, friendless Lupino? But when O'Brien and his first wife try to adopt a child, an investigator discovers the bigamy, and the case comes to trial. The judge is stern; but even he is sympathetic about the dilemmas of the heart and the complications that can arise. Each of these women loves you very much, he lectures the defendant. Now you must choose.

By 1953, Vick has married and left at least four wives, each marriage separated by intervals of four or five years. But he is about to speed it up. And I wonder if he has been, to some extent, educated by these portraits of bigamy. From the O'Brien movie alone, several lessons are to be learned. First, the women want it; they *need* a good, loving man. Second, getting found out isn't *that* bad, though it would be tough to have to choose. Possibly a third lesson is implied. Things get complicated if you stick around too long.

Even more detailed information on the subject is contained in a 1960 *Cosmopolitan* story that could well have caught Vick's eye. It's entitled "Are You Married to a Bigamist?"[2] Here, the comedic potential of bigamy, with its scenarios of bed-hopping husbands and outraged wives, is not entirely avoided. Still, the article has a serious side, reporting on how bigamists slip though the criminal justice system. Though a few accounts of men with four or five wives are included, most of the bigamists discussed in the story are men who travel for a living and who commute back and forth between two wives and two families. A cinematic version of this, as the article notes, is the 1953 movie, *Captain's Paradise*, in which a ship's captain, played by Alec Guinness, has one wife in North Africa, another in Gibraltar. On the wheelhouse wall is a reversible portrait with a wife on either side. Midway between ports, the captain takes care to flip the portrait. Such arrangements, the article claims, are on the rise with the booming economy; these days many men can afford two establishments.

Vick, I am certain, would not have been much interested in men who traveled between two women and supported two families. Surely, however, he would have looked closely at the author's claim, based on a "cross-country survey of district attorneys," that "bigamy is one of the easiest crimes in the world to get away with. Only a minute percentage of bigamists are ever discovered, only a small percentage of those discovered are ever punished, and of those punished, only a tiny percentage ever serve a year in jail."[3]

Something needs to be done, those interviewed declare; the system is not working. For Vick, however, the system would seem to be functioning almost to perfection. Perhaps, aware of these excellent odds, he really does not need to worry. Even his use of his real name, age, and place of birth is understandable. Why confuse yourself making things up?

But Vick's method, though pretty good, isn't perfect. For one thing, he seems to have a taste for new cars, which excite more attention and are more traceable than diamond rings and cash. The car companies put the pressure on the wives, and the wives locate each other through car records. And though he does seem to have taken care to get out of the state when he left a marriage, he sometimes returns a couple of years later. While he doesn't seem to have been tempted to return to Idaho, he likes the Coast and keeps circling down to California and then back up to Seattle.

Finally on February 10, 1962, the big lazy circles will come to a stop as Vick, a newlywed of two months, is picked up, driven to the King County courthouse, and booked on the charge of bigamy.

Standing in the luxurious lobby of the Mayflower Hotel in Washington, D.C., I was struck by Vick's pattern of seeking out jobs at famous establishments. With this in mind, I decide to follow up on Marie's Space Needle memory. When I write to King County Superior Court in Seattle requesting anything on Vick, I receive back a fat packet, twenty-one pages of court records documenting a 1962 case: the State of Washington versus Virgil Bailey Vickers on the charge of bigamy.

As I begin to study the court documents, I see that the warrant for Vick's arrest was outstanding for two years. The complaint, made by Odette and filed with a Seattle justice of the peace in February of 1960, charges Vick with "willfully, unlawfully, and feloniously" marrying her in Seattle, 1959, while still married to Linda, the wife from Portland. Of course, Vick was still married to Eva too, but she is not mentioned in the complaint or elsewhere in the court papers. I don't know why. I don't know if Odette has informed Eva of the case and Eva has refused to participate. Or whether, perhaps recognizing that Eva is still not ready to give up on Vick, Odette has decided it's best to leave her out.

In addition to the issuance of a warrant for his arrest, I now know that there are other events in Vick's life in early 1960 that most people would consider milestones. Though twenty-six-year-old Vick told the Canadian Army that he had no dependents or sisters and that both parents were dead, his mother was actually very much alive at that time, as were his three sisters and his four-year-old son, William. All were still alive in 1957 when Vick married Eva and told her he had lost "most of his family." But in February of 1960 Vick finally does become the orphan he has portrayed himself as for twenty years. In this month his ninety-year-old mother, Lucy, dies at the home of his sister Elinor in Wichita.

A few months later, a happier event occurs: Vick's son, William, marries in Kansas City, and within a year his wife gives birth to a daughter. Vick is in Southern California, however, and is almost certainly unaware that his mother has died, that he has become a grandfather, or that he is being sought by the police in Seattle. It will take two years for King County police to bring him in.

Even so, Odette was lucky, as I learn from Dominick Driano, the young prosecuting attorney who signed the complaint and who still practices law in Seattle. Though Driano doesn't remember the fifty-year-old case, he agrees to meet with me in Seattle to look over the court documents and help me understand how it might have been that Vick was finally captured.

If Vick hadn't returned to Washington, Driano tells me, he almost certainly would never have been arrested on the warrant; it is simply too expensive for states to go through an extradition procedure for such a relatively minor matter. And even within the state, Vick probably would not have been pursued aggressively. His mistake, Driano says, probably was applying for work at the rotating restaurant atop the Space Needle. This high-profile establishment, preparing itself for thousands of World's Fair visitors, would have taken security seriously. Quite likely the FBI was involved. When applications were scrutinized, Vick's name would have come up on a wanted list.

And Odette was, in a sense, lucky in another way. A case of bigamy with merely two wives would probably not have found its way into court, Driano tells me. Though bigamy is illegal, it is seldom prosecuted: those involved are expected to settle matters themselves out of court. But, Driano says, the highly unusual "chain of marriages" Vick was charged with probably influenced the judge to issue the warrant.[1]

So on February 10, 1962, a King County deputy sheriff drove eighteen miles to make the arrest at the suburban home of Vick's wife of two months, Janice Kavenaugh. Vick would have been handcuffed, driven back to the King County courthouse, and taken up to the twelfth floor to be booked. Probably because of his known tendency to take off, the bail was quite steep, three thousand dollars, the equivalent of about $22,000 today. From what I have seen of Vick, he wouldn't have had anything close to that kind of money. And Janice—who may or may not have yet understood that her own marriage was not legal—did not come forward to bail her new husband out. Vick would spend his first night in jail.

Today the twelfth floor of the King County courthouse no longer houses the main jail, and large windows afford views of sparkling Elliott Bay. In Vick's day, however, as I am assured by a deputy sheriff who remembers earlier times, the cells were small and dark—no windows and no views. As I stand up here, I try to imagine what Vick was thinking as the cell door slammed behind him. Was he remembering all the modest but cozy and well-kept homes that had been offered to him? Was he wondering if his days at the cherished center of some woman's life were over? Was he perhaps afraid of becoming a forgotten nobody, suddenly glimpsing himself as a two-bit chiseler whose luck had run out?

Vick spent Valentine's Day in jail. Then on February 19th, he appeared before Seattle Precinct Justice of the Peace John Croome. His plea: not guilty of the charge of bigamy. Three days later Linda, the wife from Portland, now remarried, and Odette, still single and living in her little bungalow in northwest Seattle, were subpoenaed to appear in court. Then on February 26 a reunion of sorts took place with Odette, Linda, and Vick all gathering in the same courtroom. Linda testified, no doubt, to the fact that she married Vick in 1956 and was still married to him when he married Odette in 1959. The state offered three exhibits. These, a note in court papers indicates, are "marriage certificates."

While I have a summary of the proceedings in Justice Croome's courtroom, there is no transcript, and I don't know to whom the third marriage certificate might belong. It wouldn't have been Marie, it seems; as far as anyone seems to know, Vick wasn't married to anyone else at the time he married her in 1948. The women will never know about Edna (Kansas, 1935), Ada (British Columbia, 1940), or Kathleen (Washington, D.C., 1953).

Possibly the third marriage certificate was that of the ninth Mrs. Vickers, Janice, who, by now has to know that her marriage was bigamous on at least two counts: Vick was still married to Mena in L.A., who has not yet managed to get an annulment, and to Eva, who has not yet decided to try. Ironically, Eva's delay in getting an annulment or a divorce, her refusal to give up on Vick—if that's what it is— means that since he left her, his every marriage has been bigamous.

Whether or not the marriages to Eva, Mena, and Janice are part of the formal charge against Vick, it seems undeniable that when Vick married Odette, he was still married to Linda. So I can't image how Vick's lawyer expects to make a case that his client is innocent of bigamy. Maybe there *is* no case because two days after Linda testifies and the marriage licenses are submitted into evidence, Vick's lawyer files a new motion. In it, he asks that the court allow Vick to be examined by Dr. Richard B. Jarvis, a psychiatrist.

Sanity

The fact that Vick's lawyer arranged for him to be seen by a psychiatrist requires me to take up a question that has begun to nag as the marriages pile up: Was Vick sane?

The name of the doctor brought in, Richard B. Jarvis, rings a bell: he gained a measure of fame in the 1970s when young women in the Seattle area were being abducted, sexually assaulted, and horribly murdered. Jarvis, described by Seattle crime writer Ann Rule as "specializing in the aberrations of the criminal mind," correctly "described" the age range and sexual psychopathy of Ted Bundy before the killer's identity was known.[1]

Vick, as far as we know, had no interest in violence; he didn't even like to leave dirty dishes in the sink. But could he still have been a psychopath? Is that why Jarvis was called in?

While some psychopaths—especially the famous ones like Bundy—are violent, most aren't. And most violent people aren't psychopaths. Rather, the distinguishing characteristic often attributed to psychopaths, thought to be some 4 percent of the population, is not violence but an unusual blankness concerning the feelings of others, accompanied by a smooth ability to deceive and manipulate. Several of Bundy's victims, for example, appear to have stopped to assist the well-spoken young man who had his arm in a sling or hobbled on crutches.

There are a number of recent books on psychopathy, both scholarly and popular, but one of the best-known writers on the subject continues to be Dr. Robert Hare, who, as a prison psychologist in British Columbia, began to observe a certain, distinctive group of inmates. In his 1993 book, *Without Conscience*, he lists characteristics he identified as those of the psychopath. Not only were these individuals glib, deceitful, and manipulative, but they had "little aptitude for experiencing the emotional responses—fear and anxiety—that are the mainsprings of conscience." Despite their unusual emotional emptiness, they still appeared to be completely rational, "aware of what they [were] doing and why."[2]

Hare was particularly struck by the "unflappable" nature of those he studied, an attitude they retained even when their deceit was uncovered. In fact, he came to believe that a "signpost" for the psychopath was the "smooth lack of concern at being found out." And he identified another trait: the tendency "to live day-to-day and to change their plans frequently," giving little thought to the future and worrying about it even less.[3]

Hare also noticed that those he identified as psychopaths were different from the "normal" criminals in the prison. The latter sometimes practiced deceit and manipulation, of course, but their actions were informed by moral standards, even if they were not the same moral standards of mainstream society.[4] Despite socially deviant lifestyles, Hare observed, the nonpsychopathic criminals were still "capable of feeling guilt, remorse, empathy and strong emotions," as well as intense loyalty to "groups, codes or principles."[5] None of this, Hare writes, would make sense to their psychopathic cellmates.

While Hare was most interested in the insouciant lack of conscience he observed in some of his imprisoned subjects, Dr. Hervey Cleckley—whose 1941 book, *The Mask of Sanity*, is one of the first to extensively detail the condition—was fascinated by something else. As a psychiatrist who saw patients in Georgia mental institutions, Cleckley was amazed at the ease with which utterly untruthful individuals could convince others to believe their lies. Even Cleckley himself sometimes had difficulty holding on to what he knew to be the facts of a patient's case.

The "genius" of the performance, Cleckley began to believe, could be attributed to the fact that these individuals did not in any normal way understand that they were doing anything wrong or insincere.[6] As a result they did not give off the usual signals of dishonesty, and even seasoned professionals could be tricked.

These people were, Cleckley posited, emotionally "colorblind," their strange sense of sincerity "a little like the report of a color-blind man," who says in all honesty "that the horizon is gray," though it actually "blazes with all colors of sunset." At the same time, the psychopath has been living among normal people his whole life and has become quite good at mimicking their emotional "tone."[7]

One of the men profiled in the book—Cleckley calls him Max— reminds me of Vick. Among other things, reading about Max gives me a hint of how Vick might view his own capture. In Max's case, a long career of bigamy and forgery had finally caught up with him. Jailed, he claimed that he had suffered a head injury in World War I combat, and, though the story varied in its telling, it worked to get Max transferred to a mental hospital. Examined there by Dr. Cleckley, Max was "entirely rational in conversation, alert, [and] above average in intelligence." He "talked entertainingly and with enthusiasm about his many adventures. He denied all misconduct on his part but admitted that he had often been in trouble because of his wife and others." It was not, Cleckley writes, the denial of a man who is eager to show himself innocent "but the casual tossing aside of matters considered irrelevant or bothersome to discuss." After laughing off all the things he was accused of, Max "at once shifted the subject to his many triumphs and attainments."[8]

Because the attitudes and motivations of such people are not those of the normal criminal—their actions cannot be understood as the result of greed or need, passion or rage—authorities often feel that they don't belong in jail. But in a mental institution they "stood out arrestingly from the delusional babbling and the blank-faced, staring inertia" of their "psychotic fellows."[9]

If it does not seem right for them to be in jail, it soon becomes equally clear that they are not "insane" in the way usually understood. As a result, they are often released from mental institutions and go back into an unsuspecting world, where, as Hare writes, "a good-looking, fast-talking psychopath and a victim who has 'weak spots' is a devastating combination."[10]

These weak spots are often located in women, and Cleckley reports on the "astonishing power that nearly all psychopaths have to win the devotion of women." The appeal is not erotic, Cleckley believes; in his experience psychopaths were not as interested in "really erotic aims as most men." Rather, the psychopath arouses the "impulse to mother," as women sense that here, "beneath the appearance of maturity, is a baby . . . a spiritual baby." What they fail to understand, Cleckley writes, is that the baby will never grow up.[11]

I'm suspicious of the notion, hailing from the early 1940s, that women's lives are dominated by their "maternal instinct." But Cleckley's view gets some support in a recent book written from a woman's perspective. In *Women Who Love Psychopaths*, social worker Sandra Brown, who treats female victims of psychopathic relationships, does not, to be sure, put the attraction down to maternal instinct. Still, the passion her patients feel for their psychopathic partners does resemble ferocious, unconditional maternal love. The women profiled here are not weak or passive. Rather they are strong and determined, with a great capacity for loyalty, passionate involvement, and empathy. Such women are ready to sympathize with "stories of woe": they are sure they have what it takes to stabilize that "wounded inner little boy."

The women Brown sees share another characteristic. Often they are free-spirited, excitement-seeking women, who can't bear a boring life or boring men. Though the women are not themselves psychopaths, they are often bold and extroverted, traits they share with their psychopathic partner. When two such people meet, the relationship feels intense; and it seems to the women that they have at last found the soul mate they have always sought. Once they find their grand passion, they refuse to let it go.[12]

✧ A lot of this reminds me of Eva, the obedient, demure farm girl changed over a couple of supercharged wartime years into a jaunty working gal who never came home at night. Many women, of course, had a similar experience, then returned to the life of homemaker. But Eva was young during the war, part of a seventeen- to twenty-five-year-old group that some call "transitional"—women for whom the wartime work experience did not represent "discontinuity" but was rather "taken in stride as a natural part of their development."[13] Though marriage and family were aggressively sold and though many women, including those Eva's age, bought that vision, others, as oral histories reveal, felt themselves changed in "private and subtle ways" by their wartime experience.[14] Whatever happened after the war, one woman remembered, "it was a breakthrough . . . because we knew we could do things." Another found, "I could take care of myself. . . . I think I probably learned from that experience that I could always manage."[15]

Eva, I believe, was one of these. She certainly was not, I hasten to say, a feminist. She would, I am sure, have disdained feminism as did most of her class at this time, suspecting that women who went in for such stuff just didn't have what it took to get a man.

Though she would never have consciously subscribed to any such theories, however, the life she lived was all about freedom from women's traditional roles. Seeing this, I can better comprehend the lively cigar stand in the hotel lobby, the bare apartment, even Vick. Clearly Eva was horribly torn between the love of independence and the need for conventional security and respectability that would have been best represented by marriage to bossy Dave. When her deep ambivalence finally drove him away, she picked the feckless Jimmy. Now, she was married, yes. But, if Jimmy was chosen, on some level, for his disinclination to control her life, the fact that he couldn't control his own meant the project was doomed from the start.

Divorced and "free" again, she patterned her life on the only model that she knew: her life on Swan Island during the war. I can see now that the bustling, exciting shipyard canteen where she met dozens of new people a night was to some extent replicated by the cigar stand in the busy hotel lobby. And the barren apartment in Boise, which many would have thought grim, bore a strong resemblance to the utilitarian rooms built for young women at the Swan Island shipyard. In these rooms, as in Eva's apartment, you could not cook a meal, do a wash, or run up a pair of drapes. You could care only for your own personal needs—nothing more. And in such a small bare space, it seemed to be expected that you would spend every night out.

And then came Vick. Though he could clearly earn a living, he was still a freewheeler, who loved the nightlife. With him she could keep her job and her bachelor girl's pad, though now with a handsome, loving man sharing her bed and her teeny kitchen table. And yet it's perfectly respectable—she's married! Now both she and Grace can hold their heads up. In her own way, with Vick, Eva has it all.

When Vick leaves, she simply refuses, as Brown suggests, to let go. I see this in the letters Eva sent to Mexico as she demonstrates her tenacity, her capacity for devotion, and even a kind of confidence, the sense that she can work as hard as is needed to fix whatever is wrong. Further, in those letters to Mexico, she hastens to renounce any thoughts that may have crept into her mind about "settling down," children, and so on. She never really wanted that. She wants nothing but Vick. Couldn't they just live in a little house trailer?

∽ If the profile of women who love psychopaths bears some resemblance to Eva, the description of psychopaths themselves provides a possible explanation for some of the puzzling things about Vick. Why did he always use his real name? Why did he leave behind identifying documents and allow his wedding picture to appear in the newspaper? Like the psychopaths described by Hare, Vick appears to have that "unflappable" lack of concern about being caught or found out. He just doesn't worry about such things.

The discussions of psychopathy also help me develop a theory for how these smart women could have fallen for what was clearly a very shallow imitation of love and devotion. If Vick didn't know what "being in love" meant, then he wasn't knowingly pretending. As a result, the telltale signs of insincerity were nowhere to be seen.

Perhaps, as Cleckley suggests, Vick was "acting," taking his cues from those around him, even from people in the movies. Certainly in the postwar years when marriage was an obsession, he would have had plenty of opportunity to observe people who were excited to be in love, who relished the glamour of the wedding and the romance of the honeymoon. Is it possible that Vick—like the color-blind man who couldn't know why people were raving about the beauty of the sunset—didn't really know what any of it meant on an emotional level but thought it looked like fun? Was he less like a man entering matrimony and more like a man getting dressed up to go to a party? Then, when the party seemed to be winding down, well, it had been fun but now it was over.

And what did he think about the women he left behind, at least two of them pregnant, a third with an infant? If he really didn't understand such concepts as love, devotion, and responsibility, maybe he assumed that others were the same and that the women experienced things in the same shallow way he did. When it was time to go, he didn't feel much; maybe he couldn't imagine that they did either. And if they spoke of their feelings? Well, he spoke of his feelings too. That's what people did. They said things like "I love you." They signed themselves, "Yours, forever."

What about the children? Well, women always said they wanted babies. Vick himself had said he wanted a baby. It was another thing people were always saying. That shouldn't—in a logic that I'm trying to grasp—mean you had to stay around doing things you had gotten tired of doing.

So is that it? Was Vick just born a good-looking, happy-go-lucky psychopath, one of those people who through some, as yet unclear, combination of nature and nurture have missing emotional parts?[16]

Some of the descriptions of psychopaths seem to resemble Vick; yet some things about him don't fit the profile. For one thing, I've found no evidence of the early behavior problems that are so frequently attributed to psychopaths, who, even in childhood, don't see the world the way others do. Nor does Vick go in for the random acts of antisocial behavior that are often observed; he doesn't steal from the till or rip off his friends. Further, as Dr. Weinberger noted, Vick does not have the simmering malice toward others that is often typical of those considered psychopaths or sociopaths. Indeed, aside from his marital irregularities, he appears to be a great guy whom everyone likes. He does not seem to have had trouble holding down a job. And his long and successful service in the Army is most atypical: the psychopaths I'm reading about are seldom awarded good conduct medals.

The psychopathy theory is weakened even further by Pamela Rogers, a mitigation investigator for the Washington State courts. Her job is to investigate convicted criminals and to develop a report that goes to the judge before sentencing; these reports try to explain what made the criminal act as he or she did. Despite all the press psychopathy gets, she tells me, such a diagnosis is very seldom considered sufficient to explain the actions of a criminal.

"Look again at his childhood," she says.

Eva and Vick in Seattle, Spring 1962

Though Eva's name is not mentioned in the court documents, by mid-March, 1962, she has found out that Vick is in jail. And exactly four years after the day that Vick walked out, Eva takes the bus from Portland up to Seattle.

I know this because her visit resulted in a correspondence that I now have, six letters written by Vick in the spring and summer of 1962. The letters provide the best glimpse I have into Vick's mind. And, perhaps, into Eva's as well. Because Eva is *still* not ready to give Vick up.

Of course, we don't know what is said when Eva and Vick meet in the visiting room of the King County jail, but when she gets back to Portland after her visit, Eva sits down to write Vick. Although I don't have her letter, I do have his response, which makes it clear that she has left the door open to a future for the two of them. And his message to her is equally clear: Eva has always been special to him. Now he hints of something that I have seen her trying to convince herself of—despite everything, she has been the "only one."

> Dearest Eva, Your letter came yesterday and you will never know how much it meant to me, and also the time we spent talking together. I felt so much better after seeing you and for the first time have peace of mind, for, at least I feel that you understand me. I have always felt that way about you. And I too had the most wonderful months with you.
>
> I can never tell you how sorry and ashamed I am that I have hurt you so much and can't tell you why.

Then that's pretty much it on the question of why he married her bigamously, left her with a string of bad checks to cover, disappeared with the car, then went on to marry three more women in rapid succession.

I don't know if Eva is able to make more of this than I can. Maybe she still thinks it was wartime trauma that made Vick unable to stay with her, even though he wanted to. Perhaps she really can read his successive marriages as acts of despair and desperation: having blown the one good thing he had, he just didn't care anymore. Maybe his brief marriages to other women were a little like Eva's "going steady" with Bud.

Now Vick seems glad to enlist Eva in his support and to hint—carefully—of what the future might bring. They have, apparently, discussed the lawyer's strategy, and Vick agrees with Eva's belief that the lawyer wants to help. As a result, Vick has gone along with the lawyer's wish to bring in the "head doctor," though this is "not to my way of thinking."

The examination has left him uneasy. I know that Dr. Jarvis sometimes administers "truth serum" in criminal cases.[1] Perhaps he has done so now, and Vick isn't sure what he may have said. Perhaps he's worried that he will be judged a "head case" and confined to a mental hospital. For once, Vick seems really worried. "Eva, as you know, he sent a Doctor up to see me and I am not sure just what is going to happen. I want you to keep in touch with the lawyer, and if this gets out of hand try and get things back on an even keel."

In addition to soliciting Eva's help, Vick is also working to show how responsible he can be; even his handwriting is clearer than in the earlier letter I have from him, the one to Marie ten years earlier, telling her "I'll look after Vick and you look after Jr." Then, he was in a big hurry; there were a lot of cross-outs and scribbled additions. He even botched his own name twice. But now, writing in pencil on cheap jailhouse tablet paper, he's as careful as a third-grader, the handwriting slowed down with no scratch-outs. And the letter is carefully organized, dutifully responding to every topic Eva has brought up.

She has apparently heard that Vick's latest wife, Janice Kavenaugh, has also visited the jail, and Vick undertakes to explain. It is perhaps here that he most reveals his thinking about his relationships, as two stunningly disparate notions coexist quite comfortably: the first is that he has done his best to "help" Janice; the second is that he may have destroyed her forever.

> I am quite sure you received the right information about Janice. I know she is going along with the lawyer's suggestions, however, she came to see me <u>once</u> (so I could give her my pay check) and wrote <u>one</u> letter, and, I

can feel what little we ever had is gone (mostly through her children) as they were wonderful.

She has started drinking again and I know how your life was before I met you. I knew she had that problem and if I never did any good in my life I can say that for a few months I did help her. However the shock of all this and being a very unstable person in reference to drink—it is all over—because she knows and I know she will never believe in anything again.

I'm trying to understand why he wants to tell Eva this. If I were trying to win someone's trust, I don't think I would underline the fact that, thanks to me, another person will "never believe in anything again." Surely it doesn't help his case to paint himself as a man who not only destroys women but *knows* he destroys them. Wouldn't this make Eva reflect on how devastated *she* has been? Wouldn't she possibly imagine him saying to someone else, "I tried to help Eva. But I know that after me, she probably won't trust anyone again."

Maybe the logic of the letter goes like this: Vick is in jail and is being called upon to explain himself to, among others, his lawyer and the court. Probably he understands that "remorse" needs to be part of the picture. So here he's expressing remorse about Janice. But, as this passage seems to suggest, he doesn't really see that he has been at fault, that he has energetically and aggressively gone outside every moral and legal convention and *caused* the problems. Rather Janice's misery is attributed to "all this"; "all this" has wrecked an already "unstable" person, who, in a certain sense, Vick was only trying to help.

I notice something else about this passage. Besides giving a practical reason for Janice's visit to the jail, Vick adroitly compares Janice to Eva's alcoholic first husband, Jimmy. In doing so, he compares himself to Eva, both of them good people who did what they could before finally giving up on a hopelessly drunken spouse. And a final part of the message: Janice is history. Vick is "free" now to focus on Eva.

I puzzle over why he seems so avid to get Eva's help and, as it seems, to get her back. Why does he want to take up with one of the women he has abandoned and whose failure to get an annulment has complicated his situation?

I suppose when you are in jail, a visit from someone who seems to care about you is welcome. Surely it would be good to have someone helping from outside, looking things up, writing letters. Even now, Vick notes in a postscript, she can help by enclosing stamps in her next letter. Also, I suppose, lovely, respectable-looking Eva could come across as a good character witness, perhaps helping to persuade Vick's lawyer to believe in him, to work hard for him. Perhaps her appearance in court as a loyal wife could favorably influence the judge.

Maybe, shaken by his incarceration and the mental examination, Vick understands that he needs to be—or at least needs to play the part of—a man who wants to go straight. Resuming the marriage with Eva could demonstrate that, despite his failings, he is capable of fidelity. Or—could it be possible that what Eva seems to be holding onto is true? Somehow, and despite everything, she is his one true love?

Whatever Vick's reasons or feelings might be, it is clear that he is reaching out with both hands for what Eva is offering. And he elaborates upon the theme, subtly, of Eva being the only one. He apologizes that he even had to mention Janice at all. "I am sorry to be writing you this type of letter, but I do want to be honest with you if nothing more. I have wanted to tell you every day since the night I left you. If I had only known I could have????"

On its face, this is so ridiculous. What on earth was it he wanted to tell her every day for the last four years? Whatever it was, he doesn't spill it now. But maybe what Eva is reading—maybe he said this when they met—is that he always wanted to come back to her, to confess to her the things he was somehow compelled to do. But he just didn't dare.

In addition to "honesty," Vick also introduces the subject of constancy and promises that he will write every single day. The mail goes out only on Monday and Thursday, but he explains that he will still write something every day and then collect the pages to send twice a week. The letter is apparently begun on Saturday, because the fourth page is headed "Well Another Day—Sunday." And on page five, "Here it is Monday—so a few more lines."

See? Every day.

In the later pages of the letter, with all the important matters covered, Vick ventures to mention how nice Eva looked when she visited and how he enjoyed her letter and "hearing all the little things." He's glad her eye problems are better. He urges her to write again when she can "as I am looking forward—!!!!!"

Now he allows himself to become a bit more upbeat, not only about life in jail but prospects for the future. He's had a visit from the union agent, who has brought him some "cigs." The union guy talked to a couple of people, and now Vick is allowed to cook for the prisoners. This means they eat better, and Vick has more privileges. Also the union man has told Vick that there will be a job for him when he gets out and that in the meantime he'll pay Vick's union dues. ("At least one person has faith in me. Ha!") And Vick is excited to hear what the wages are expected to be during the World's Fair, $24 a shift! If he could just get out there and get to work.

> I hope all of this mess is over soon and I can get back on my feet and try to do some good besides hurting people. I have thought of you all the time and now I feel you are the only one who really has any faith in me. I don't see how you could after all this. Well, must close for now. All my love always, <u>Vick</u>.
>
> P.S. Put a couple of stamps in your letters. <u>Vick</u>

And soon it *will* be over. Perhaps, as he has done in other cases, Dr. Jarvis, his examination complete, has assured the court that Vick recognizes the error of his ways and wants to reform. Whether it is a result of the doctor's recommendation of clemency or for some other reason, Vick changes his plea to guilty and is released on two years' probation. In addition, the court requires Vick to undo some of the harm he's caused.[2]

First, he is ordered to pay Odette five hundred dollars in monthly ten-dollar installments administered through the court. Though the records do not say so, this is the exact amount that Odette had to spend on her backstreet abortion. Vick must also clear up his marriage record. To do this, he will have to obtain annulments from the wives he remains married to: Mena, Janice, and Eva.

✐ Eva has always used the back of envelopes to jot memos to herself, check spellings, and save phone numbers. "Middle of April," she writes on one now. "Vick was released and went to work."

The Seattle World's Fair has just opened, and Vick is getting out at the perfect time to start raking in the big wages. The day after the fair opens, April 22, 1962, is Easter Sunday, and down in Portland, Eva has received a holiday greeting card from Bud. At the bottom of the card Bud has added an inscription in his bright green ink: "Wish I were with you so we could enjoy it together. Will be someday I hope."

On the oversized envelope containing Bud's elaborate card she has written,

19th–23rd in Seattle
27th & 28th in Seattle
4th–13th of May—Bud in Portland.

And off to the side in an uncharacteristically jagged scrawl she has written, "impossible."

Before long Eva apparently comes to a decision, and in late May she writes to Bud, telling him that Vick is back. What she is feeling about his return is reflected in a last letter from Bud, though he begins with the usual report on his personal arrangements: he's just taken his bath; he's hoping the weather will be good the next day so he can get some sun. The previous day he belatedly took the annual post office exam; he almost forgot. He guesses he must have a lot on his mind. Finally, he gets on with it, responding to her letter, which he has read "at least ten times." This is his fifth attempt to reply; the previous four drafts have gone into the wastebasket. Bud's stationery is decorated with a different woodland animal on each page, a duck, a deer, a leaping trout. But the silly green ink is gone; now Bud writes in black.

He begins by assuring her that he will do anything possible to help her and that he doesn't want to "make things any worse for you or hurt you in any way." Then he faces it like a man. A boring man, perhaps, but an extremely decent one all the same:

You mentioned in your letter of the great love you and "Vick" once had for each other and that you still had feelings for him but could not determine of what nature and that he still loved you.

I could write my personal opinion of the above paragraph or part of it but I refuse to do so because I feel that I don't want anything I write, do, or say to have any influence on your thoughts or personal feelings, because I feel that I just do not have the right to do so. This is something only you and you alone can work out, because only you know the true feelings in your heart.

But I do know that true pure love can not be divided or shared with another or third party, and I feel as though I am the third party in this case.

I suppose I have been all along but did not want to admit it to myself, so really if that is the case I have nobody to blame but myself.

Here the letter breaks off; and when it resumes, Bud writes that he was just too tired to continue and had to go to bed. Then he couldn't get to sleep; too many things on his mind, he supposes. The sleep that finally came, however, must have done him good because now he's able to wrap it up. He has to go to work soon and needs to get the letter in the mail. The main thing he wants her to know is that she shouldn't worry about anything because he is sure that "all will turn out for the best for all you have gone through."

She has mentioned something about going to church, and he closes with a memory. It's as if he understands that's all Eva is now: "Remember when we used to go to church here in 'Boise.' You always looked so sweet with that cute little hat on, I could hardly resist saying what was in my heart all through the sermon."

So. Sayonara to Bud. And by June, Eva and Vick are making plans for their future together.

"Ha! Ha! I Just Laugh and Tell Everyone a Different Story," Seattle, Summer 1962

In the early summer of 1962, the World's Fair was big news in the West; and though it was our busiest time, my father got away from the farm long enough to take us to Seattle. We had been hearing about the Space Needle and its fabulous rotating restaurant for months. Of course, a place like that would be much too expensive for people like us. We did, though, stand in line for the elevator to the observation platform at the top of the Needle. I remember that the view was fabulous on that clear day. Off to the east were the Cascade Mountains that separate the rainy coast from the arid inland; to the west, beyond Puget Sound, was the wild Olympic Range. And there, to the southeast, was the great ice-cream cone of Mt. Rainier, immense and startlingly close.

Standing on that platform, we marveled at all we saw—not only the mountains and the ferries crossing Puget Sound, but the World's Fair laid out below us, the graceful white spires of the Science Pavilion, and the flashing lights of the amusement park. Somewhere down there too, though we couldn't have known it, was Vick, out of jail, and making good money in a city full of visitors. If we had been the type of people to go into a fancy hotel bar, we might have seen him. We might even have seen Eva, for now she was regularly traveling up to Seattle on her days off.

I couldn't see Eva from the top of the Space Needle back then, but I am trying hard to see her now. I have to realize, of course, that Eva may have known things that I don't. Perhaps, for example, she has seen the psychiatrist's report, and its findings have allowed her to believe that Vick had not wanted to behave as he did, that, as she had always felt, he *was* battling internal demons. Perhaps the report indicated that he wanted to change, could change. Perhaps in person Vick was more convincing than he is in letters that this was so.

Perhaps. But as I have, in a sense, lived Eva's life with her, I think I can see that she may simply have decided that she would reach out to embrace, however fleetingly, the happiness she once knew. Right or wrong, he is the only man she has ever really loved.

She is aware that within a few weeks she will turn forty. Maybe after this milestone there will still be other nice, conventional men like Bud to marry; maybe not. At this point, I don't think Eva cares all that much. By now I think she understands that has never been—at least not since she left the farm in 1943—what she really wants.

I wonder, too, if it may be getting a bit easier to live as she's always done, for by now, the frantic selling of domestic bliss has eased up. The trauma of war and depression—a time during which, as Betty Friedan writes, "women as well as men sought the comforting reality of home and children"—is beginning to subside.[1] Word is now beginning to leak out that a life devoted entirely to homemaking is not paradise for every woman. A recent *Redbook* article, for example, entitled "Why Young Mothers Feel Trapped," struck such a chord that editors received twenty-four thousand pieces of mail.[2] And just this year people are talking about a movie, *The Days of Wine and Roses*, that puts a very different spin on the life of the homemaker. Though the lonely single girl does find a man, get married, and have a baby, this does not produce magical happiness. Rather, trapped at home, she drinks and watches cartoons.

Of course, Betty Friedan is even now putting the finishing touches on *The Feminine Mystique* and will herself be deluged with letters from those who recognize themselves in her description of women trapped and infantilized by the demands of postwar culture. Many, as Brett Harvey puts it, are beginning to "understand and deplore their retreat into the 'cozy cocoons' of family life."[3] Also, the rate of marriage has actually begun to decline for the first time since the beginning of the war.[4]

Eva, whose life has certainly been no "cozy cocoon," could not help but notice this shift. Maybe this new cultural mood contributes to her decision to cut Bud loose and, just because she wants to, get on the bus up to Seattle.

In June, however, something changes. Grace comes to Portland, supposedly to see the annual Rose Festival. Since she stays with Eva in her little apartment, Eva can't get up to Seattle. Then it appears that Grace is not well, heart trouble, and she stays on. Perhaps she is remaining in Portland to see a specialist.

By now she knows that Vick has resurfaced; and Vick suspects, as he writes to Eva, that Grace is having "things to say" about him. Undoubtedly he is right. Though Grace believed so completely in her good, sweet girl twenty years earlier, she has now learned through wretched experience that terrible things can happen, even to a girl as carefully and lovingly raised as Eva. And perhaps over the years, Grace has agonized that she did not do enough to guide Eva as the war wound down, did not help her to salvage Dave or at least to avoid the disastrous marriage to Jimmy. Perhaps now she has resolved to do whatever she can to save her daughter from this new, horrendous situation.

Despite Grace's disapproving presence, Vick and Eva are still in touch throughout June. They talk on the phone, and the letters go back and forth. Vick is pursuing Eva, respectfully, carefully, but passionately. His letters express how anxious he is to hear from her and to see her. "I was so glad to hear you on the phone and that everything was OK. I kept waiting each day last week to hear from you, thinking maybe you would come up."

The letters continue to be packed with assurances of his love. In the six letters from Vick to Eva, the same phrases appear over and over: "I think of you all the time" and "all my love always." In one letter, I notice, "always" appears three times on the same page. In numerous small references, he paints himself as a man who is not taking anything for granted, but who is allowing himself to hope that they just might find a happy future together.

> You know what my lawyer said? Cause I told him I had been seeing you, writing, etc. He said I should marry you legally when this is all over as he thinks you are one fine person and of course he knows how I feel about you. I think he knows how much I need you and without you I don't have anything. (He's pretty smart.) And he also knows that I have peace of mind I haven't ever had for a good many years. Of course we all know it is up to me to prove myself because I would never want you to have any doubts and I never want to hurt you anymore.
>
> If your mother goes back on the 18th, you could come on up as I can

get off Mon, Tues, or Wed plus Sunday any time I want it. I sure wish you could work up here this summer. Write when you can and I will do the same. So much to talk about.

One thing they have to discuss is his legal situation. In addition to the charge of bigamy, he has now been sued for child support by Marie in California. Vick writes,

> All that happened June 6, the court ordered me to pay $36.00 dollars a month support to California. I didn't even go to court, Mike went up and took care of it. I payed the court cost of twenty-five dollars and that was that. I have $62.40 court cost for the other times I went to court to pay. I have several months to pay it as that is tied up with the deferred sentence. All I have left is what Mike is going to charge me and he won't say. I have been paying him twenty dollars a week every week since I went to work, so I know it won't be long until I'm squared away.

So. all this "mess" will be cleared up soon, and Vick—perhaps with Eva at his side—can look toward to a bright future. If what he writes is true, Vick has won over the lawyer, who believes Vick can sustain a real relationship. And, as always, Vick appears to be popular at work; he boasts to Eva that his boss came into the kitchen, took him and another guy aside, told them not to tell anyone, and then gave them each "a bonus check for twenty-five dollars."

He has been saving his money and has "some stuck away for us to do with whatever we decide. I have been living a quiet life and believe it or not I enjoy it." Vick has never come across as a man with especially expensive tastes—except, perhaps, in new cars—and it does seem now that he is living economically. He writes on stationery from the Hotel Reynolds ("Specializing in Courtesy and Low Rates"), which was, and still is, literally across the street from where prisoners first enter the King County courthouse. The Reynolds, now a work-release residence, is old and crumby, but it doesn't seem to have ever been very grand. On the residential floors are tiny rooms off a bare hallway; the rusting communal bathroom is undoubtedly the same one that Vick used back in 1962.

Even if Vick is saving his money and devoting himself to the "quiet life," however, and even though he has vowed to "prove" himself, he is still managing to have a pretty good time in World's Fair Seattle. Though it's no palace, the Reynolds has a good location, only a few steep blocks up from the waterfront, which, during the fair, is festive with ships. Vick describes for Eva how he has gone down to see the *HMS Bounty,* the ship that was built for the movie, *Mutiny on the Bounty.* Vick got a laugh when the ship ran into a buoy and a tug had to be sent to take it off. "I wonder if Captain Blithe would have called up a tug company in his day." Vick has also gone to a football game and seen "old Hustling Hugh in action. He still is pretty good and believe me San Francisco gave him a rough time. Ha!"

While Vick seems to have settled into a carefree bachelor existence, Eva worries about the still unresolved issue of Vick's marital status and, correspondingly, her own. One thing she is wondering is if her name is still "Mrs. Vickers." Twice he responds to this concern, assuring her that "I would like for you to have the name of Mrs. V—always, and not just in name. If you want??"

Eva has also been asking about the plan for Vick to get annulments from the three women—one of them herself—to whom he is known to be still married. Vick replies that the lawyer hasn't sent the papers out yet, perhaps "stalling" until he sees "what you and I want to do, etc."

I'm not sure what this means. Is Vick suggesting that his marriage to Eva could still stand if the other marriages are cleared away, even though it was, when entered into, bigamous? Whatever the considerations, I do know that there is a decision to go ahead with the annulments, and on June 20 Vick signs a "complaint" against Eva, Janice in Tacoma, and Mena in Glendale, California, alleging that his marriage to them was not legal since he was already married. (I notice in the court papers that two of the women's first names are misspelled: Jenice rather than Janice; Dena rather than Mena. I don't know if this is due to clerical error or Vick's difficulty in keeping all the names straight.) In July summonses are served upon the three women, with Eva getting hers in Portland on the sixth.

I have a copy of the complaint, and, as has happened a few other times, I am brought to a standstill by what this document represents. I try to imagine how it felt for these women to be served at their homes with a legal complaint on Vick's behalf, summoning them to appear in court with themselves named as defendant. I understand—and no doubt the women understood—that this is a court-ordered procedure, designed to bring the case to a close. I understand that the women are free to ignore the summons as all do, thus allowing the annulments to be granted.

Still. It's horrifying that the system is such that Vick is allowed to present himself as the guiltless party—something that, on some level, he seems to feel himself to be.

During July, Eva stays in Portland, dealing with some issue that Vick alludes to but does not name in his letters. The problem is, no doubt, Grace: her heart trouble and her continued opposition to what Eva is doing. It is likely that the two conditions are related. Undoubtedly, Grace's anguish is taking its toll, as is Aub's shocked disbelief. Vick, he has said, belongs not in a cell but in a cage.

Indeed, it is hard to imagine that anyone Eva knows would be anything but appalled by the idea that she would go back to Vick. And now, Eva herself is beginning to ask a few questions. In one letter, Vick responds to her complaint that he has not been writing enough. He has a good explanation. He knows Grace is there and thought it would be better that she not see a letter arriving from him. "Honey, I will keep writing, you know now why I didn't as I thought maybe with other people around they would just have more to say to you about me."

His letters are still filled with professions of love and constancy. At the same time there seem to have been some recent slipups on his end that have to be explained:

> I sure feel like kicking myself for not calling Sat or being home Sunday, but I thought you wouldn't be home Sat and Sunday you wouldn't feel like answering any phone. Dick the other cook I work with had breakfast together, goofed around, went out to Sand Point and seen the "Blue Angels" air show. Then we stopped for Chinese food so was about ten o'clock when I got in. I still feel like kicking myself.

The description of the day spent with "Dick" is pretty good. But the suggestion that Eva would not want to answer the phone on a Sunday is so lame that it makes me wonder if Vick's attention is wandering.

Additionally, there is confusion as to where Vick is living. His post-jail letters have been written on stationery from the Hotel Reynolds. But now Vick tells Eva she should write in care of his buddy, Jim, who lives at the Holland Hotel. He gives no explanation of where he is, in fact, living. The only information he provides: "Jim is the guy I told you about who lost his arm in France."

By mid-August, Eva is still in Portland. Grace is still not well though she has gone back home to eastern Oregon. With Grace gone, Vick can now visit. He was, he writes, thinking of coming down the previous weekend. In the end, however, he stayed in Seattle; and he gives a detailed explanation of how he spent his time: he got home late from work, was really beat, slept until noon, tried to call but no answer, took a walk, and went to see *The Music Man*. "The music was good and it was rather funny." He assures Eva that she is missed in Seattle among the people they know. But Vick knows how to handle inconvenient questions. "Everyone asks about you here and at work they are dieing of curiosity. Ha! Ha! I just laugh and tell everyone a different story."

Dr. Jarvis is deceased, as is Vick's lawyer, and the report on Vick's mental state almost certainly has not survived these many years. But I'm more convinced than ever that Vick needs a shrink. And New York City psychoanalyst Dianne Kaminsky agrees to take on the project.

When I arrive at her elegant Upper East Side apartment, she has the man spread out on a long table: there's a timeline of his activities, letters from his wives, and photographs of his weddings. Kaminsky also has my report on Vick's parents, their financial difficulties, and clippings about the family from their hometown newspapers. And she has the three Vickers family photographs, sent to me by one of Vick's great-nieces, whom I've located online. Finally, Kaminsky has read the letters Vick sent to Eva in the spring and summer of 1962, first from jail, then after his release.

It's an unusual case, Kaminsky says. Vick doesn't have a problem with commitment in the ordinary sense. In her opinion, he's not faking when he tells a woman that he's deeply in love, that she's made him the happiest man in the world. He *is* in love—but not really with her. Rather, he's in love with the admiration and idealization that she offers, something he seems to need desperately. "As long as she believes in him and everything looks so beautiful, he's glowing with happiness, real happiness."

Of course, Kaminsky doesn't have the actual man on her couch, and she is careful to say that she can't know with certainty that he wasn't born with some kind of brain anomaly as is posited by some of the recent work on psychopaths. But, based on the evidence I've given her, she doesn't believe a brain disorder accounts for Vick's pattern of marriage and abandonment. Nor does she believe Vick suffered from Post-Traumatic Stress Disorder as a result of his military service. "I don't think that his pathology is because he was in a tank. I think this started much earlier."

In fact, Kaminsky suspects, the Army was good for Vick, giving him a structure that allowed him to function more or less normally. "He's a bright guy and he could do what he was told to do. He could get admiration from his buddies because he's good at things. He could get medals. And there were no women around to idealize him."

What was going on with Vick, Kaminsky believes, was a version of attachment disorder, the inability to sustain deep emotional attachment with others, a pathology that begins before the age of two. The cause is usually some disconnect between the child and the adults who care for him, and Kaminsky gives as an example the case of children who spend their earliest years in foster care or orphanages, who form no emotional connections during that time, and who, in later life, have difficulty sustaining relationships.

I point out that Vick wasn't left in an orphanage or put into foster care. Rather he was born into a large, intact family. It's true that the parents, Wilbur and Lucy, had rather devastating financial reversals when Vick was a toddler. Still, the Vickerses seem have been a sociable, respectable family. I show Kaminsky the 1938 obituary noting that Wilbur "will be missed by his many friends."

Furthermore, I argue, it would seem that the Vickers children were valued by their parents. Here, again, is the 1914 photograph of the infant Vick perched on his father's knee. Somebody has bothered on this wintry day to bring a chair out from the house and to dress the baby in a frilly gown and cap.

A later photograph, probably taken around 1917, shows the Vickers children standing in front of a big tree, with farm buildings in the background. By now, Vick's sister Clara, twenty-three years older than he, has been married and gone for two years, and Clark has recently died. But here are the remaining four: and if the Vickerses have come upon hard financial times, you can't see it in the children. These are no barefoot, half wild, farm kids in ragged overalls and shapeless dresses. Rather, Vick's young teenage sisters, Esther and Elinor, stand together in high-button shoes and snugly fitting dresses of a dark shiny material; their hair is done up in back with large white bows. Beside them is cheerful-looking, string-beany, twelve-year-old George in a jacket, knickers, and long stockings. And there is baby Virgil, about three, standing in front of George; he is dressed up in a short pants outfit with dark stockings and a ruffled necktie. The photograph was apparently sent to friends or family at a distance, because on the back someone, surely a doting mother, has identified the children and written, "Do you see any boys and girls that look like these out in Kansas? We think these look very nice."

I show Kaminsky one more family photograph, this from around 1926. By now George too is has moved away. But Esther and Elinor, both in their twenties and married, stand together in front of a Model T. Their arms are around each other, their heads close, their hair blowing. In front of them is a little blonde boy of about four. I take this to be the son of one of the sisters, and that they have driven home for a visit. They all look happy to be standing out in the sun and the wind. Off to the side is Vick, a husky twelve- or thirteen-year-old wearing a white shirt and tie and a suit that is a bit too tight. He smiles, head a little down, squinting against the light.

In addition to the attractive appearance of the family, I suggest to Kaminsky that a good deal of evidence seems to show that Wilbur and Lucy raised solid and stable children, at least when it came to their three daughters, all of whom stayed in Kansas. The eldest, Clara, married a bank bookkeeper, and by 1930, the Depression notwithstanding, the couple owned a home worth $3,000 and had three children.[1] Today Clara and her husband are buried side by side in the western Kansas town where they lived their whole lives. Clara's gravestone, inscribed "Mother," has been photographed by her descendants and put up on a genealogy site. Esther, twelve years older than Vick, was teaching school at eighteen and went on to become a dietician. At twenty-three she made a lifelong marriage to a Kansas farmer. A third sister, Elinor, was married to a butter maker and was the mother of a one-year-old daughter by the age of twenty-one. Her obituary shows that she was still married to the same man at her death. Certainly she hadn't abandoned the family, for it is at Elinor's home in Wichita where her mother, Lucy, was living when she died at the age of ninety.

I know less about Vick's brother George, but I do know that, like Vick, he went West, ending his life in Lake Hughes, California. When he dies at seventy-seven, a 1983 obituary gives as his survivors a wife, an adult son, and daughter.

ᴥ Kaminsky and I study the pictures of the family and consider the lives fashioned by Vick's siblings. Doesn't she agree that Vick appears to have come from a normal, healthy, and fairly successful family?

"Outwardly," Kaminsky says, "they look like pretty okay people." The question, however, is how emotionally available the parents were to Vick, their sixth child. "The fact that Vick was born seven years after his next-oldest siblings to parents who were forty-five and fifty-one, suggests he was not planned. And if his parents were worn out by years of child rearing, Vick may not have had the type of emotional connection to them that the others did." Also, it's possible that Vick was a menopausal baby, in which case the mother may have been depressed or unable to breastfeed.

"Perhaps," Kaminsky says, "as is often the case in large families, older siblings played parental roles. Perhaps it was the sisters who raised Vick, and then, in what might have felt like abandonment to a little child, they left to live their own lives, to raise their own children." This sense of abandonment could have begun with the marriage of the eldest sister, Clara, when Vick was eleven months old. By the time Vick was two, Clara had her own baby.

The family's financial troubles and death of the twenty-year-old Clark when Vick was three may have "magnified" the situation, Kaminsky says, but she believes that if Vick had already formed normal emotional attachments, these family traumas would have been sustained, even if he had temporarily responded with temper tantrums, nightmares, and depression. Vick, though, may not have had any of these symptoms. A child who has failed to attach emotionally doesn't act out in this way, Kaminsky says. Instead he "simply detaches. On a superficial level he probably seems fine."

Kaminsky is still interested in Vick's sisters and looks again at a studio portrait I have located of his sister Esther, made on the occasion of her 1925 wedding. For fourteen-year-old Vick, it was his third sister to marry and the second wedding in a couple of years. His sister Elinor had also recently married. In the portrait, Esther is trim with Vick's dark good looks, and she seems remarkably fashionable for a Kansas farm girl. She wears a long fitted dress with three-quarter-length sleeves and a cone-shaped hat with a wide white band and a tiny black feather. Her hands are lifted slightly as if she is smoothing the fit of her elbow-length, black leather gloves. Her head is high, and she glances to the side with the casual attitude of somebody who is used to the admiring glance.

"They are a nice middle class family," Kaminsky says. "This picture, along with the pictures of the nicely dressed children, shows that it was important to the family to present themselves well." She turns back to her long table and picks up the picture of Vick and Marie on their 1948 wedding day in California; both bride and groom are as elegant as magazine models.

"The women he marries resemble the well-turned-out sisters, who may have been mother figures to him," Kaminsky muses. "I think he tries to recreate an idealized early family. Over and over."

I ask Kaminsky why she thinks Vick lied so pointlessly about his family, telling the Canadian military that he had no living family members other than one brother, telling Eva that his mother and three sisters were dead, when in fact all would live for many more years. And why did he tell Eva that he had *two* brothers, when one of the brothers had died when Vick was three?

"People aren't real to him," Kaminsky says. "He cuts them off." Concerning the dead brother, she speculates, Vick may have created some kind of fantasy of his continued presence. Similar fantasies of an idealized family may have been behind Vick's claim that his father was a hotel owner in Newton and his obsession, as Marie remembers, with a family coat of arms.

We turn to the packet of letters that Vick wrote Eva in 1962, beginning with his first letter from jail.

"When Eva contacts him," Kaminsky says, "it's the honeymoon all over again. 'No matter what,' she seems to be saying, 'you're the love of my life.' He gets caught up in the romantic fantasy. He believes that she loves him and that he loves her. That they will love each other 'always.' Because that is how a romantic fantasy works. He doesn't really discuss what has happened, what he has done. Romantic fantasy doesn't require any of that."

But doesn't he know how much he is hurting the women he loves and then leaves?

"For me to understand I'm hurting you," Kaminsky says, "I have to identify with you and know that you are hurt. Once I am able to empathize with your pain, I feel bad or at least guilty. But Vick isn't able to empathize with the women. They are real only as romantic fantasies. This is why I don't think it was PTSD. This type of disconnectedness starts early."

And the women Vick chose?

Those Vick picked, Kaminsky says, were especially ready to share in a fantasy of perfect love. "Any couple is a co-construction. Not every woman would have gone for this. They would have seen through it, challenged it, looked for the ground underneath. Vick can smell out nice-looking women who are looking for a nice-looking man to idealize. They sense it in each other."

Still, Kaminsky believes the women were much healthier than Vick and would probably have been able to stay with the relationship, to allow it to move through its successive phases, as demonstrated by their other successful relationships. For Vick, however, when the honeymoon was over and reality began to intrude on the idealized romantic fantasy, the bubble of happiness burst. This would especially be true if a child were involved. "I don't think he could tolerate being a father and having a child. *He's* the child; he's the one that needs to be idealized. Having a baby is real life, not playing house any more. So he splits."

And Eva?

"She had failed several times at love and marriage," Kaminsky says. "For her, Vick was perfect. Finally, the dream of head-over-heels love and a perfect marriage had come true."

If Kaminsky is right that Vick was happy as long as the relationship remained a magical romance, her theory could explain why Vick stayed with Eva longer than with the others. For one thing, she didn't get pregnant. And maybe too, the way Eva liked to live kept the honeymoon excitement alive longer than in the other marriages. Though the letters to Mexico show that Eva had started to think about a house and a baby, she wasn't in a rush. Like Vick, she enjoyed the nightlife, getting dressed up, working in the exciting hubbub of a fancy hotel.

I look again at Eva's frantic letters to Mexico, where she assures Vick that she needs "no home, no family, friends, or so called worldly possessions." On some level, it seems, Eva understood and was willing to accept that Vick couldn't live a normal grown-up life. It's not, as I've begun to see, something she herself really wanted. But if Eva still holds out hope that she and Vick are meant for each other, she's not, finally, completely blind.

"She wants to believe," Kaminsky says, as she looks through Vick's letters. "Maybe she can at first. But she does begin to ask questions."

Before Kaminsky and I finish our session, I bring out something I've been saving, something I find so remarkable that I want to see the effect it has on her. It's a cartoon that Vick clipped from *Argosy* magazine, signed, and enclosed in one of his letters from jail. In the drawing, a dark-haired man is sitting in an armchair, his feet on a hassock. He's reading a newspaper, holding it up so that it obscures his face and chest. In front of him stands a woman. She is an early sixties housewife, attractive enough in a dress, little apron, high heels, and the jutting breasts all *Argosy* cartoon women must have. But her mouth is turned down in a look of dismay, and her eyebrows are raised in bewilderment. For, still hidden behind his newspaper, the man has reached down to pull a lever installed at the side of his chair. This has activated a large sign that rises up behind him. The sign reads, "YES, I REALLY LOVE YOU!!"

Kaminsky is suitably impressed. "It's fascinating that he sends her this cartoon when he's trying to get her back. How much awareness does he have of what the cartoon says? Does he know that he really is cut off?"

Kaminsky studies the cartoon a bit more. "Maybe he sends it because Eva is nagging a little, making demands. 'Am I the only Mrs. Vickers? What about the annulments?' He wants women to love and admire him, not ask a lot of questions. He's getting a bit bugged."

Is he sane? I ask.

Kaminsky shrugs. "He wouldn't be accepted into a mental institution."

Wing Valley, August 1962

By August of 1962 Grace has returned to Wing Valley. Shortly after returning home, she has a heart attack and is taken to the hospital in Baker. Eva hurries home from Portland and remains in eastern Oregon for several weeks, caring for Grace. While she is there, one last letter comes from Vick.

Dearest,

Gee honey it has been so long since I have heard from you is something wrong? If so surely you can let me know. I miss you and love you so much. I wonder just what has happened.

Same old thing going on here so not much news to write about. The weather turned lousy last day or two.

Honey, write please and let me know whats what.

All my love *always*, Vick.

But Eva is finally finished. Maybe she has at last faced the fact that something is missing in Vick. Maybe she hasn't. Maybe she just can't kill her mother by going back to him.

To Follow the Heart, 1943–2002

Not so very long after Vick's final exit from Eva's life, a man named Warren became her third husband. He was another one of the six-footers she favored, a red-faced man with big plans for his future, who came out to eastern Oregon dressed up in a dark blue double-breasted suit and shiny city shoes. They had met, I believe, in the restaurant business. But he was another alcoholic, and before long he and Eva were separated.

As I got older, I saw less of Grace and did not see Eva at all, so I am surprised to discover, as I go through Eva's things, that there is a good-sized packet of letters from me, filled with news of my acceptance to college, my summer job in Washington, D.C., another summer working in the Netherlands.

In one of these letters from Europe, I comment on a breakthrough with Eva's eye problems. For the first time in her life, doctors have been able to fit her with spectacles that enable her to do close work. She has enrolled in what was then called "business school" and, her studies complete, has gotten an office job at the Bonneville Power Administration in Portland. In her papers I find a photo I.D. of a hugely smiling, middle-aged Eva. She is sitting at a desk covered with papers, and she has not removed the thick glasses for the photo, though they give her cinnamon-colored eyes a weird magnified look.

In my letter I congratulate her, though I could not then have understood what it must have meant to Eva, now in her late forties and on her own again, to have a job with benefits and one that did not require her to walk around all night in high-heel shoes.

As the sixties come to a close, I write to tell Eva of my plans to marry one of my University of Oregon classmates. We had, of course, come of age in the Vietnam era and, as did many others, felt deeply alienated from our parents' World War II certainties, as well as their fifties aspirations. Now, as I write Eva, we are planning to go to

Canada to escape the draft. We have fitted up a Volkswagen bus to live in; we'll try to get on teaching in Saskatchewan.

My parents, not surprisingly, are horrified; my father can barely speak to me. In fact, the only person from home who seems happy that I am in love and excited about a life of adventure is Eva. And one summer night my fiancé and I hitchhike from Eugene to Portland, where Eva throws an engagement party in her apartment, an even tinier and barer version of the one on Jefferson Street in Boise.

It's just the three of us sitting at her little kitchen table, feasting merrily on Cornish game hen—the one thing that will fit in Eva's doll-sized oven—and on chocolate cupcakes from a bakery, decorated with pink hearts. Though Grace would have been scandalized, Eva has gotten a bottle of rosé for the occasion; it just fits sideways in the miniature fridge, which is right at Eva's elbow. She can reach it without getting up.

On that festive night, I have no idea, nor would Eva have mentioned, that she too came of age in a world turned upside down, one in which her parents' beliefs seemed only dimly relevant and that— right or wrong—she too had tried to follow her heart.

A few weeks later Eva is present at my rather grim little wedding. In the photographs, I see myself in a white minidress; my new husband has put on a suit and tie but is still groovy enough to appall my father with his wild hair and wire-rimmed glasses. Eva, who has stood up with me as matron of honor, is wearing her new spectacles, and she has her arm through mine.

In the years that followed, my husband ended up avoiding the draft, and we drove the VW bus to Mexico instead of Canada. From time to time, we would swing out to Wing Valley, where my dad had made his peace with my decision and was now willing to inspect my traveling home with interest. Everything was so convenient, I explained to him. We could reach out and make coffee on our little camp stove without even getting out of our sleeping bag.

I always went down the road to see Grace, though it was mostly out of duty. Grace was growing more religious with every passing year. As we sat, she tried to make me look at articles in her Billy Graham magazines, and the question of whether or not I was saved seemed to be the only topic that interested her.

I heard, at some point, news of Eva. She had finally divorced Warren; and her divorce lawyer, Lester, had become her fourth husband. Everyone, I expect, raised an eyebrow at this development; it had all the earmarks of another of Eva's losing propositions. However, the marriage to Lester, a man I never met, apparently worked. They were together until Lester's death in 1988. And it says a lot that after the funeral Eva brought Lester out to eastern Oregon to be buried in the family cemetery alongside Eva's father, Wes, and Grace's pioneer forebears.

When Lester's will was opened, it turned out that some stocks he owned—accepted once in lieu of legal fees and then apparently forgotten—were worth a lot of money. A whole lot of money. Surely no one was more shocked than Eva, who, now in her midsixties, found herself a millionaire.

Now Eva too got the chance to travel, visiting the hot and exotic countries she had always dreamed of. In Guatemala she saw the Mayan temples at Tikal. In Hawaii, with Grace as her guest, one of them scooped up a packet of grey sand from the beach, and I find it in Eva's things. In Africa she went on safari and visited the home of Isak Dinesen, the writer who abandoned a bourgeois life in Denmark for one of high adventure and fascinating, unreliable men in the Kenyan highlands.

Though she had an apartment in Portland and a house in Arizona, Eva also kept a rustic cabin on the Oregon coast. Situated on twenty old-growth acres, it was where she and Lester and the three dogs they called "the boys" had lived after his retirement.

By this time, I had left the West, the boy in the wire-rimmed glasses, and the Volkswagen bus and had moved to New York City. I got out to Oregon most summers, though, and once I made it out to the coast to see Eva. She was there alone, thin as always, long-legged in the standard costume of the place: boots, blue jeans, and a flannel shirt. It was one of the rare, glorious sunny days on the coast, and Eva and I sat on the porch, talking and drinking coffee.

Grace and Aub were both dead now, Aub recently. Freed, I understood, by some promise she had made, Eva had something she wanted to tell me, a secret that had never been breathed: in the first year of her marriage to Jimmy, she had had a baby. With Jimmy "out on a spree somewhere," Eva, drugged and dazed after a long, difficult labor, had signed papers to give the baby up. There was a doctor's wife, she'd been told, who'd lost her own newborn and who wanted to adopt. Eva's child would have the best of everything. Later she tried to undo what she'd done, to get the baby back. But it was too late.

"It was a little girl," Eva told me. "She was only a year older than you."

❧ The summer after 9/11, with a new husband and my own daughter, I drove across the country from the East Coast to Oregon. Something about the attacks near where I was working in downtown Manhattan made me want to go home. Also, my daughter was turning twelve, and I thought it could be my last chance for a while to show her the country where I had grown up and to introduce her to people I had known. We drove through Kansas corn and up through the Sandhill country of Nebraska and into Wyoming. Then we wound down through Idaho and the Hells Canyon region to Wing Valley, still as lost in time and heartbreakingly beautiful as ever. Once there, we went down to visit the graves, Grace's and that of my dad, then on to Portland, where we looked up Eva.

We were picking her up to take her to dinner, and I was curious to see where she lived, now that she was a millionaire. But the little apartment in a nondescript building was surprisingly familiar, very much like the ones I had known in Boise and later in Portland, plain and spare as a dorm room. Eva, by now, was much too thin, her legs like sticks. Still, after we'd eaten, she, with the old conspiratorial smile, took my daughter over to the dessert case, where they picked out a gooey chocolate concoction called Midnight Sin. When we weren't looking, Eva picked up the tab.

A year or so later, I got word that Eva was dying of emphysema. I flew out to Portland and sat beside her hospital bed while she dozed and tried to breathe. When she was awake, we reminisced a bit, talking about Grace. In her labored whisper, Eva told about the time she introduced her mother to a man she was dating, a big Russian, a terrific dancer. The Russian, trying to make a good impression, offered Grace a swig of vodka from his flask.

The old merry look was in Eva's eyes, but she didn't have enough breath to laugh.

Eva had been on the phone with her daughter, Judy, a woman in her fifties, who lived in the Midwest, and who, after a long search, had found Eva two decades earlier. But Eva, I gathered, had not wanted Judy to come; the little hospital room, Eva suggested, would be too crowded.

Although I think Eva was glad I had come, after a couple of days she let me know that she would just as soon be left alone. When I turned the pages of my book, she said, the rustling woke her. And she was tired of waking up.

So I said goodbye, and in a few days Eva was gone, soon to return home at last to lie beside her family in the well-watered cemetery overlooking the dry hills of eastern Oregon.

✑ Eva named me executor of her will, and it was my job to dispose of her things. In the boxes and bundles of papers, I found handsome studio photographs of Eva and Jimmy on their wedding day. I also found a snapshot of Eva and her daughter Judy standing with their arms rather awkwardly around each other, both looking silly in sixties miniskirts. These I sent on to Judy, and we talked a bit on the phone. She and Eva had visited each other several times, I learned. Eva had met Judy's children, and Judy had met Grace, even traveling, though surreptitiously, to Wing Valley. Judy's tally of Eva's marriages, she told me, stood at three; she had never heard of a man named Vick.

It would take a couple of years for the lawyer to work through Eva's bequests and send me the papers to sign. There was still a lot of money, and Eve had bequeathed a dozen or so sizeable gifts to environmental and animal rights funds. But the bulk of Eva's fortune, by way of atonement I am sure, went to Billy Graham, Grace's favorite evangelist.

Epilogue

Dave Johnson sent his last letter to Eva on Paramount Studios stationery, but he does not seem to have stayed in the movie business. A 1966 obituary for his mother indicates that Dave had rejoined the service and was stationed at an Air Force base in North Carolina.

To my surprise—since none of this was mentioned as the elder Johnsons agonized over Dave's World War II service—I learned that his father was seriously wounded in World War I. While convalescing, he married a French girl, Dave's mother, Marie. To my even greater surprise—remembering Grace's horror of Catholicism—I read that at Marie's funeral a rosary was recited.

Jimmy Wright, like a lot of Alaska hands, eventually came down to Seattle, where, not surprisingly, he died fairly young, at fifty-six. It doesn't appear that he ever married again.

Bud, once Eva was out of his life for good, married an Idaho widow with three grown children. He continued to work at the post office; and once, buying stamps in Boise in the 1970s, I found myself face-to-face with him. I saw the name on the uniform and recognized him immediately, though the glossy dark hair had gone gray. He didn't recognize me, of course, and he looked old and tired. I didn't bother him with who I was.

Warren lived on in Portland until his death in 1996. Today someone has memorialized Warren on a genealogy web site, putting up snapshots from the 1960s, and I see again the man I met, the double-breasted suit and the long, red, hopeful face.

୶ William, Vick's son, lived in Kansas all his life. He and his wife Jeanette had five children and thirteen grandchildren. When Jeanette and I spoke, the count on great-grandchildren stood at four.

It took William's mother, Edna, fifteen years to recover from her youthful marriage to Vick, Jeanette told me. He'd taken her and the baby down to Mississippi and abandoned them there; Edna had to write her folks for money to come home. Eventually though, she married again.

Hearing that I was interested, Jeanette went out to the nursing home to ask her mother-in-law, now ninety-five, what she remembered about Vick. Edna thought and then said, why, she could not remember a thing.

୶ Vick, after his correspondence with Eva breaks off, remains in Seattle. He's been on probation, of course, since his release from jail and is not allowed to leave the state. And he has court-ordered responsibilities to fulfill. On November 29, 1962, he makes, through the court, the first ten-dollar payment to Odette on the five hundred dollars he owes; and he begins to pay Marie the nine dollars a week child support that has been ordered.

Also in November, Vick's suit for three annulments reaches court and is picked up by a *Seattle Times* police reporter, who, under the headline "Cook Asks Court to Annul 3 Marriages," writes a lead that undoubtedly gets a laugh on the copy desk. "A Seattle restaurant cook convicted of bigamy here last April has asked the Superior Court to straighten out his complex marital affairs." The article names not only Vick but the three remaining wives—Eva, Mena, and Janice—and notes that Vick was arrested on a fourth wife's charge of bigamy with yet another wife, a fifth.

The annulments will not come through until February. On December 23rd, however, Vick—who probably can't wait for Christmas to pop the question—takes the car ferry to Langley on Whidbey Island. Here in a 1:00 P.M. ceremony in the Community Methodist Church, forty-nine-year-old Vick marries thirty-eight-year-old Leda Henault, an office manager in a Seattle carpet brokerage. She is—though, of course, she does not know—the tenth Mrs. Vickers.[1]

Leda does not seem to have been married before, and the Polk

Directories from 1959 to 1962 have her living alone in a house in the Magnolia section of Seattle. Then in 1962, the directory shows, she has moved to an apartment building on Olympic Place in the Queen Anne District. It's a nice art deco building, with a fabulous location, near downtown, still high on a bluff overlooking Elliott Bay. Formerly listed in the directory as "Leda Henault," she is now listed—perhaps conviction and probation have made Vick just a tiny bit cautious—as "Mrs. Leda Henault."

It would be only a month after the wedding that another article appeared in the *Seattle Times*, this one headlined "Cook's Marital Tangle Partly Unraveled." Vick's annulments from Eva and Janice have come through, the article reports; but, for reasons not given in the court papers, the judge has refused to grant the annulment from Mena, the wife in Southern California. Again, the *Times* plays it for laughs: "Vickers was told a divorce was needed to lose a third wife."

Perhaps Leda noticed the item, for in February of 1963, Leda's own annulment is listed in the *Times*. And the city directory shows that she has moved back to the house in Magnolia, becoming once again plain "Leda Henault."

By this time, of course, Vick was long gone. After paying Odette a total of twenty dollars on the judgment of $500 and Marie a total of $243 in support of their now ten-year-old daughter, his payments ceased. In March of 1963, King County issued a bench warrant for his arrest. He was, however, never apprehended.

∽ ∽ ∽

After World War II, Americans spent a great deal of imagination and energy creating a fantasy. It was a fantasy that embodied all they had dreamed of during the privation, loss, and upheaval of Depression and war, a vision so strong that it took on a doctrinaire quality. *Everyone* had to have the storybook romance and marriage; everyone needed the glowing home, where a loving husband made a lucky woman joyously happy.

Vick spent much of his own imagination and energy inserting himself into this fantasy. Time and again he became the adoring groom who would provide the perfect ending that the times required and that every woman sought. Surely Vick would not have been so successful, so *swift*, in creating one blissful marriage after another if the postwar years had not presented him with such a compelling role, one so superbly fitted to his looks, his demeanor, and even the simple pleasure he appears to have taken in lending a hand around the house.

Indeed, I suspect one aspect of Vick's smooth success was that he grasped the true nature of fantasy better than normal people. During these years, urged on by the magazines and the movies and the new social conventions, men and women alike appeared to accept that a fantasy could be real, that it could live on and on in glowing Technicolor. Of course, even the most perfect and romantic marriage would take on a more realistic coloring after six months or so. And undoubtedly some women confined to the home did not experience the total bliss they'd expected. Meanwhile, some husbands and fathers read *Playboy* in secret. Still, it would be a decade before society in general dared to openly question the magical, magazine-ad perfection that was supposed to bathe the fifties marriage and home.

Vick, on the other hand—lacking, for whatever reason, the usual range of human emotion, the usual set of desires and beliefs—was never suckered. From the beginning, he seemed to know, at least in some part of himself, this stuff wasn't *real*. Which was, perhaps, what allowed him to become the most brilliant dream-spinner of them all.

And Eva? Certainly she bought the romance part of the fantasy, clinging ferociously to the idea of the movie-star-handsome lover who adored her and wanted only her forever. Certainly too, she wanted to be married, to be safe and respectable, in part so that her mother could breathe again. But she never fell for other key elements of the fifties fantasy. For her, I believe, as for some other women who came of age as war work ramped up, the experience of self-sufficiency, independence, and excitement jammed the fifties message—pervasive as any wartime propaganda—that woman's only fulfillment was in the home.

To be sure, other women noticed how radically things had changed, how the women's magazines, for example, which not long ago had promoted recipes you could make in ten minutes, now featured dishes that took a day to prepare. Some raised an eyebrow as "you can do it" became "you'd better not." Though most women bowed to the times, some undoubtedly embraced the new normal wholeheartedly, others perhaps less so. But whatever a woman felt deep within herself, it was not easy to go against what everyone around her—including all the experts in all the books and magazines—said was a woman's necessary place. Only a real maverick would dare contemplate supporting herself when jobs for women were limited and low paying, especially if you planned to grow older than thirty-five or forty.

Eva was one of the mavericks: in a time when women were told that it wasn't in their nature to function out in the world, that the only conceivable life was home and children, she knew better. She didn't set out to be a rebel. She just knew better. Yes, she wanted the perfect lover/husband. And her affection for me suggests a yearning for the child she had lost. Still, time and again she declined to make the choice that would have placed her in the three-bedroom home where she could keep busy changing diapers, doing laundry, and cooking complicated meals. Instead she spent her life in the bare little apartments that resembled the liberating dorm rooms of her youth.

As so often happens to those who break all the rules, Eva had it tough. Though she thrived on the nightlife, she grew tired, I know, of hotel work. I remember, for example, how she groused about the greasy restaurant meals that were considered part of her pay. And she had to know that, even in this poverty-level job, a day would come when she would be edged out by someone new and fresh.

By 1956, on her own and not getting any younger, she was the perfect target for Vick, who seemed to offer the mix of romance, security, and freedom she wanted; and her obsession with him took up the prime years of her life.

Yet I don't see Eva as a victim, and I'm just about positive she didn't see herself that way either. At a time when the women's magazines were bursting with portraits of infantilized women who received an "allowance" from their husbands, she took care of herself and pretty much lived the way she liked. She made her own decisions, took her own lumps, and always landed on her own two feet. Even in death, she preferred, as she let me know, to be on her own.

ᝌ Eva's letters, along with those of Grace, Aub, and all the others are reunited now, packed together in green cardboard filing boxes with tightly fitting lids. I am not sure what I should do with them. Perhaps I should offer them to a historical society. Perhaps I should offer them to Eva's daughter. Or to my own daughter who, in an age of electronic communication, will never know the heart-stopping thrill of beloved handwriting on an envelope. Will never weep onto the pages within until the blue ink runs like a river.

For now, I will leave the letters in peace, stacked in the back of my attic—though occasionally I may climb the stairs to pry into one of the green boxes, breathing again the unsettling, yet bracing aroma of lives lived to the hilt.

Notes

PART 1

MARCH 1958   Boise, Idaho

1. *The Idaho Statesman*, December 21, 1930.
2. *His Girl Friday*, 1940.
3. *Picnic*, 1955.
4. *I Want to Live*, 1958.
5. *Blue Gardenia*, 1953.
6. Kuhn, "You Ought to Get Married," 15–20.
7. *The Man in the Gray Flannel Suit*, 1956; *High Wall*, 1948.

1940–1942   Wing Valley

1. Gaffen, *Cross-Border Warriors*, 46.

1942   "If the Fair Sex Were to Replace Men"

1. Costello, *Virtue Under Fire*, 175.
2. Ibid., 178.
3. Chafe, *The American Woman*, 136.
4. *Oregonian*, January 14, 1942.
5. Goodwin, *No Ordinary Time*, 317, 318.
6. Kesselman, *Fleeting Opportunities*, 13.
7. For a discussion of the role of the *Bo's'n's Whistle* in "framing women in sexual language as oddities on male turf," see Jane Marcellus, "*Bo's'n's Whistle*: Representing 'Rosie the Riveter' on the Job," 83–108.
8. *Bo's'n's Whistle*, March 26, 1942.
9. Humbird, "Oregon Women Already Signed Up for Defense."

1942–1943   War in Europe

1. Pyle, *Here Is Your War*, 38.

2. Atkinson, *An Army at Dawn*, 4.

3. Ibid.

4. Terkel, *The Good War*, 117.

5. Thanks to Burt Kimmelman for this insight.

1943 ⁓ "One Woman Can Shorten This War"

1. Chafe, 137.

2. Gregory, *Women in Defense Work during World War II*, 15.

3. Chafe, 147.

4. Yellin, *Our Mothers' War*, 45.

5. Hartmann, *The Home Front and Beyond*, 82.

6. Rupp, *Mobilizing Women for War*, 153.

7. Gregory, 33.

8. Chafe, 147.

9. Honey, *Creating Rosie the Riveter*, 36.

10. Ibid., 48, 52.

11. Ibid., 35, 144.

12. *The Saturday Evening Post*, May 1943. Rockwell's masculine Rosie—massive but pinheaded—is very different from the icon of women's war work that most of us has have seen on the well-known "We Can Do It!" poster. This "Rosie" is a trim, attractive woman in a fitted shirt who stares at us with dark eyes, fiercely but calmly flexing her bicep. Sarah Palin, Hillary Clinton, and Michelle Obama, among others, have been pictured in the "We Can Do It!" pose.

But this image, widely assumed to express attitudes toward working women during World War II, would not have been seen by Eva or most other women of the time, according to Gwen Sharp and Lisa Wade ("Secrets of a Feminist Icon"). Rather the "We Can Do It!" poster was part of a Westinghouse in-house promotion, displayed for a few weeks in 1943. It was probably not aimed specifically at women but designed rather to discourage labor unrest. Furthermore, wartime security would have ensured that its audience was limited to workers and management.

Only since its revival in the mid-1980s has the poster become well known. Its unambiguous appreciation of women's strength and determination is, I believe, far more representative of the women's movement of the 70s and 80s than of the 1940s.

13. "Hats Off to the Girls in the Factories," 98.

14. Giles, *Punch In, Susie!*, 123.

15. Chafe, 150.

16. Lingenfelter, *Wartime Jobs for Girls*, 157.

17. Rupp, 159.

18. "The Margin Now Is Womanpower," 98.

WINTER 1956 ⁓ Vick Hits Boise

1. Harvey, *The Fifties*, 69, 70. Ehrenreich, *The Hearts of Men*, 15.

2. "The American Woman," *Life*, December 24, 1956.

3. Women are still working. Thirty percent of the workforce is female, the *Life* issue on "The American Woman" reports. But the fact of women working is not a problem, as several writers make clear, as long as women's first focus is on home and family.

4. "The American Woman," 23.

5. Written by psychiatrist Marynia Farnham and journalist Ferdinand Lundberg, *Modern Woman: The Lost Sex* was popularized in numerous magazine articles. The views expressed are even stated almost verbatim by Debbie Reynolds in the 1955 movie, *The Tender Trap*. Reynolds plays a twenty-one-year-old, who, despite her success as a singer and actress, wants to get married right away since "women are not fulfilled without marriage and children."

A decade and a half later, Betty Friedan will write that the "literal application of Freudian theory" by Lundberg and Farnham was paraphrased "ad nauseam" in the magazines and marriage courses, "until most of its statements became a part of the conventional, accepted truth of our time" (*Feminine Mystique*, 187).

6. Lundberg and Farnham. Quoted in Buhl, *Feminism and Its Discontents*, 175.

7. Mead, "On a Pioneer Past," 27. Many were distressed at Mead's "retreat from the unyielding culturalism of her youth." Her shift "reflected a sweeping turnaround in the behavioral sciences at large" (Buhl 196).

8. Ehrenreich, 20–24. Miller and Nowak, *The Fifties*, 154.

9. Vincent, "So You Want to Stay Single?"

1943 ⁓ Shipbuilding Boomtown, Portland

1. Goodwin, 206.

2. Ibid., 332.

3. Oregon Blue Book.

4. Davies, "Henry Kaiser Shows His Ships."

5. Goodwin, 318.

6. Skold, "The Job He Left Behind," 159.

7. Kesselman, 14.

8. *Oregonian*, November 4, 1943.

9. *Oregonian*, June 2, 1943.

10. *Oregonian*, January 11, 1942.

11. "When Your Soldier Comes Home," *Ladies' Home Journal*, October 1945.

1944 ✍ Swan Island, Portland

1. Oregon Ship, the first of the Kaiser yards in Oregon, was built in 1941 and absorbed most of the unemployed men. After Pearl Harbor, Kaiser built a second yard (named Kaiser) across the Columbia in Vancouver, Washington. In March of 1942 a third Kaiser yard went up on Swan Island (Skold, "Job" 159). Kaiser also has four shipyards in the San Francisco area.

2. Thanks to Portland historian Bob LaDu for his most generous assistance in showing me around the present day site of Swan Island, explaining the Kaiser operation there and sharing memories of World War II on the Island and in Portland. Also, thanks to his sister, Therese Klein, who shared memories of being a young motorcycle messenger on Swan Island.

3. Goodwin, 318.

4. Herman, *Freedom's Forge*, 184.

5. Davies.

6. Kesselman, 14.

7. Davies.

8. Goodwin, 318.

9. Ibid., 450.

10. Herman, 176.

11. For example, an ad in the June 2, 1943, *Oregonian* trumpets, "500 WOMEN NEEDED THIS WEEK. Earn at least $49.40 a Week in War Production as an Electrician's Helper. No experience necessary. Learn Free—the Federal Govt pays tuition."

12. Lane, *Ships for Victory*, 257.

13. Rieke, Oral History. Courtesy of the Oregon Historical Society.

14. Connie Field, *The Life and Times of Rosie the Riveter*.

15. Skold, Papers. Courtesy of the Oregon Historical Society.

16. Courtesy of the Oregon Historical Society.

17. *Bo's'n's Whistle*, June 17, 1943.

18. Merrill, *Social Problems on the Home Front*, 101.

19. Archibald, *Wartime Shipyard*, 19.

20. *Bo's'n's Whistle*, April 19, 1943.

21. Gluck, *Rosie the Riveter Revisited*, 229.

22. Ship Launchings. Meyer Sound Recordings. Courtesy Oregon Historical Society.

23. *Bo's'n's Whistle*, January 14, 1944, 15.

24. Oral History. Courtesy of the Oregon Historical Society.

25. Photograph courtesy of the Oregon Historical Society.

26. *Bo's'n's Whistle*, September 2, 1943.

27. One such job, held down by a pretty brunette named Norma Jean Dougherty, was that of parachute stuffer. After an Army newsreel team spotted her and her photos "created a sensation" in *Yank* magazine, she moved to Hollywood, dyed her hair, and became Marilyn Monroe (Herman 264).

28. Skold, "The Job He Left Behind," 169–171.

29. Elizabeth Field, "Boom Town Girls," 296.

30. Hartmann, *Home Front*, 80.

31. Photo from *Oregon Journal*, September 26, 1943. Courtesy of the Oregon Historical Society.

32. Kesselman, 28.

33. Interview, University of Southern California Collection. Quoted in Goodwin, 367.

34. *Oregonian*, June 10, 1943. The decision to deny contraceptives to women was made, the article reports, after a discussion of the health of women in uniform, during which there was "a determined feminine punch to smash through any outmoded double standards of the day."

35. Rieke, Oral History.

36. Terkel, 117.

37. May, "Rosie the Riveter Gets Married," 128.

38. Chafe, 154.

1944–1946 ⚓ Swan Island Shipyard and Fort George Wright Convalescent Hospital

1. "Shell Shocked Men Not Shell Shocked," 24.

2. Painton, "There Is No Such Thing as Shell Shock."

3. The term we know today, PTSD or Post-Traumatic Stress Disorder, is not yet in general use.

4. Atkinson, 405.

5. Ibid., 405.

6. Ibid., 406.

7. Rosten, *Captain Newman, M.D.*, 7.

8. Painton, 60.

9. Ibid., 63.

10. This account of harsh treatment resembles that of Grinker and Spiegel in *War Neuroses.*

11. Painton, 59, 60.

12. Ibid., 61.

13. Ibid., 62.

14. Ibid., 63.

15. Grinker and Spiegel, 94.

16. Culbertson, Oral History. Courtesy of the Oregon Historical Society.

17. Grinker and Spiegel, 78–81.

18. Hartmann, "Prescriptions for Penelope," 227.

19. Ibid.

20. "When Your Soldier Comes Home," *Ladies' Home Journal,* October 1945.

1944 ∽ "The Taste of Independence," Swan Island

1. Between 1940 and 1945 the number of women working grew by 50 percent. The number at work outside home jumped from 12 million to 18.6 million. By 1945, women accounted for 36 percent of the civilian labor force (Hartmann, *Home Front,* 21).

2. Goodwin, 369.

3. *Bo's'n's Whistle,* September 29, 1944.

4. *Bo's'n's Whistle,* May 12, 1944.

5. *Bo's'n's Whistle,* June 1, 1945.

6. *Bo's'n's Whistle,* April 14, 1944.

7. *Bo's'n's Whistle,* May 12, 1944.

8. *Bo's'n's Whistle,* April 21, 1944.

9. *Bo's'n's Whistle,* March 31, 1944.

10. *Bo's'n's Whistle,* March 19, 1944.

11. *Bo's'n's Whistle,* March 31, 1944.

12. *Bo's'n's Whistle,* July 27, 1945.

13. *Bo's'n's Whistle,* March 10, 1944.

14. Herman, 338.

15. *Bo's'n's Whistle,* April 7, 1944.

16. *Bo's'n's Whistle,* March 19, 1944.

17. Quoted in Honey, 23.

18. "Females in Factories," *Time,* July 17, 1944.

19. "American Women," 28.

20. Courtesy of the Oregon Historical Society.

1945 ≈ Sunday Punch

1. *Bo's'n's Whistle*, June 1, 1945.
2. *Bo's'n's Whistle*, August 17, 1945.
3. *Bo's'n's Whistle*, August 24, 1945.
4. Chafe, 180.
5. Anderson, *Wartime Women*, 162.
6. Ibid., 162–163.
7. Honey, 23.
8. *Christian Science Monitor*, June, 1945.
9. *Bo's'n's Whistle*, May 11, 1945.
10. Quoted in Kesselman, 95.
11. Hartmann, *Home Front*, 24.
12. Connie Field.
13. Kesselman, 112–115.
14. Hartmann, *Home Front*, 24.
15. Skold, "Job," 174.
16. Chafe, 178.
17. Furnas, "Meet Ed Savickas," 59–63.

PART 2

Odette, March 1959

1. Since I have been asked so often if Vick was a Mormon, let me point out that bigamy and polygamy are two very different things. Male polygamists want a number of wives and families at once and, in some religious teachings, believe they have the right and duty to maintain several families. But a number of wives and families to support was the last thing Vick wanted. He's a bigamist, one who gets married even though he's already legally married to one or more others.

Tessa, Baltimore

1. McClinsey, *Washington, D.C.'s Mayflower Hotel*, 54–55.

Why?

1. Soothill, et al. "The Place of Bigamy in the Pantheon of Crime?" 70.

2. Jones, *From Here to Eternity*, 112.

3. Fifties family-living author Paul Landis estimated that 92 percent of all Americans were or had been married, the highest record in national history (Miller and Nowak, 147).

4. Gilbert, *Men in the Middle*, 63.

5. Ibid., 66.

6. So pervasive is the idea of marriage and family, however, that the teenagers played by James Dean and Natalie Wood set up a "mock family" where they try to care for the distraught boy played by Sal Mineo (Miller and Nowak, 171).

7. Kerouac, *Dharma Bums*, 29.

8. Kerouac, *On the Road*, 195.

9. Quoted in Ehrenreich, 47.

10. Yoder, "A Way with Women."

Vick's War, 1940–1951

1. http://www.army.gc.ca/iaol/143000440001622/143000440001624/index-Eng.html.

The Vickers Family, Kansas, 1910–1930

1. This distinction is claimed by Lebanon, Kansas, about one hundred miles northwest of Newton.

2. Smurr, *Harvey County History*, T2.

3. *Newton (KS) Journal*, August 22, 1913.

4. The federal census was taken in 1910, 1920, and 1930. Kansas conducted a census in 1915 and 1925.

5. Hess, *Anatomy of a Town*, 145–155.

6. Thompson, *A Garden of Sand*, 192, 194, 109, 119.

7. http://www.newtonkansas.com/index.aspx?page=191.

8. Thanks to Harvey County historian Pam Navrat for this information.

9. Generous help was provided in locating these newspapers by the Riley County Historical Society.

Portland, 1960–1961

1. Saccharin was a habit learned during the war when sugar was scarce. Many women continued to use it after the war.
2. Both movies were made in 1955.

Mena and Janice, 1961

1. Washington State Digital Archives.

The Bigamist, 1953–1962

1. Tolbert, "The Taming of Bigamy Jones," 54.
2. Douglas, "Are You Married to a Bigamist?"
3. A notorious contemporary bigamist, the "Irish Casanova" Oliver Killeen, seems to prove this rule. Though credited with nineteen bigamous marriages, Killeen has served only brief prison stints in Ireland and Canada. In interviews, Killeen has explained his method. "Conning women is easy. . . . I studied psychology and behavior patterns. I presented myself as a dashing, suave sort of guy and women fell for it." Unlike Vick, who appears never to have been unpleasant, Killeen was verbally abusive and didn't wait until he was on the way out the door to write bad checks. Life with him was "pure hell," one woman reported.

On a comment page attached to the *Irish Central* article, several men have written in to say Killeen should be left alone and the law should stay out of the bedroom. http://www.irishcentral.com/news/Irish-man-who-admits-he-was-married-to-19-women-is-convicted-of-bigamy-141726993.html.

King County Jail, Seattle, 1962

1. Of all those who helped me pursue this research, none was more gracious than Dom Driano.

Sanity

1. Rule, *The Stranger beside Me*, 112–113.
2. Hare, *Without Conscience*, 76, 22.
3. Ibid., 14, 35, 59.
4. Ibid., 83.
5. Ibid., 69, 85.
6. Cleckley, *The Mask of Sanity*, 149.

7. Ibid., 40, 150, 133.

8. Ibid., 57, 37.

9. Ibid., 73.

10. Hare, 145.

11. Cleckley, 198.

12. Brown, *Women Who Love Psychopaths*, 110.

13. Gluck, 267.

14. Ibid., 269.

15. Kesselman, 133.

16. The causes of psychopathy continue to be debated. As is often noted, the outgoing and carefree psychopath presents himself very differently from the person who was neglected or abused as a child and who often suffers from depression and anxiety. Even the pioneering Cleckley noticed that the families and siblings of psychopaths often appeared perfectly normal.

In their efforts to discover a physiological factor, researchers have made the claim that the brains of psychopaths function differently from those of normal people. For example, experiments have shown that when a psychopath is asked to make a decision that involves "emotional words," there is "increased blood flow to the temporal lobes," whereas "normal people" might have "such an increased cerebral blood flow if asked to solve a mildly challenging intellectual problem" (Stout, 125). The implication is that emotions are a puzzle for these individuals.

Some also claim that psychopathology has a genetic element. In their book, *The Psychopath: Emotion and the Brain*, James Blair and his coauthors at the National Institute of Mental Health suggest that, in psychopaths, genetic-based brain anomalies result in impairment of "aversive conditioning, instrumental learning, and the processing of fearful and sad expressions." As a result of these impairments, it is argued, the individual "does not learn to avoid actions that cause harm to other individuals" (139).

Eva and Vick in Seattle, Spring 1962

1. Gerassi, *The Boys of Boise*, 166–167.

2. Dr. Jarvis recommended clemency in another case of socially unacceptable behavior, as recounted in John Gerassi's *The Boys of Boise*. In the mid-1950s, Jarvis traveled to Boise amid a homosexual scandal. The psychiatrist was brought in to perform examinations on men accused of homosexuality, using the "truth serum" sodium amatol. In at least one case he concluded that the accused person desired to change his inclinations,

which he now understood to be "contrary to public welfare"; and in a letter to the court, Jarvis agreed to treat the prisoner if probation or suspension of sentence was found to be justified (166–167).

"Ha! Ha! I Just Laugh and Tell Everyone a Different Story," Seattle, Summer 1962

1. Friedan, 120.
2. Harvey, 226.
3. Ibid., 227.
4. Ibid.

Psychoanalyzing Vick

1. United States Census, 1930.

Epilogue

1. Washington State Digital Archives.

References

ORAL HISTORIES

Baker, Marie. In Gluck, *Rosie the Riveter Revisited.*
Culbertson, LueRayne. Oregon Historical Society.
Gleason, Marie. Oregon Historical Society.
Hahne, Dellie. In Terkel, *The Good War.*
Rieke, Forrest E., M.D. Oregon Historical Society.
Sauer, Inez. In Goodwin, *No Ordinary Time.*

BIBLIOGRAPHY

"The American Woman: Her Achievements and Troubles." Special Double Edition. *Life*, December 24, 1956.
"American Woman's Dilemma." *Life*, June 16, 1947, 112.
"American Women." *Life*, January 29, 1945, 28.
Anderson, Karen. *Wartime Women: Sex Roles, Family Relations, and the Status of Women during World War II.* New York: Greenpoint Press, 1976.
Archibald, Katherine. *Wartime Shipyard.* Berkeley: University of California Press, 1947.
Atkinson, Rick. *An Army at Dawn: The War in North Africa, 1942–1943.* New York: Henry Holt, 2007.
Blair, James, Derek Mitchell, and Karina Blair. *The Psychopath: Emotion and the Brain.* Malden, MA: Blackwell, 2005.
Brown, Sandra. *Women Who Love Psychopaths.* Penrose, NC: Mask Publishing, 2009.
Buhl, Mari Jo. *Feminism and Its Discontents: A Century of Struggle with Psychoanalysis.* Cambridge: Harvard University Press, 1998.
Chafe, William Henry. *The American Woman: Her Changing Social, Economic, and Political Roles, 1920–1970.* New York: Oxford University Press, 1972.
Cleckley, Hervey. *The Mask of Sanity: An Attempt to Clarify Some Issues about*

the So-Called Psychopathic Personality. 5th ed. Augusta, GA: Emily S. Cleckley, 1988. http://cassiopaea.org/cass/sanity_1.PdF.

Costello, John. *Virtue Under Fire: How World War II Changed Our Social and Sexual Attitudes.* New York: Fromm, 1987.

Davies, Lawrence. "Henry Kaiser Shows His Ships." *New York Times Sunday Magazine,* January 24, 1943.

Douglas, Adam. "Are You Married to a Bigamist?" *Cosmopolitan,* October 1960, 68–73.

Ehrenreich, Barbara. *The Hearts of Men: American Dreams and the Flight from Commitment.* New York: Anchor, 1983.

Erenberg, Lewis A., and Susan E. Hirsch, eds. *The War in American Culture: Society and Consciousness during World War II.* Chicago: University of Chicago Press, 1996.

"Females in Factories." *Time,* July 17, 1944, 60.

Field, Connie. *The Life and Times of Rosie the Riveter.* Berkeley, CA: Clarity Films, 1980.

Field, Elizabeth. "Boom Town Girls." *Independent Women,* October 1942, 296–298.

Friedan, Betty. *The Feminine Mystique.* 1963. New York: Norton, 2001.

French, Brandon. *On the Verge of Revolt: Women in American Films of the Fifties.* New York: Ungar, 1978.

Furnas, J. C. "Meet Ed Savickas: His Chances of Complete Recovery Bring Hope to Thousands." *Ladies' Home Journal,* October 1945, 59–63.

Gaffen, Fred. *Cross-Border Warriors: Canadians in American Forces, Americans in Canadian Forces.* Toronto: Dundurn, 1995.

Gerassi, John. *The Boys of Boise: Furor, Vice, and Folly in an American City.* 1966. Seattle: University of Washington Press, 2001.

Gilbert, James. *Men in the Middle: Searching for Masculinity in the 1950s.* Chicago: University of Chicago Press, 2005.

Giles, Nell. *Punch In, Susie! A Woman's War Factory Diary.* New York: Harper & Brothers, 1943.

Gluck, Sherna Berger. *Rosie the Riveter Revisited: Women, the War, and Social Change.* New York: Plume, 1988.

Goodwin, Doris Kearns. *No Ordinary Time: Franklin and Eleanor Roosevelt—The Home Front in World War II.* New York: Simon & Schuster, 1994.

Gregory, Chester W. *Women in Defense Work during World War II.* New York: Exposition, 1974.

Grinker, Roy R., and John P. Spiegel. *War Neuroses.* 1945. New York: Arno, 1979.

Hare, Robert D. *Without Conscience: The Disturbing World of the Psychopaths among Us.* New York: Guilford, 1999.

Hartmann, Susan M. *The Home Front and Beyond: American Women in the 1940s.* Boston: Twayne, 1982.

———. "Prescriptions for Penelope: Literature on Women's Obligations to Returning World War II Veterans." *Women's Studies* 5 (1978): 223–239.

Harvey, Brett. *The Fifties: A Women's Oral History.* New York: HarperCollins, 1993.

"Hats Off to the Girls in the Factories." *Ladies' Home Journal,* October 1942, 98.

Hegarty, Marilyn E. "Patriot or Prostitute? Sexual Discourses, Print Media, and American Women during World War II." *Journal of Women's History* 10, no. 2 (Summer 1998): 112–136.

Herman, Arthur. *Freedom's Forge: How American Business Produced Victory in World War II.* New York: Random House, 2012.

Hess, Mary. *Anatomy of a Town: Heston, Kansas.* New York: Carlton, 1976.

Hickey, Margaret. "What's Ahead for Women Who Earn?" Speech, March 14, 1946. "Conferences, Labor Advisory Committee, Women's Bureau, Postwar 1945–52," WBA accession, no. 58A, 850, container 3.

Honey, Maureen. *Creating Rosie the Riveter: Class, Gender, and Propaganda during World War II.* Amherst: University of Massachusetts Press, 1984.

Humbird, James. "Oregon Women Already Signed Up for Defense." NEA Service. *Ironwood (MI) Daily Globe,* May 22, 1942.

Jones, James. *From Here to Eternity.* 1951. New York: Dell, 1979.

Kaiser Ship Launchings. Meyer Sound Recordings. Oregon Historical Society.

Kerouac, Jack. *Dharma Bums.* 1958. New York: Penguin, 1986.

———. *On the Road.* 1957. New York: Viking, 2007.

Kesselman, Amy. *Fleeting Opportunities: Women Shipyard Workers in Portland and Vancouver during World War II and Reconversion.* Albany: State University of New York Press, 1990.

Kuhn, Irene Corbally. "You Ought to Get Married." *American Mercury,* November 1954, 15–20.

Lane, Frederic C. *Ships for Victory: A History of Shipbuilding under the U.S. Maritime Commission in World War II.* 1951. Baltimore: Johns Hopkins University Press, 2001.

Lingenfelter, Mary Rebecca. *Wartime Jobs for Girls.* New York: Harcourt Brace, 1943.

Lundberg, Ferdinand, and Marynia Farnham. *Modern Woman: The Lost Sex.* New York: Harper & Brothers, 1947.

Marcellus, Jane. "*Bo's'n's Whistle*: Representing 'Rosie the Riveter' on the Job." *American Journalism* 22, no. 2 (2005): 83–108.

"The Margin Now Is Womanpower." *Fortune,* February 1943, 98.

May, Elaine Tyler. "Rosie the Riveter Gets Married." In Erenberg and Hirsch, *The War in American Culture*.

McClinsey, Keith. *Washington, D.C.'s Mayflower Hotel*. Mt. Pleasant, SC: Arcadia, 2007.

Mead, Margaret. "On a Pioneer Past." *Life*, December 24, 1956, 27.

Merrill, Francis E. *Social Problems on the Home Front: A Study of Wartime Influences*. New York: Harper, 1948.

Miller, Douglas T., and Marion Nowak. *The Fifties: The Way We Really Were*. Garden City, NY: Doubleday, 1977.

"More Women Go to Work." *Newsweek*, September 6, 1943.

Oregon Blue Book. http://www.bluebook.sta.or.us.

Painton, Frederick C. "There Is No Such Thing as Shell Shock." *Reader's Digest*, October 1943, 59–63.

Pyle, Ernie. *Here Is Your War*. New York: Henry Holt, 1943.

Rockwell, Norman. "Rosie the Riveter." *Saturday Evening Post*, May 1943, cover.

Rosten, Leo. *Captain Newman, M.D.* New York: Harper, 1961.

Rule, Ann. *The Stranger beside Me*. 1980. New York: Pocketbooks, 2009.

Rupp, Leila J. *Mobilizing Women for War: German and American Propaganda, 1939–1945*. Princeton: Princeton University Press, 1978.

Sharp, Gwen, and Lisa Wade. "Secrets of a Feminist Icon." *Contexts* 10, no. 2 (May 2011): 82–83.

"Shell Shocked Men Not Shell Shocked; There's No Such Thing, Say World Medics, Who Claim 'Shell Shocked' Vets Were Always Neurotics." *Pittsburgh Post-Gazette*, July 29, 1931, 24.

Skold, Karen Beck. "The Job He Left Behind: Women in the Shipyards in World War II." In *Women in Pacific Northwest History: Essays*, edited by Karen J. Blair, 107–129. Seattle: University of Washington Press, 1988.

———. Papers. Oregon Historical Society.

Smurr, Linda. *Harvey County History*. Dallas: Curtis Media Group, 1990.

Soothill, Keith, Elizabeth Ackerley, Barry Sanderson, and Moira Peelo. "The Place of Bigamy in the Pantheon of Crime?" *Medicine, Science, and the Law* 39, no. 1 (1999): 65–71.

Stout, Martha. *The Sociopath Next Door*. New York: Broadway Books, 2005.

Terkel, Studs. *The Good War*. New York: Pantheon, 1984.

Thompson, Earl. *A Garden of Sand*. New York: Carroll and Graf, 1970.

Tolbert, Frank X. "The Taming of Bigamy Jones." *Colliers*, February 19, 1954, 54–63.

Vincent, Haywood. "So You Want to Stay Single?" *Cosmopolitan*, August 1954, 58–61.

"When Your Soldier Comes Home." *Ladies' Home Journal*, October 1945.

Yellin, Emily. *Our Mothers' War: American Women at Home and at the Front during World War II.* New York: Free Press, 2004.

Yoder, Robert M. "A Way with Women." *Saturday Evening Post*, May 7, 1955, 36, 146, 148.

Index

Note: This is a true story based entirely on some eight hundred letters and other primary documents, on site visits and interviews, and on archival and library research. However, since there are those who still live with the legacy of these events, the author has undertaken steps to protect their privacy. For this reason the names of people and places have sometimes been changed.

financial state of, 170–71, 173, 215; and marriage license of Vick, 148; Vick's false claims about, 189, 218

Vickers, Virgil "Vick": appearance of, 138, 145; arrest and prosecution for bigamy, 188, 189–92, 200–4, 228; attachment disorder theory, 215; and Aub, 74–75, 212; author's initial impression of, 58–59; birth certificate of, 134; birth of, 171, 217; brothers of, 127–28, 173; cars of (*see* automobiles taken by Vick); and census records, 133; checkbook of, 9–11; and coat of arms, 142; date of birth, 134; drinking of, 126; duration of marriages, 158; empathy of, 219; employment at Hotel Boise, 6, 44–45, 47–48, 147; employment at Mayflower Hotel, 146–47, 189; employment at prominent establishments, 147–48, 189; employment at United Airlines, 138; employment of, in Seattle, 205, 207, 210; employment sought at Space Needle, 190; Eva deserted by, 7–9, 89–91, 157–58, 197–98; Eva's devotion to, 157, 197–98, 200, 219–20; Eva's early relationship with, 48; Eva's engagement to, 57–59; and Eva's family, 57–59; Eva's honeymoon with, 99–100, 124, 159; Eva's marriage to, 6, 74–76, 101; Eva's renewed relationship with, 200–6, 207–8, 209, 218; Eva's search for, 13–18, 127–28 (*see also* Mexico); financial damage left by, 125, 126–27, 139, 141, 154; frugality of, 154; girlfriends of (*see* Nesbitt, Tessa McKee); health issues claimed by, 120–21, 143; idealized family fantasies of, 218; intelligence of, 138, 162, 165; and intervals between marriages, 186, 187; jealousy of, 142; Kansas as birthplace and early home of, 130, 133, 134, 148, 166–67; legal trouble of, 142, 148; letters from, 200–4, 209–10, 212–13, 214, 218, 221; lifestyle of, 48; and marriage annulments, 204, 211–12, 228; marriage licenses of, 59, 130, 133–34, 148–49, 183–84, 191; military service (*see* military service of

Vick); motives of, 129, 145, 151, 218–19, 229–30; move to Boise, Idaho, 42–45; photographs of, 144–45; in Portland, 42; probation sentence of, 204, 228; psychiatric evaluation of, 192, 193, 201, 204, 207; psychoanalysis of (modern), 214–20; and psychopathy theory, 198–99; romantic fantasies of, 218–19, 229–30; school records of, 173–74; search for records on, 129–33; sexuality of, 151; shoebox of, 9–12, 18, 146, 148; as soldier, 11; VA records of, 11, 130, 148; warrants for arrest of, 189–92, 229; and wartime trauma theory, 15, 126, 145, 156–57, 159, 161–65, 200; wedding pictures of, 11, 12, 74–75, 156, 198; widower claim of, 59, 117, 125, 134, 148, 159, 184; wives (*see* wives of Vick); youth of, 215–18

Vickers, Wilbur (father): and birth of Vick, 171, 217; and census records, 133; children of, 167–68, 216; civic work of, 174; death of, 174, 175; farming of, 168; financial state of, 170–71, 173, 215; and marriage license of Vick, 148; property pur-chases of, 172; property sales of, 170–71, 172, 173

Vickers, William Wilbur (son), 175–76, 189–90, 228

Vickers Family, 166–76; and birth of Vick, 171–72, 217; and census records, 167–68; children of, 167–68, 171, 215; Eva's search for, 173; farming of, 168; financial state of, 168–69, 170–72, 173, 215, 217; frequent moves of, 168, 171, 173; and idealized family fantasies, 218; photographs of, 214, 215–16, 217; and Vick's bigamy, 218; Vick's false claims about, 142, 189, 218; and Vick's youth, 215–18

Wade, Lisa, 234n12
war bonds, 52
War Neuroses (Grinker and Spiegel), 81, 85, 238n10
wartime employment of women: and ability to make money, 52; acceptance and appreciation of, 50, 92–93; advertisements for, 236n11; and

attitudes about career ambitions, 178; attractive work attire for, 63; and campaign to register/recruit women, 30–31, 37–38, 40; and domestic responsibilities, 62, 93, 95, 96; early reactions to, 29–31, 50, 93; and effects of wartime experience, 196–97; and end of war, 103–5; and femininity, 62–63, 104; and Grace, 31, 38–39, 40, 54; and Great Depression, 26; hesitations regarding, 37–38, 67–68; husbands' reactions to, 37; and independence, 103–4; and manpower crisis, 29, 37, 54; and mass migration of workers, 49–50; and morality concerns, 63–64; number of women employed, 92, 105, 235n3, 238n1; opportunities for, 39; patriotic component of, 63, 97; in popular culture, 38, 39; positive response of women to, 67; postwar attitudes about, 178, 231; and postwar desire to continue working, 95, 103–4; and postwar employment worries, 95–96, 105; and sexual promiscuity, 71–72; and welders/riveters, 61, 64, 105, 117

Wartime Jobs for Girls, 39

"A Way with Women" (*Saturday Evening Post*), 154–55

We Build Tankers (promotional film), 97

"We Can Do It!" (promotional poster), 234n12

Weinberger, Larry, 164–65, 199

welding and welders, 60–61, 62, 64, 105

West Coast, 49–50

Whistle. See Bo's'n's Whistle

"Why Young Mothers Feel Trapped" (*Redbook*), 208

Wing Valley, Oregon: author's visits to, 223; church community in, 51–52; and Dave's letters, 55, 111; and Dave's return from the war, 77–78; and Eva's appeal, 179; and Eva's daughter, 226; and Eva's engagement to Dave, 19–21, 98; and Eva's engagement to Jimmy, 112–13; and Eva's engagement to Vick, 57–59; and Eva's move to Portland, 53; Eva's prolonged absence from, 70, 98; and Eva's youth, 14; familiarity in,

59, 89; and Grace's heart attack, 221; isolation of, 166; and Vick's desertion of Eva, 89–90; and wartime employment of women, 31; and World War II, 27–28, 178

Without Conscience (Hare), 193–94

wives of Vick: communication between, 120–27, 157–58, 183–84, 188; duration of marriages, 157–58; lives of, after Vick, 177; and marriage annulments, 228, 229; number of, 123, 164, 174, 176, 228; and romantic fantasies of Vick, 218–19, 229–30; and sisters of Vick, 218; traits shared by, 149–50; and Vick's trial for bigamy, 191–92, 204. *See also* Ada; Cimmiotti, Mena Z.; Douglas, Marie; Eldridge, Eva; Foster, Edna C.; Greerson, Linda; Henault, Leda; Kavenaugh, Janice; Olsen, Odette; Rittenhouse, Kathleen

Wolf, Peggy, 103

women: and birth control, 71–72, 237n34; and children outside of marriage, 71–72; dissatisfaction with homemaking, 208; and domestic responsibilities, 93, 96; and equality, 96; and expectations for marriage, 45–47; and fantasy cultivated by postwar Americans, 230–31; and Friedan's *Feminine Mystique*, 208; and independence, 103–4; malaise among, 45–46; and motherhood/family life, 24, 45, 46; postwar portrayal of, 151–52; and psychopaths, 195–96, 198; role of, in home, 26, 95, 96, 104, 106; and social pressures to marry, 35; and soldiers' transitions to civilian life, 86–87; "transitional" group of, 196–97; and the war effort, 29–31, 37–38; and women's movement, 234n12. *See also* wartime employment of women

Women Who Love Psychopaths (Brown), 196

Women's Advisory Committee to the War Manpower Commission, 105

World War I, 78

World War II: Battle for Hill 609, 34; and bombing of Bath, 32; as central event in adults' lives, 178; and combat

fatigue of soldiers, 79–81, 84–85, 108–
9; and contraceptives for soldiers, 71;
and Dave's military service, 25–26, 27,
32–36, 55, 81, 161, 227; and disruption
of Eva's rural life, 113–14; invasion
of Italy, 35–36; long-term impact of,
46; and Pearl Harbor attack, 27–28,
46, 49; and postwar employment
worries, 94–95; and postwar literary
portrayal of women, 151–52; rationing
during, 50, 62; and shell-shock
theory, 11, 78–79; and shipbuilding,
60–61, 65–66; and social pressures to
marry, 35; and transition to civilian
life, 85, 86–87; and Vick (*see* military
service of Vick); victory declared
in Europe, 102; and war bonds, 52;
and wartime employment, 49 (*see
also* shipbuilding and shipyards of
Portland); women's contributions to,
67. *See also* wartime employment of
women

Wright, Jimmy: desire for second chance,
181–82; drinking of, 110, 112–13, 157,
182, 202; Eva's child with, 224–25,
226; Eva's courtship and engagement
with, 110, 112–13; Eva's divorce from,
178, 181; and Eva's engagement to
Dave, 82; Eva's marriage to, 113–14,
157, 197; and Grace, 112–13, 178, 181;
later life of, 227; wedding pictures
of, 226

Yank magazine, 33, 237n27